Regional Economic Development in the European Union and North America

MORRIS L. SWEET

PRAEGER

Westport, Connecticut
London

Library of Congress Cataloging-in-Publication Data

Sweet, Morris L.
    Regional economic development in the European Union and North
America / Morris L. Sweet.
        p.   cm.
    Includes bibliographical references and index.
    ISBN 0–275–95617–2 (alk. paper)
    1. European Union countries—Economic policy.   2. North America—
Economic policy.   3. Regional economics—European Union countries.
4. Regional economics—North America.   I. Title.
HC240.9.E85S93   1999
338.94—dc21   98–33547

British Library Cataloguing in Publication Data is available.

Library of Congress Catalog Card Number: 98–33547
ISBN: 0–275–95617–2

First published in 1999

Praeger Publishers, 88 Post Road West, Westport, CT 06881
An imprint of Greenwood Publishing Group, Inc.
www.praeger.com

Printed in the United States of America

To my wife, Sally,
without whose encouragement and
cooperation completion of this work
would not have been possible.

Contents

Tables

Preface

This publication is the product of a longstanding involvement in studying the components of location (public and private). In this study, my emphasis is on the regional aspects of industrial location. I have sought to bring together the history, institutions, policies and programs of regional development in one volume, with a view towards increasing awareness of this subject and as a basis for policy and subsequent programs.

The importance of the public sector in spatial economic development has not necessarily disappeared in the United States. There has been a change in the character of the involvement. It now functions in a more indirect and complex manner, as witnessed by the World Trade Organization and North American Free Trade Agreement influence on subnational regions with the national governments as principals. Another aspect is the direct involvement in their regional economies of the European Union and Canada, in sharp contrast to the policy of the United States where involvement is measured by comparable direct federal expenditures and concern with subnational competition is minimal.

I am grateful to the officials and staff members of the various institutions and organizations for their assistance, which made completion of this book possible. The author is especially indebted to the individuals whose crucial contributions are too numerous to single out for special recognition.

Further acknowledgment is extended to colleagues and coauthors who sharpened and broadened my analytical perspectives. Another debt is due those who edited, reviewed and typeset the manuscript.

PART I

BACKGROUND

Chapter 1

Introduction

Practically all government policies and programs have a geographic impact, but in this review the focus is on those government activities that have a specifically targeted spatial or regional economic development basis. The term "region" as used in this volume fundamentally connotes subnational entities but covers the impact of supranational organizations on regional economies. The goal of regional economic development policy in this volume refers to maintaining and encouraging policies and programs leading to economically viable regions. The study takes a comparative viewpoint of the European Union (EU) and North America within a historical context and examines such supranational entities as the North American Free Trade Agreement (NAFTA) and World Trade Organization (WTO).

The historic analysis offers a systematic method for understanding the changing context of regions and their place in national and global systems. Regional development is not static and overemphasis on the present can lose sight of the direction of policy and programs. Historical analysis provides an awareness of the interrelations of technical, social, cultural and political factors.

There is a dual or overlapping aspect: supranational organizations that may be regional in terms of groups of nations as components, in contrast to regions that are subnational entities but may overlap national boundaries. Supranational arrangements have implications extending beyond free trade. They eventually require harmonization or coordination of domestic economic and political policies with those of other members. For example, subsidies that were once primarily a domestic matter become subject to international scrutiny and may be of dubious legality. The broadening range of domestic activities that are covered by international economic agreements can unsettle national and subnational relations. Subnational regions may attempt to bypass the national governments and influence the supranational policies as well as seek greater independence, for example, the Committee on Regions in the EU. In the United States a national policy of devolution of responsibilities to the states and a series of Supreme Court decisions could mean greater powers for the states. Yet devolution is paradoxical in view of the concern with globalization. From a practical standpoint, can fifty states with separate agendas and competing with each other or the national government be the most effective representative for the country in the supranational organizations? Subnational efforts (state, regional, community) individually are limited in their effectiveness if contrary to or separated from national policies.

By reducing the effects of international boundaries, the supranational organizations can integrate the economic territories of the member nations, producing a consolidated unit that forms a new spatial context for economic activity. A new economic entity is formed and the shape, contiguity and structure become factors in corporate investment and locational decisions, such as the Canada-U.S. and Mexico-U.S. borders.[1]

GLOBALIZATION

Economic development programs are faced with the globalization or internationalization of investment and production. There is increasing fluidity in the location of economic activity as well as more rapid and more unpredictable changes in patterns of regional development. The capability for any government, national, regional or local, to act independently is curtailed.

Decisions about investment, production and sales are made at corporate headquarters, as multinationals seek efficiency without regard to national or regional boundaries or to the company's employees or communities in which they have facilities.[2] Yet spatial factors have to be considered in locational decisions. There has to be a division between activities that require limited investment in facilities and personnel and thus are free to move quickly and those that have some fixed economic activity and thus are impervious to spatial considerations. Not all regions are equal in terms of their locational value, and regional economic development consists of maximizing their advantages. Globalization does not make regional economic development superfluous.

How will regional development be affected and adapt to ongoing or likely change? Competition has to be considered in terms of scrutiny and compliance with supranational guidelines. A parallel situation is the matter of internal subsidies, in states in the United States and provinces in Canada. Given the mobility of industry, economic development is increasingly an ongoing activity necessary for survival, even for prosperous regions.

Regional and urban economics and economic geography have been given insufficient attention by mainstream economics.[3] Though the constantly increasing internationalization affects virtually all countries and industries, geography and location still are important: "We hesitate to refer to such a trend as globalization, since the term conjures up images of firms released from the bonds of geography and hence is at odds with the more prosaic reality of foreign and direct investment." [4]

TECHNOLOGY

To what extent will new technologies replace prevailing regional industrial and residential patterns? Can advanced technology erase the contingencies of place and time? "The cliche of the information age is that instantaneous global telecommunications, television and computer networks will soon overthrow the ancient tyrannies of time and space. Companies will need no headquarters, workers will toil as effectively from home, car or beach as they could in the offices that need no longer exist, and events half a world away will be seen, heard and felt with the same immediacy as events across the street—if indeed streets will have any point."[5]

Communications improvements will change the nature of spatial relations but companies that have gone furthest in linking their global operations electronically state that an increase in face-to-face contacts is necessary to keep operations functioning well. The social cohesion of personal relations becomes more crucial.[6]

According to neo-classical economics the world should move away from concentration toward an optimum dispersion of people, skills and economic competence. Other than for transport costs, the production source of a tradable good or service should not be a matter of concern. Yet, clustering has survived and thrived in particular industries along with technological change.

COMPARATIVE PROGRAMS AND POLICIES

A comparison of U.S. regional programs and policies with the EU, Canada and Mexico strikingly reveals how far the United States, with the exception of Mexico, lags. Furthermore, knowledge in the United States of the range of EU, Canadian and Mexican activities is limited. In terms of population, the EU with 371 million is closest to the U.S. 261 million; Mexico has a population of some 92 million and Canada, 28 million.

Though the EU has a high profile in the United States, less is known of its regional development programs, which consist of a variety of innovative approaches, related political institutions and the decision-making process. In the United States, interest in the EU has been focused largely on trade and monetary matters. While the EU is actively formulating policy, the United States has no semblance of any federal regional policy or even any concern expressed by the executive branch. In considering the two entities, factors to consider are different political parties and alignments, priorities, industry mix, culture, traditional government support and public intervention. Thus, the EU, its history, institutions programs and policies, are reviewed with respect to regional aspects. In addition, the Canadian and Mexican approaches are examined. What guidelines can be derived from this comparative review?

FEDERAL ACTIVITIES IN THE UNITED STATES

Federal activities affecting economic development fall into different categories: fiscal and monetary policies with broad national goals; programs and policies that do not have direct economic purposes but have critical economic implications, for defense, education, environment, and the category with which this study deals—federal policies and programs whose purpose is directly concerned with economic development spatially. Though there are critics of direct federal involvement in economic development, this study acknowledges the need for responsibility and a direct role by the federal government.

Disparities among different geographic regions and economic sectors, often related, are obscured by an overall satisfactory level of economic activity. In a period of relative economic prosperity, should regional economic development be overlooked or ignored? Needs exist and this is the most propitious time to resolve them. "The question that remains is whether [the president], and Americans in general are making the most of these extraordinary times. Economic booms bring governments more revenue, as well as more breathing space. These can be frittered away, or they can be used to tackle deep-seated problems and invest in future growth. America at present, like the proverbial summer grasshopper, is doing more frittering than stockpiling."[7]

It is an opportune time to invest in infrastructure on a regional basis and eliminate barriers to interregional cooperation. Ideally there should be no need for government concern and involvement but encouragement by the federal government can bring about regional convergence at a high level. A program that has long-term benefits but requires immediate expenditures would cut across political boundaries; however, infrastructure is not considered a prime federal concern.[8]

NEED FOR A REGIONAL POLICY

Regional economic development brings about an increase in the economic well-being of businesses and residents, (e.g., profits, income or employment), with an increase in the tax base and revenues. Rather than concentrating on improving the economic fundamentals of a region, the emphasis is all too often on purchasing or bidding for jobs and would be even more so with deregulation and free markets. The constituency for economic development comes from those with a stake in the well-being of the region: regionally based businesses, elected officials, labor, and real estate interests, including homeowners.[9]

Whatever federal regional programs existed in the United States barely survived after the advent of the Reagan administration in 1980. A regional policy for the United States in the 1990s cannot merely replicate what previously existed. Problems exist such as curtailing overbidding for industry and assisting regions lacking adequate financial resources to face deindustrialization. Regional and sectoral approaches have to be combined.

BENEFITS

A consideration in formulating a regional policy is the ensuing benefits and costs between different regions. A national regional policy should not merely be an instrument for redistributing resources within a nation. Regional expenditures for research and development, education, and highway construction have positive spillover effects for other regions and the nation as a whole.[10]

A backward or declining region becomes an area in which social problems are found in greater numbers or intensity than in other parts of the country. Regional economic development can alleviate or mitigate social problems by increasing job opportunities. Thus social programs cannot be independent of economic development and a concomitant increase in job opportunities. Successful regional economic development does not necessarily alleviate poverty and social programs do not necessarily lead to long-running, self-sustaining regional economic development. This leads to recognition of the need for two separate programs.

This study encompasses a wide-ranging examination and review of a number of facets of regional economic development with a view toward contributing to an improved understanding of regional economic development, encompassing both national and subnational levels. In the United States both federal and state policy and programs are reviewed. In what direction should the president and Congress guide economic development? The review is based on an examination of the United States, Canada, Mexico, EU and supranational organizations and their impact internally on regions.

NOTES

1. Max Barlow, "A Geographical Perspective on Integration," in Glen E. Lich and Joseph A. McKinney, eds., *Region North America: Canada, United States, Mexico* (Waco, Texas: Baylor University, 1990), p. 88.

2. George C. Lodge, *Managing Globalization in the Age of Interdependence* (San Diego: Pfeiffer and Company, 1995), pp. 7, 15.

3. "If we want to understand differences in national growth rates, a good place to start is by examining differences in regional growth; if we want to understand international specialization, a good place to start is with local specialization" (p. 3). "Regional comparisons offer a huge, almost untapped source of evidence about how our economy really works" (p. 9). "Economic geography is also of considerable policy relevance. Regional issues are important in and of themselves" (p. 99). Paul Krugman, *Geography and Trade* (Cambridge, Mass.: MIT Press, 1991).

4. Steven Thomsen and Stephen Woolcock, *Direct Investment and European Integration* (London: Pinter Publishers, 1993), p. 9.

5. "Does It Matter Where You Are?" *The Economist* 332 (July 30, 1994), p. 13.

6. Ibid.

7. "Bill Clinton's Golden Moment," *The Economist* 343 (June 21, 1997), p. 16.

8. Fred R. Bleakley, "Infrastructure Dollars Pay Big Dividends State City Projects," *Wall Street Journal*, August 12, 1997, p. A2.

9. Harold Wolman and David Spitzley, "The Politics of Local Economic Development," *Economic Development Quarterly* 10 (May 1996), p. 115.

10. Timothy J. Bartik, "The Market Failure Approach to Regional Economic Development Policy," *Economic Development Quarterly* 4 (November 1990), p. 368.

Chapter 2

The Region

DEFINITION

In terms of this study, it is necessary to define the terms "region" and "regionalism." There are no accepted definitions.[1] Are the boundaries fixed historically or do they adapt to changing conditions more quickly today?[2] Regionalism presupposes that there is a regional solution for economic, political or social difficulties. Regionalism acknowledges that area-wide problems and their solutions transcend the boundaries and capabilities of local governments. Regionalism calls for broad governmental arrangements extending beyond local governments.[3]

Another definition discussed separately looks to regionalism to extend beyond national borders. Regionalism also can be used "to characterize a broad array of different economic and political processes. Typically, it is used to identify the formation of a supranational economic region (i.e., a region in which governmental policies at the national level play a diminishing role in constraining international exchange among participating countries)."[4] The European approach to defining regions as contrasted to one more relevant to the United States grows out of the differences in historic patterns. "The regions are what they are, and that is all there is to it. That is to say that history has created them thus and they must be accepted as such, with their differences because they are not born in an institution factory, they are born of history, of culture, of traditions, they have lived through particular historic events, they have lesser or greater powers."[5]

Yet interest in European regional problems is not old. Prior to the 1930s global economic crisis, the prevailing wisdom was that in respect to economic development the spatial distribution was set by natural events and that it was useless to attempt to alter that distribution. From a theoretical standpoint, regional disequilibrium was considered to be only a temporary misadjustment in a generally self-correcting mechanism of economic equilibrium.[6]

Mainstream economists have traditionally ignored regional analysis because it is a messy discipline that borrows from some half-dozen other disciplines "within the economics profession, where academics since the birth of modern economics have pretty much ignored anything smaller or larger than a single nation. But as traditional macroeconomic approaches to policy are again found wanting the study of individual regions—long a backwater of a profession that worships at the altar of elegant theory—is attracting more notice."[7]

Solving the problems of particular regions may call for more than the simple application of broad-brush macroeconomic policies. Many younger economists agree that the key to understanding everything from economic development to international trade is location, location, location.[8]

The following definition of a region still has applicability except that there currently is more unity among regional entities:

The largest territory of common concern of a functioning pattern of human settlements, which has the greatest opportunity to match problems and potential with resources—whether or not there is presently a unified regional government. Typically, regions in this country are multicounty or multistate, without focused representation, skilled research, organized decision making capacity or adequate regional policy dialogue.[9]

According to William Dodge, the term "region" is limited to areas that fall within a common or integrated development area with an independent identity in the national and international marketplace. Other definitions are a regional economic commons or a citistate.[10]

Regions in this study are subnational units of variable size, and a functioning region may not necessarily be confined within national or provincial boundaries or in the United States within a particular state. Their *raison d'être* is multipurpose and interwoven. The definitions of regions are flexible, depending on the variables to which regional policy is addressed. The focus in this review is on the economic development of subnational or substate regions in which the central government has an important role.

Regions contain remnants of features (e.g., natural physical phenomena) established in earlier periods that determined the formation of the region. The existence of natural resources and the physical limits imposed by mountains and waterways and the similarity of customs, traditions and language cannot be ignored in the establishment of regions. Yet the physical criteria upon which the region was initially formed may lose their importance over time as these natural boundaries become less significant and economic regions transcend natural and political boundaries.

Boundaries of political or administrative regions are based on government decisions that often arise from physically related regions. Political units serve to perpetuate regional boundaries. The data provided by governments delineate regions along the lines of the political boundaries, which may not necessarily coincide with a *de facto* economic region. Governments may create special purpose or functionally defined units, interjurisdictional bodies, to cope with regional matters such as transportation, water, and public safety.

The formation of regions can be influenced by establishing systems for gathering and analyzing data on a regional basis. Existing boundaries are confirmed or new configurations are established. United States federal agencies such as the Census Bureau and Bureau of Labor Statistics can issue information in a regional perspective. If a region is totally identified with a specific political entity, economic development programs stand a better chance of succeeding. The difficulties of placing responsibility and obtaining cooperation from overlapping jurisdictions may be insurmountable in terms of obtaining funding to solve regional economic problems. Also, there are few self-contained economic regions.

Static natural assets and political boundaries are less important in forming economic regions than are dynamic economic patterns such as trade, investment and programs in developing a skilled labor force, advanced infrastructure and technology. Yet political boundaries will still have meaning. However, the economic region has become the most important unit of analysis and the focus for economic development strategy. This new concept of region spans multiple political jurisdictions. This trend has required and will increasingly require new forms of collaboration among nations, states, counties and cities.[11]

REGIONAL IDENTITY

Differences in economic development within a country bring about a demand for national governments to take steps, which in turn bring about a heightened sense of regional identity as regional politics are strengthened to obtain what is considered a fair share of funds.

In addition to the economic component—the major focus of this study—regionalism has socio-psychological and political components. In its socio-psychological dimensions, regionalism refers to a set of attitudes and feelings: an identification with an area; a sense of a distinctiveness from other areas; an attachment to a territory, its people and institutions. It is the culmination of a process whereby a particular geographic space is transformed into a social space, one infused with significance and emotional connotations not attributed to other spaces.[12] The existence of local ethnic, linguistic, cultural and historic differences contributes to a sense of regional identity. As compared with Europe, ethnic and linguistic differences in the United States have not been as widespread; however, with massive immigration, there has been a geographic effect with enclaves dominated by these groups.

POLICIES

Regional policies have taken many forms, and their success has varied considerably. But the economic processes with which these policies have been concerned are changing in terms of their underlying causes. As a consequence, traditional regional policies have to be reviewed constantly.

Regional economic policy consists of public actions that affect the geographic distribution of economic phenomena such as infrastructure, population, income, government revenues, production, transport, and subsequently political power. A goal is to eliminate economic inequality.[13]

Is a regional policy necessary or desirable? According to the neoclassical theory of regional development, free competition and factor mobility tend to equalize factor returns across regions, and therefore regional differences in economic development cannot be sustained. However, in practice the anticipated results from neoclassical theory are not always realized. For example, labor and capital are not totally mobile and persistent disparities among regions may continue. Lower costs are not the only basis for location. Development or growth may tend to favor certain regions whose attraction is the existence of industry and trade with the necessary infrastructure, associated services and a more accessible market for production. Relatively well-developed areas continue to grow while more backward areas experience continued economic decline. Regional growth thus tends to be concentrated in areas already advantaged.

On a less theoretical level there is opposition to involvement by the government affecting market decisions. It is considered futile and counterproductive to interfere with secular economic trends; the investment in particular locations should be freely chosen without government incentives or inducements. According to this argument, government should not be involved in supporting regions or concerned with industry's location decisions or hindering firms from moving plants to less costly or more satisfactory locations. Regions have become increasingly reliant on national government decisions as well as those made outside the country by supranational organizations (e.g., trade arrangements such as NAFTA and WTO).

One caveat in any government involvement is that assistance should not be used merely to subsidize the relocation of industry and to reallocate resources. Before migration is encouraged or aided, the need for such migration should be evaluated in terms of whether existing resources in an area are adequate or can be upgraded at a lower cost than that of relocating.

Regional inequalities have economic and social implications and costs. The economic and social problems of less prosperous regions tend to be transmitted into other regions and to affect the overall activity of the country. A consideration is the spillover effect on other regions. Favoring one area can reduce employment or create fiscal problems elsewhere. On the other hand, growth in a region makes it a market for services and products from other regions. Technological innovation can be applied outside the source of the innovation.

Programs to assist poorer regions at the expense of richer ones can result in the poor in richer regions being overlooked while the rich in poorer regions benefit. Worker displacement or plant closing is just as likely to take place in a growth region as in a declining region. Though many displaced workers cannot easily move into new occupations or industries, regional policies can offer an avenue for attracting investment or retaining existing industry in the region and can provide an opportunity for absorbing these workers.

Regions with a large share of declining industries may suffer from an aging infrastructure and work force as well as superannuated plants and equipment and may experience intense competition from producers abroad at same time. Ossified management, deficiencies in innovation and insufficient opportunities in large, old companies for the rise of entrepreneurship are seen as impediments for overcoming the problems with ease. Depressed activity rates and low growth of per capita income are the results.

What priorities should be assigned to regional policies? When the national economy is depressed with high rates of unemployment throughout the country, regional development programs have to be secondary to macroeconomic policies designed to bring about economic recovery.

An important issue in regional policy is the role of technology. Technology has to be seen as crucial in the competitive ability of regions. How can advances in technology be made available to help less favored regions overcome their handicaps?

Regional policy at the national level traditionally has attempted to reduce socioeconomic disparities among regions by raising the level of the regions most in need of assistance. It is based on the principle that market forces alone cannot produce the necessary degree of economic growth, and this implies government involvement. If regional economies are healthy, the entire nation can benefit when social costs such as welfare are reduced.[14]

METROPOLITAN AREAS

The pattern of large dense central cities with downtowns as centers for everything from commerce and manufacturing to culture, surrounded by adjoining suburbs that in turn were surrounded by rural areas and small towns, is obsolete. The dispersion of population has led to the formation of new spatial units such as metropolitan areas.[15]

There are 330 metropolitan areas in the United States in which eight out of ten Americans reside. Over half reside in the thirty-nine metropolitan areas with populations of 1 million or more. Urban economies account for 83% of national income and virtually all employment in the advanced technical and service sectors of the future. The United States is increasingly a system of metropolitan-oriented regional economies that transcend municipal and state boundaries: "America's metropolitan regions are the engines of our national economy."[16]

The question arises as to the future of metropolitan regions because of the increasing use of information networks, communications technology and improved transportation networks. According to Michael Stegman and Margery Turner, the concentration of expertise and economic interchange in urban centers is crucial to the continued existence of knowledge intensive industries. Communications and transport costs are lowered where there are clusters. The infrastructure costs of spatial dispersion are high.[17]

Metropolitan regions are not usually a single political unit, instead consisting of mixed jurisdictions. As with other regional arrangements, there are inherent problems in finding agreement by the different component governments on policies and coordinating activities, including responsibility and sharing public expenditure. If there is a metropolitan government, it is limited in its ability unilaterally to take initiatives and assume responsibility for following through on decisions. Interdependence in terms of economic linkages varies. A major problem is that component entities continue to seek businesses from other entities.

Eighty percent or more of the goods and services in the EU and North America are produced in the urban economies that embrace cities and their suburban regions. As national trade barriers are lowered, these "city regions" in the EU and NAFTA are the real arenas for global economic competition. Another viewpoint is that region-states not city regions, are the real arenas.[18]

GLOBALIZATION

A growing share of national economic activity is affected by transactions and factors external to national borders as a decreasing share of goods and services are produced and consumed entirely within any particular national economy. The relationship between regions and nations is changing. With globalization, the role of national borders is diminished as the volume of international trade grows rapidly with progress in communications technology and new modes of transportation. Global investment and widespread corporate and personal mobility are transforming regions around the world.

Globalization challenges traditional regional policies designed to attract industry to depressed areas through spatially selective subsidies. Such policies assumed that locational choices were largely restricted to sites within the country. But with globalization, these policies have lost a degree of influence in determining the location of industry. In terms of foreign investment within a particular country, there are substantial alternative options worldwide that could negate efforts to direct investment to a particular region within a country. Furthermore, as in the United States, there is internal competition for this investment. A mitigating factor is the concern of the EU and WTO on state subsidies.

Yet there still remains a regional focus to the production of goods and services and a need for publicly financed regional infrastructure. Regional economic development programs have to adapt to these new forces. National governments will have to reconsider how the allocation of resources to backward regions can attract foreign investment which is attracted to the most favorably endowed locations. Thus, regional policy has to be adjusted not only to enhance international competitiveness but to raise the competitive level of depressed or backward regions.

Industries differ in their degree of mobility; a problem is the growth of "footloose" industries for which physical locations are irrelevant. Yet in terms of relocating from their home country, certain multinational companies have become aware that their local roots can be very valuable assets. Different countries and regions have different competitive strengths.[19] Many multinationals move no farther than their local regions, attractedby the ties of language or culture and close contact. Some modern management techniques reinforce the trend toward regionalization: a preference for keeping low inventories of finished goods (lean manufacturing) and for having suppliers deliver only when needed (just in time).

Companies utilize regional resources, the education system, infrastructure and political system and external economies also strengthened by competitors. These resources are fairly immobile. Thus a region has to offer a physical and social infrastructure superior to that offered by international competitors.[20]

REGION-STATES

Some contend that a new kind of human settlement is emerging with its own unique physical, economic and social form.[21] "The forces of globalization have made it possible to breach the territorial, social and cultural integrity of the nation-state on a daily basis....[The] need [is] to develop a new set of norms or interstate relations, a set of rules that recognizes the realms of production, exchange and consumption have largely escaped from the effective regulation of the territorial nation-state, while the people who make up that state remain largely attached to it."[22]

A well-publicized thesis espoused by Kenichi Ohmae is that as a byproduct of globalization, region-states will replace national states. National states are diminishing in importance as the foci of economic activity and their replacements are the natural economic zones, region-states. The primary linkages of these natural economic zones are not to their host countries but to the global economy. Businesses will organize their international activities on the basis of region-states rather than national states. "Region states have thus become the primary units of economic activity. It is through region-states that participation in the global economy actually takes place, largely because they are the only human scale political entities whose economic activities put the global logic of individual well-being ahead of cheap nationalism and the interest of national political elites. These region states may in fact stretch across national borders."[23]

A regional economy is a unit of about 5 million to 20 million people with a distinct skill base and industrial profile that cause it to trade not only goods and services but also people, information, technology and capital with other regional states around the world.[24] As a rule they are small enough to share a limited set of economic and consumer interests, but large enough to justify the infrastructure necessary to participate effectively in the global economy.

A viable regional economy has to be based on a community of interests, such as infrastructure, communications and industry. Fundamental to the existence of these regions are clusters of related firms. Even in an information age that facilitates dispersion, external economies, a skilled labor force and suppliers work to sustain a regional economy.

A likely source of region-states is agreement, such as NAFTA, that facilitate formation of binational regional states (e.g., between the United States and Mexico) without clear boundaries and administration. Between Canada and the United States, economic regions such as around the five Great Lakes have become very important. According to Ohmae, it will become impossible for Ontario to become the center of Canadian industry; rather it will become part of the Great Lakes industrial region. And in that context, whether regions belong to the United States, Canada or Mexico does not really matter. As national borders continue to fade, the winners of the future will not be nations but regions such as Alsace-Lorraine, Wales, Kansas, Orange County or North Carolina.[25] But rather than remain part of a national state, regions are demanding independence as a national state (e.g., Quebec, Northern Italy, Spanish provinces, and Flanders and Wallonia in Belgium).

A factor in the formation of region-states is location, proximity to a border or to the sea. Proximity to a border leads to economic ties between regions in the adjoining countries. Where there are arrangements such as the European Union, national borders are easier to transcend. Another factor is size, which makes possible a high degree of self-sufficiency. Efforts to strengthen the role of regions in a national state or a state within the United States are moderated by the threat to the power of these existing governmental entities.

CLUSTERS

A key consideration receiving increasing attention in the study of regional economies is geographic concentration in the same or related industries and the advantages gained by linkages between them and the potential for increased efficiency through specialization and the relationship to globalization. "Economic activity commonly clusters in space. Of that there can be no doubt."[26] Industry clusters are geographic concentrations of similar industries sharing technical, skill, financial or distributional advantages; specialized buyer-supplier relationships and dependencies; and evolving to duplicate competitive advantages in the marketplace over time.[27]

A U.S. Department of Commerce Report optimistically identifies 380 clusters that drive the U.S. economy.[28] They employ 57% of the U.S. work force, generate 61% of the nation's output and produce 78% of its exports.[29]

Agglomeration economies arise from geographic concentration of a large number of economic activities served jointly by different facilities, such as transportation, a skilled labor force, financial institutions, proximity of markets for their output and the potential for technological breakthroughs.

Preceding the interest in clusters was the preference for diversification of industry. Traditionally, policy strategists have favored a diversified industry base rather than a specialized one. Specialization was generally seen as a disadvantage in regard to a region's susceptibility to drops in employment in the major sectors in slow growth periods. This premise led to demands for increased diversification as the best long-run industry structure and the best potential for a sound regional economy, avoiding too great a reliance on a few fast but transitory growth industries. There would be a cushion to offset downturns in employment in particular industries. Thus, the ideal industry mix would contain an employment mix that minimizes instabilities in the regional economy.[30]

This conventional viewpoint of the dependence of a regional economy on diversification has been questioned. Highly diversified regions could have an economic base of industries whose standard production techniques reflect the mature stage of the product cycle. With deindustrialization, globalism, technology, transportation and locational patterns, depth rather than breadth becomes crucial. A limited number of key sectors becomes the goal. Hence the standard assumption that industry diversification is a precondition for high growth potential may be misplaced, challenging conventional arguments for diversification.[31]

A differing view stresses the importance of diversification in clustering. Diversification in terms of external economies is particularly important to smaller companies and is "less strongly related to the proximity or density of clusters of similar businesses."[32] Clustering is not a new concept. Alfred Marshall (1842–1924) coined the term "industrial district" for the regional clustering of firms from the same industry with complementary and competing products and services, and its most prominent proponent has been Michael E. Porter.[33] The cluster theory is just as applicable to smaller areas such as the inner city as it is to relatively large areas such as nations and states.[34]

Less attention should be paid to interest rates, trade statistics and industrial policy than to studying geography. Porter questions the conventional wisdom that global markets, computer networks and modern communications have obliterated the importance of geography in business. A firm prefers to locate where there are concentrations of skilled labor, important suppliers, markets and sources of technological progress or innovation such as universities or laboratories. Geographic proximity of competitors enhances the growth of the cluster's competitive advantage; cost of infrastructure is spread over a wider base. There is evidence that eye-to-eye contact is more important than ever.[35] He contends that concentration in industries is occurring despite the electronics and telecommunications revolutions that make possible instant communication between widely dispersed technicians. Physical proximity is still an asset.[36]

There is a difference between industries that rely chiefly on cost factors regardless of location and those that rely on a supply of skills and networks of specialized firms. Regional policy will be more effective if based on the principle of building on clusters. Magnets for clusters in the form of universities, research laboratories, specialized infrastructure or trained labor pools are much more effective than subsidies. The most effective regional policy determines the bases of industry strength and utilizes them to build spatially concentrated clusters. One industry can create a climate conducive to other industries. This approach is by far superior to attempting to persuade unrelated groups of firms to establish facilities in a location in which there will be no upgrading or expansion.[37]

Regional policy is less effective when it involves generalized subsidies to induce firms to locate plants or other facilities in a region. Depressed areas do not become a true home base; it is necessary for one firm to reinforce competitive advantage in others and to stimulate new business formation.[38] There are benefits in employment from clusters. Firms have access to a labor force with suitable skills. Qualified individuals know if they lose their jobs, they have a better chance of finding new jobs and there are more opportunities to advance by changing their jobs. The need for uprooting and relocating families is minimized.

PUBLIC POLICY

One view is that public policy toward economic development should emphasize existing and growing clusters of firms that have a competitive advantage in their industries. Public policy should abstain from subsidies that seek to establish clusters where they do not naturally take place.[39] Public sector participation in clusters should focus on the most productive firms in a region. Such firms are characterized by high levels of investment to sustain their productivity and market shares. From the standpoint of the public role, assisting the efforts of the most productive firms will ensure that subsidies are not given to aid inefficient operations, poor locational choices or short-lived gains.[40] Under this approach declining regions will have even more difficulty reviving. A more equitable approach should be to use the cluster concept to assist distressed regions.

Porter offers little support for targeted federal assistance to critically important industries. Growth of industries into competitive powers usually depends more on local factors. He prefers non-intervention by government in creating clusters. However, once a cluster begins to form, government at all levels can play a role in reinforcing it and a state and local role is essential.[41]

Central government policy on cluster formation is best directed toward encouraging and supporting many localized efforts rather than a few centrally chosen ones. Governments have a poor track record in selecting sectors where subtle conditions of national advantage are present.[42]

The government concern with regional industrial clusters should be with state and local governments, which are best able to provide the physical and educational infrastructure required by industry.[43] The missing ingredient is funding; the federal government rather than state and local governments is a better source of such funding. Even some of those who accept Porter's analysis contend that there is a need for much more direct support from the federal government than Porter favors.[44]

Government has an important role in the formation and support of clusters such as support of universities and research facilities, in providing infrastructure and in enforcing regulations. "The clusters of the future will be induced by national strategies," said Porter's Harvard Business School colleague, George C. Lodge. "To have clusters soon enough and strong enough, government will have to have a role."[45] Clusters are magnets that can become home bases for foreign as well as U.S. companies thereby attracting jobs, investment and technology to the U.S. The federal government can help mainly by promoting the conditions under which clusters flourish.[46]

Industry clusters should be targeted investment. Sustainable economic development comes from industry clusters and not from the usual practice of supporting individual businesses. Thus, instead of investing public funds in efforts to attract individual companies, states should develop comprehensive strategies designed to meet the particular needs of industry clusters. In addition, incentive and development programs should not favor new firms at the expense of existing firms, but rather should support entire clusters by filling critical gaps in the ranks of core industries, support firms or specialized economic foundations.[47]

CLUSTERS AND TECHNOLOGY

Considering the advanced and highly developed communications and transportation systems and the existence of a national market for skilled labor and capital goods in the United States, it could be expected that the United States would "approach the limiting case of immediate, costless diffusion of technology." But proximity is a vital consideration[48]: "Geography does make a difference in the speed of adoption of advanced technologies. Proximity to other users of technology is associated with higher rates of adoption, and this effect remains apparent even when industry and other plant characteristics are taken into account."[49]

Labor or human capital appears to be a key component of the proximity; it apparently affects positively not only the productivity used in a given stock of physical capital but also the incorporation of technology in the capital stock. Almost no evidence was found in 1993 that compared with smaller and less urban areas, the center-city counties of large metropolitan areas had a significant disadvantage in respect to technology use. To the contrary the data suggest that between 1988 and 1993 there was a positive association between a core urban location and an increase in the number of technologies used. Certain new technologies may be particularly suited to urban manufacturing.[50] A study of locations within urban or metropolitan areas is warranted to provide information on the location variables that determine site selection.

Clusters vary in terms of how they grow or stagnate. Silicon Valley in California and Route 128 in Massachusetts, two technology-based clusters, had similar origins, post–World War II spending and university research. Silicon Valley recovered from the 1980 downturn while Route 128 was not able to recover as quickly: "The simple fact of spatial proximity evidently reveals little about the ability of firms to respond to the fast changing markets and technologies that now characterize international competition."[51]

Despite their similar origins and technologies unique industrial systems evolved in Silicon Valley and Route 128. These distinctions reveal the importance of the components of industrial adaptation. Silicon Valley has a regional network-based industrial system that promotes learning and mutual adjustment among the specialist producers of a complex of related technologies. On the other hand, Route 128 is dominated by "autarkic" corporations that internalize a broad range of productive activities. Silicon Valley has greater external communication, while Route 128 is more internally focused.[52] In both clusters technology firms have shifted their routine manufacturing operations to lower-wage areas.

This comparison of Silicon Valley and Route 128 industries highlights the analytical leverage gained by treating regions as networks of relationships rather than as collections of atomistic firms. By transcending the theoretical distinction between what lies inside and outside the firm, this approach offers important insights into the structure and dynamics of regional economies. It directs attention to the complex networks of social relationships within and between firms and local institutions....

The Silicon Valley experience also suggests that the network form of organization flourishes in regional agglomerations. Proximity facilitates the repeated, face-to-face interaction that fosters the mix of competition and collaboration required in today's fast paced technology industries. Yet the case of Route 128 demonstrates that geographic clustering alone does not ensure the emergence of regional networks. Competitive advantage derives as much from the way that skill and technology are organized as from their presence in a regional environment.[53]

There has been a shift in the utilization of the facilities on Route 128. The 1991–1992 recession was strengthened by technological shifts and reductions in defense spending, leading to the subsequent conversion of former research and industrial facilities into high-priced office space with a variety of occupants.[54]

A more cautious viewpoint about clusters and technology is expressed by Bennett Harrison et al.: "While clustering may promote interfirm learning about technologies, its is unlikely to be sufficient—and may even be relatively less important than had been thought—once characteristics of the individual firm's relationship to its more complex organizational environment are taken into account. The question can be explored only by simultaneously studying the impacts of technology, business organization and location on innovative behavior."[55]

Is technology eliminating the need for face-to-face or human contact? Clusters belie the belief that they are no longer important. Advanced technology does not make place unimportant, but it does facilitate a sorting-out process in which certain functions can be decentralized.[56]

COMMENTS

Clustering is not necessarily applicable nor beneficial to all firms. The relevance of clustering as a determinant of location varies by industry, as exemplified by the exodus of production to locations outside the United States. Yet clustering has been a key consideration in the concentration of certain industries.

A distinction has to be drawn between those parts of corporate activity where spatial proximity is important and where it is not. The view of those…who have studied this is that commercial (sales, strategic, or financial) and basic scientific networks can work well at a long distance. However, dealing with practical, production-related issues, such as designing software or making product adjustments or applications, tend to be geographically a clustering phenomenon. Trust is built between lower managers, and the networks that they build are kept going for as long as possible until they are destroyed by mergers or acquisitions.

The practical nature of network relationships is echoed in a second important spatial dimension of successful systems of networks, which is the fact that local and regional context matters. If the relationships between public and private organizations concerning business services, finance, innovation, and training are cooperative then the overall performance of firms situated in such a regional milieu is better than it would otherwise be.[57]

There is the contention that technical and competitive forces are at work in the geographic distribution of jobs. Technical changes are freeing work from its geographic restraints while competitive realities are concentrating jobs in networks of metropolitan areas.[58] There are a variety of forces encouraging the dispersion of jobs. As raw material becomes a less important ingredient in production, proximity is less important. In addition, location near major transportation nodes becomes less important as networks are connected more by information and communications technology and less by physical transport. Moreover advances in air transport reduce the importance of location near land and water transport sites. Finally, the technical ability to reach far-flung domestic and global markets has resulted in a self-propelled extension of competitive networks beyond local markets.[59]

But at the same time, new competitive requirements tend to concentrate job growth in population centers. The increasing service content of economic competition encourages proximity to allow personal contact both inside and outside the firm. Concentration of partners among and within metropolitan networks is further encouraged by access to rapid transportation and a high concentration of customers in urban areas. Moreover, centrality of learning in the new economy encourages location in population centers with access to educational and research and development infrastructure. Therefore, most jobs are being created in the extensive networks of the densely populated metropolitan areas. In the South and West most new jobs are in urban areas. Urbanization of job creation does not preclude rural or small town development. The ability of smaller communities to develop their economies depends more on their ability to find a niche in a broader network and less on their ability to develop independently.[60]

A criticism of the cluster theory is that the clustering or concentration of an industry in a region has a potential downside. When a key industry in a region weakens, there is overdependence on this industry and the period of recovery is prolonged.[61] An economic base of firms involved in both innovative and mass production may offer the soundest foundation for actual and future growth.

As industries shift production abroad to take advantage of low-cost foreign labor and to gain footholds in protected foreign markets, the importance of clusters may be declining. Michael Porter acknowledges that industries are becoming globalized in this way. But he states that the increasing importance of flexibility and innovation in the fast-moving economy of the 1990s has made regional clusters even more important.[62]

Spatial clustering alone does not create mutually beneficial interdependencies. An industrial system may be geographically agglomerated and yet have limited capacity for adaptation. This is overwhelmingly a function of organizational structure, not of technology or of firm size.[63]

Charles Sabel of MIT supports a plan to expand networks of regional technology centers. More is involved than merely transferring technology. Small businesses face a multitude of problems, such as finding appropriate organizational structures for training and product development, that they can no longer solve in isolation. Yet vehicles for interindustry cooperation and dialogue, such as trade associations, are moribund. The industrial future lies in promoting flexible clusters or networks of companies that compete, while benefiting from many formal and informal links. This is the type of industrial structure that seems to account for the continuing dynamism of Silicon Valley.[64]

STRATEGIES

Regions have become the primary units of economic geography in the new global economy. Regions compete with each other not only internally but also globally. To compete in this new arena calls for a parallel restructuring of economics and governance at the regional level.[65]

Empowerment zones and local community development, rather than regions, have become the focus of economic development efforts in the United States. Changes are most visible at the local level and are thus easy to mobilize politically. However, the separation of the place of employment from the place of residence subordinates local economic development to regional development. Thus, in reality there is a closer connection to the region in terms of employment and income than to the neighborhood residence.

Small area multipliers tend to be very low in terms of income flows, regardless of whether the residents are rich or poor. Neighborhoods generally reveal more economic dependence than autonomy. Particularly in the generation of income, they are dependent on the larger urban and regional economies within which they function.[66]

For a regional economy to function effectively, it is desirable to reduce the barriers among governmental entities in the region and to make residents aware of the importance of the region for their economic welfare. Their efforts are better directed at improving the housing stock, education, environment and municipal services.

In the discussions of diversification versus clustering or specialization, economies at all spatial levels cannot rely on the status quo. There is a need to search continually for new industries and to support existing industries. Once production becomes standardized or routine, with globalization it is apt to be transferred to countries with the lowest costs of production. The only means of preserving the economies of well-developed, mature regions is for them to place their resources constantly in the creation of new industries that add wealth to the local economy before they begin to expand globally, the "get smart" strategy. The other option is to attempt to maintain the existing industrial structure, as it declines when confronted by external innovation and competition, the "get poor" option.[67] This approach may overemphasize new industries while resources might be devoted to upgrading existing industries.

Though a region may have an unbalanced industrial structure and seek to correct that by bringing in new firms, there should be a logical basis for recruiting industry in terms of the soundness of the new industry and its compatibility with the region. Unfortunately, in some situations there may not be any options or choice in rejecting industry. This applies to severely distressed areas.

From a long-range standpoint, an effective regional development policy must be flexible and adaptable in the face of changing conditions. Conditions within a region change with time. Predicting the future shape of regional economies and the sort of problems that will arise requires ongoing monitoring to detect prospective change. Policies and programs may have to be altered, dropped or replaced. Likewise, regional priorities may have to be shifted. One problem is that too many regions have a short-term focus. Political officials are primarily concerned with the effect of economic development on their election prospects; the immediate is preferred over the long range.[68]

Central governments cannot remain indifferent indefinitely to the changing economic geography of the country, to the consequential problems that arise and to the economic opportunities that might be lost without their intervention. This applies both locally and over wide geographical areas. No government can long escape its responsibility to take strategic views of interrelationships between its international and national policies on one hand and local and regional development issues on the other. Even the least interventionist administration requires the means to interpret these interrelationships through formal dialogue and information exchange. It also needs the ability to reconcile those elements that are contradictory.[69]

NOTES

1. "Region" is almost as elusive a word as "planning." Presumably a region is a geographical area defined by certain common and distinguishing characteristics. But as the word is so broadly interpreted, it is too elastic and flexible to be of much value. Paul Conklin, "Intellectual and Political Roots," in Erwin C. Hargrove and Paul K. Conklin, *TVA–Fifty Years of Grass-Roots Bureaucracy* (Urbana: University of Illinois Press, 1983), p. 26.

2. On the historical derivation of the term "region," see Perry Anderson, *The Invention of the Region 1945–1990* (Florence, Italy: European University Institute, 1994), Working Paper EUF, Number 94/2.

3. In the United States regionalism as a concept for meeting problems and

26   REGIONAL ECONOMIC DEVELOPMENT

needs was recognized and enunciated in 1927. A need existed for developing regional planning and regional government, that is, the formulation of regional plans and the creation of regional legislative and executive institutions to carry them out. Alfred Bettman, "How to Acquire Parks and Other Open Spaces," in *City and Regional Planning Papers, Harvard City Planning Studies, Vol. 3* (Cambridge: Harvard University Press), 1946, p. 80. Cited in William Bonner, "Rural Development," in Frank S. So, Irving Hand and Bruce D. McDowell, *The Practice of State and Regional Planning* (Chicago: International City Management Association and American Planning Association, 1986), p. 366.

4. Andrew Hughes Hallett and Carlos A. Primo Braga, *The New Regionalism and the Threat of Protectionism* (Washington: The World Bank, International Trade Division, International Economic Department, August 1994), Research Work Paper 1349, p. 3.

   5. Carlo Bernini, president of the Assembly of European Regions, Minutes of General Meeting, December 5 and 6, 1990.

   6. Norbert Vanhove and Leo H. Klassen, *Regional Policy: A European Approach*, 2d ed. (Teakfield, UK: Saxon House, 1987), p. 1.

   7. Sylvia Nasar, "New Debate on Regional Economics,"*New York Times*, December 30, 1993, p. D1.

   8. Ibid., p. D11.

   9. William R. Ewald, *Information, Perception and Regional Policy* (Washington: National Science Foundation, Research Applications Directorate, Division of Intergovernmental Science and Public Technology, 1975) Grant No. GI 41666, p. 24.

   10. William R. Dodge, *Regional Excellence: Governing Together to Compete Globally and Flourish Locally* (Washington: National League of Cities, 1996), p. 38; Neal R. Pierce with Curtis W. Johnson and John Stuart Hall, *Citistates How Urban America Can Prosper in a Competitive World* (Washington: Seven Locks Press, 1993) and Robert A. Beauregard, "Denationalizing Cities," ECSA Review 11 (Fall, 1998), p. 7.

   11. Mary Jo Waits and Karol Kahalley, "Organizing Economic Development in the 1990s: The Price of Prosperity." Paper presented to the American Society of Public Administration/CASU 54th National Training Conference, San Francisco, July 1993, p. 19.

   12. Jacques Vandamme, "Regionalism in Europe," Chapter 3 in David Cameron, ed., *Regionalism and Supranationalism* (Montreal and London: Institute for Research on Public Policy and Policy Studies Institute, 1981), pp. 58–59.

   13. Niles Hansen, Benjamin Higgins and Donald J. Savoie, *Regional Policy in a Changing World* (New York: Plenum Press, 1990), p. 1.

   14. Organization for Economic Cooperation and Development, *Regional Policy Developments in OECD Countries* (Paris: 1989), p. 16.

   15. For an early study of this phenomenon see S. George Walters, Morris L. Sweet and Max D. Snider, "When Industry Moves to Interurbia,"*Sales Management* 82 (February 20, 1959), in S. George Walters, Morris L. Sweet and Max D. Snider, *Marketing Management Viewpoints: Commentary and Readings* (Cincinnati: South-Western Publishing, 1970), p. 89.

   16. Michael A. Stegman and Margery Austin Turner, "The Future of Urban America in the Global Economy," *Journal of the American Planning Association* 62 (Spring 1996), p. 157.

   17. Ibid., p. 160, and Kelly Ragan and Bharat Trehan, "Cities and

Productivity," *Journal of Commerce* (September 21, 1998), p. 5a.

18. *Divided Cities in the Global Economy: Human Strategies,* European-North American State of the Cities Report (Washington: German Marshall Fund of the U.S., 1992), p. i.

19. The terms "multinational" and "transnationals" have been defined differently but are now used interchangeably.

20. "A Survey of Multinationals," *The Economist* 335 (June 24, 1995), p. 10.

21. "Global City Regions: Searching for Common Ground," *Landlines,* Newsletter of the Lincoln Institute of Land Policy, January 1996, p. 1.

22. Michael Hart, "A Multilateral Agreement on Foreign Direct Investment: Why Now?" in Pierre Sauve and Daniel Schwanen, eds., *Investment Rules for the Global Economy Enhancing Access to Markets* (Toronto: C. D. Howe Institute, September 1996), p. 75.

23. Kenichi Ohmae, "New World Order: The Rise of the Region-State," *Wall Street Journal,* August 16, 1994, p. A16.

24. Kenichi Ohmae, "Trade Watchers Should Focus on Regions, not Nations," *Wall Street Journal,* January 27, 1993, p. A16.

25. Kenichi Ohmae, "Beyond Friction to Fact: The Borderless Economy," *New Perspectives Quarterly* 7 (Spring 1990), p. 20; for comments see "Global Citizen Ken," *The Economist* 333 (October 22, 1994), p. 77.

26. Bennett Harrison, Maryellen R. Kelley, and Jon Gant, "Specialization Versus Diversity in Local Economies: The Implications for Innovative Private-Sector Behavior," *Cityscape, A Journal of Policy Development and Research* (HUD) 2 (May 1996), p. 84.

27. U.S. Department of Commerce, National Technical Information Service, *America's Clusters: Building Industry Clusters,* report prepared by DRI–McGraw Hill, June 1996, p. 1.

28. Ibid., p. 9.

29. Ibid., p. 11.

30. Stephen F. Seninger, *A Policy Analysis of Labor Market Dislocation and Foreign Competition* (Baltimore: University of Maryland Graduate School, Thomas M. Bradley Center for Employment and Training Education and Research, Spring 1987), p. 7.

31. Ibid.

32. Harrison et al., "Specialization," pp. 61, 84.

33. Michael E. Porter, *The Competitive Advantage of Nations* (New York: The Free Press, 1990).

34. Michael E. Porter, "The Competitive Advantage of the Inner City," *Harvard Business Review* 73 (May–June 1995), p. 57.

35. Dan Morgan, "Think Locally, Win Globally Harvard's Porter Pushes Regional Cluster as the Key," *Washington Post,* April 5, 1992, p. H1.

36. Ibid.

37. Porter, *The Competitive Advantage of Nations,* p. 657.

38. Ibid.

39. Mark S. Rosentraub and Michael Przyblski, "Competitive Advantage, Economic Development and the Effective Use of Local Public Dollars," *Economic Development Quarterly* 10 (November 1996), p. 317.

40. Ibid., p. 321.

41. Porter, *The Competitive Advantage of Nations*, p. 654.

42. Ibid., p. 656.

43. Norman Boucher, "Bends in the River: A Natural History of the Connecticut Valley Metal Trade," *Regional Review,* Federal Reserve Bank of Boston 4 (Winter 1994), p. 11.

44. Morgan,"Think Locally," p. H6.

45. Ibid., p. H1.

46. Ibid., p. H46.

47. Mary Jo Waits, Karol Kahalley and Rick Heffernon, "Organizing for Economic Development: New Realities Call for New Rules," *Public Administration Review* 52 (November–December 1992), pp. 614–615.

48. Jane Sneddon Little and Robert K. Triest, "Technological Diffusion in U.S. Manufacturing: The Geographic Dimension," *Proceedings, Technology and Growth Conference* (Federal Reserve Bank of Boston, June 1996), Series 40, p. 215.

49. Ibid.

50. Ibid., pp. 243–244.

51. Annalee Saxenian, "Regional Networks and Industrial Adaptation in Silicon Valley and Route 128," *Cityscape, A Journal of Policy Development and Research* (HUD) 2 (May 1996), p. 44, and Cynthia A. Kroll with Ashok Deo Bardhan, "A Global Reshaping of the Computer Industry," *Research Report* (University of California, Berkeley, Winter 1997/1998), pp. 1–6.

52. Ibid., p. 45.

53. Ibid., p. 57.

54. Ross Kerber, "Boston's Route 128 Back on Fast Track," *Wall Street Journal,* 30 July 1997, p. B10.

55. Harrison, et al., p. 66.

56. Todd Swanstron, "Ideas Matter: Reflections on the New Regionalism," *Cityscape, A Journal of Policy Development and Research* (HUD) 2 (May 1996), p. 9.

57. P. Cooke and K. Morgan, "The Network Paradigm: New Departures in Corporate and Regional Development," *Environment and Planning D: Society and Space* 11 (October 1993), Pion Limited, London, pp. 553–564.

58. Anthony Patrick Carnevale, *America and the New Economy* (American Society for Training and Development and U.S. Department of Labor Employment and Training Administration, 1991), p. 85.

59. Ibid.

60. Ibid.

61. Michael S. Lelyveld, "New Data Says Regional Dependence on Key Industries Poses Risk," *Journal of Commerce* (November 1, 1993), p. 14A, and Bennett Harrison, *Lean and Mean: The Changing Landscape of Corporate Power in the Age of Flexibility* (New York: Basic Books, 1994), p. 8.

62. Morgan, "Think Locally.", p. H1.

63. Annalee Saxenian, *Regional Advantage Culture and Competition in Silicon Valley* (Cambridge: Harvard University Press, 1994), p. 161.

64. Michael Prowse, "Harvard Hopefuls Hazy on Details," *Financial Times,* November 16, 1992, p. 32.

65. R. Scott Fosler, "Revitalizing State Economies," in E. Blaine Liner, ed., *A Decade of Devolution Perspectives on State Local Relations* (Washington: Urban Institute Press, 1989), p. 98, cited in Pierce, *Citistates,* p. 294.

66. Michael B. Teitz, "Neighborhood Economics: Local Communities and Regional Markets," *Economic Development Quarterly* 3 (May 1989), p. 117.

67. John E. Jackson, "Initiation and Implementation of a Creation Strategy," Chapter 8 in R. Scott Fosler, ed., *The New Economic Role of American States Strategies in a Competitive World Economy* (New York: Oxford University Press, 1988), p 134.

68. Hansen, Higgins and Savoie, *Regional Policy*, p. 291.

69. David Wadley, *Restructuring the Regions Analysis, Policy Model and Prognosis* (Paris: Organization for Economic Cooperation and Development, 1986), p. 116.

Chapter 3

Supranational Organizations

INTRODUCTION

The subject of internal economic development on a spatial basis or for specific industries has to be resolved within the framework of supranational, global, multilateral and bilateral trade agreements. In the United States subsidies now have to be reviewed in terms of the North American Free Trade Agreement and World Trade Organization. Voluntary agreements and codes of conduct of an informal nature—soft law—have become hard law, formal treaties, binding agreements between governments. For example, the WTO covers a growing body of international trade rules that govern member nations' rights, for example, controlling government subsidies.[1]

Most industries are affected, even those that function entirely within one country. With the expansion of trading agreements, the importance of tariffs is reduced and nontariff factors become more important. Their purpose may be to achieve domestic policy goals, such as internal spatial subsidies. Nontariff barriers are more complex than tariffs and more difficult to measure or control.

Do NAFTA, Asia-Pacific Economic Cooperation (APEC) and the European Union (EU) signal the triumph of multinational regionalism?

Is there a realization that global firms operating in global markets will sooner or later face global rules? How will the various regional blocs interact with their overlapping rules and structures, dual memberships? What are the possibilities of an "eventual convergence" under the aegis of the WTO?[2]

An aspect is the process of growing sovereignty of supranational organizations and the implications for subnational regions. International trade agreements reduce the ability of nations to pursue autonomous economic policies. Traditional subnational regional policy is challenged. The result is that instead of allocating resources to depressed regions, nations may increasingly feel the need to favor their most dynamic sectors and locations so as to optimize national competitiveness and therefore to enhance the chances of attracting transnational enterprise capital.[3]

The proliferation of international agreements across a broad range of policy areas could alter the internal distribution of powers in federal states.[4] As international trade agreements become increasingly important in the U.S. economy, they will play a greater role in determining the level and character of state and local policies. Trade treaties or international agreements approved by Congress or any legislation or regulations pursuant to such agreements are superior to inconsistent state or local laws.[5]

Changes in the perceived locational preferences for development and expansion and for new spatial configurations make a difference in what were formerly deemed desirable locations. Globalization, improved telecommunications, transportation, technology and provisions of WTO and regional agreements are factors that limit the influence of state and national governments. In terms of NAFTA and WTO, only national governmental entities have formal status; however, subnational entities can exert influence on the national governments and the agreements. Subnational governments in turn have sought a voice in the drafting of the agreements.

Additional regional agreements as represented by the EU, NAFTA and APEC can become increasingly important in U.S. economic life. A tripartite industrialized world is envisioned with major blocs in the EU, North America and Asia-Pacific: "It could well be that the integrated regional trading bloc would replace the nation as the principal negotiating unit in the GATT and that a formalized and recognized two tier application of the MFN principle—stronger obligations to bloc members than to other GATT members—would become a standard feature of U.S., Japanese and EC-member policies."[6]

Supranational organizations vary considerably in the degree of common decision-making. NAFTA is much less centralized and narrower in scope than the EU. A free trade area is the least restrictive along a continuum of arrangements:

1.   Free-trade areas in which free trade is established between members but each
     state retains its own independent trade policies with non-members.
     Restrictions in respect to trade between the members are eliminated or
     reduced. It is the least comprehensive of the various supranational agree-
     ments.
2.   Customs unions are free trade areas that have common trade policies and tar-
     iffs with respect to non-members. In addition to eliminating barriers to free
     movement of goods and services between members, there is equalization of
     tariffs relative to imports from third countries.
3.   Common markets are customs unions within which the factors of production
     (capital, labor and entrepreneurship) move freely. There can be a combina-
     tion of common policies and national policies with respect to non-member
     countries.
4.   Economic unions are identical to common markets except that facets of
     macroeconomic policy, rather than unilaterally retained by member states,
     are delegated to a central authority attaining a degree of harmonization of
     diverse national economic policies.
5.   Economic and monetary union adds a common currency to the economic
     union. At the end of the spectrum, economic union reaches a point of eco-
     nomic integration and national policies are unified under a supranational
     authority.

TRANSATLANTIC FREE TRADE AGREEMENT

In 1995, proposals were made for a Transatlantic Free Trade
Agreement (TAFTA) consisting of Canada, the United States and the EU;
subsequently Mexico was included. It would cover some 770 million people. Among the areas to be pursued was the strengthening of subsidy
disciplines. The regional arrangement would be WTO-compatible and
would effectively strengthen the multilateral trading system. A free trade
area would be a component.

The EU is responsible for over 50% of all Foreign Direct Investment
(FDI) in the United States while U.S. FDI in the EU represents 40% of total
U.S. FDI. Some 3 million jobs on each side of the Atlantic depend on these
investments. In 1994, 17.6% (ECUs 95 billion) of EU exports went to the
United States and 17.3% (ECUs 93 billion) of EU imports came from the
United States. U.S. exports to EU represented 22% (ECUs 83 billion) of
total U.S. exports, and imports from the EU totaled almost 16.4% (ECUs
87 billion) of total U.S. imports.[7]

A problem was the need to conform to the WTO rules, and TAFTA
could be counterproductive if it gave developing countries the impression
of a "rich men's club" leaving the rest of world behind. In order to conform to WTO rules, free-trade areas must cover "substantially all trade."[8]

One consequence of the creation of a Transatlantic Economic Space
would be to gradually render unnecessary the use of antidumping and

countervailing duty measures by one side against the other. However, they have been maintained in NAFTA.⁹ A result of the negotiations has been an emphasis on resolving particular trade issues rather than on formation of a supranational organization.

REGIONAL ALIGNMENTS

Beyond North America, Europe and Asia, other regional alignments are in the making, such as the five nations of Africa's Maghreb region—Algeria, Libya, Mauritania, Morocco and Tunisia. Chile has been considered the next member of NAFTA. South American countries have several regional arrangements. APEC includes Australia, Brunei, Canada, Chile, China, Indonesia, Japan, South Korea, Malaysia, Mexico, New Zealand, Papua New Guinea, the Philippines, Singapore, Taiwan, Thailand and the United States.

Regional blocs in Latin America include the Caribbean Community (CARICOM), the Central American Common Market and the five nations of the Andean Pact—Bolivia, Colombia, Ecuador, Peru and Venezuela. Farther south, the free trade agreement known as Mercosur consists of Argentina, Paraguay, Brazil and Uruguay.

Almost every member of the WTO is a member of a regional free trade agreement. WTO lists at least seventy-six free trade areas or customs unions established or modified since 1948. The coverage of the agreements varies considerably.[10]

Regional integration agreements have to be differentiated on the basis of reciprocal and nonreciprocal agreements. In a reciprocal agreement each member agrees to reduce barriers to trade; and a nonreciprocal agreement has been formulated by developed countries to assist developing countries without asking for reciprocity from the developing countries. Few agreements eliminate the use of nontariff border measures between members such as import licensing, antidumping and countervailing (CVD) measures.[11]

THE FEDERAL GOVERNMENT AND INTERNATIONAL TRADE

The role of the federal government in international trade derives from the U.S. Constitution, Article 1, Section 8, which grants Congress broad, comprehensive and exclusive authority to regulate commerce with foreign nations. While Congress has retained a prime role in international trade policy, it has delegated significant authority to the executive branch. In 1934, Congress gave the president the power to negotiate international trade agreements for the reduction of tariffs. Congress and the president have further delegated their responsibilities by having numerous federal agencies administer a wide variety of trade laws and programs.

The U.S. Trade Representative (USTR) and Commerce Department share major responsibilities in formulating, coordinating and implementing U.S. trade policy. The USTR has primary responsibility for developing and coordinating U.S. international trade policy and lead responsibility for the conduct of international trade.

The USTR is a relatively small agency located in the Executive Office of the President with a 1994 budget of some $22 million and a staff of some 170 people. It is headed by the U.S. Trade Representative, a Cabinet-level official with the rank of ambassador, who acts as the principal trade adviser, negotiator and spokesperson for the president on trade and related investment matters. It is responsible for developing and coordinating international trade, commodity and direct investment policy and leading or directing negotiations with other countries on such matters. USTR guides formulation of trade policy through an interagency process.[12]

Section 301[13]

Section 301 of the Trade Act of 1974 as amended is broader in scope than antidumping or countervailing actions. It covers any restraint on U.S. trade. Action by the USTR is mandated when a foreign practice or policy violates an agreement with the United States or is unjustifiable and burdens U.S. commerce. Remedies are the imposition of duties or other import restrictions, suspension or withdrawal of concessions made in trade agreements and agreements with the offending country to remove the practice or policy or to eliminate the burden on U.S. commerce.

The Department of Commerce is a much larger and more complex organization than the USTR, with a 1994 budget of some $350 million and a staff of some 2,800 people.[14] The Department of Commerce shares responsibilities with the International Trade Commission (ITC) for administering countervailing duty and antidumping laws. Under these laws the U.S. government can place a duty on imports of goods that are being unfairly subsidized or dumped (i.e., unfairly sold below market prices) in the United States to the detriment of U.S. firms. Commerce's International Trade Administration (ITA) supplies much of the information and analyses that support formulation of U.S. trade policy and strategy and is responsible for determining whether subsidization or dumping has taken place, while in a parallel proceeding in another agency, ITC seeks to determine whether injury has occurred to U.S. firms as a result of the subsidies or dumping. If subsidization or dumping and injury exists, duties can be imposed on the importers. Commerce also provides information and analyses that the U.S. Trade Representative uses in performing investigations into other unfair trade practices under Section 301.

Subsidies

In reviewing the agreements, account has to be taken of subsidies, especially for regional development. The antidumping duties (AD) and countervailing duties (CVD) of the constituent nations were crucial factors in the Canada-U.S. Free Trade Agreement (CUFTA), NAFTA and WTO negotiations. This leads to consideration of key provisions in U.S. law covering antidumping and countervailing duties. Imposition of CVD laws in many countries is subject to the policy discretion of the government, whereas in the United States it is mandatory.[15]

Antidumping

The origins of antidumping law are in Title VII of the Tariff Act of 1930 as amended. The law provides relief in the form of special additional duties that are intended to offset margins of dumping. Antidumping law acts against international price discrimination (sales at a lower price in the United States than in the home country of the exporter) and sales below cost. Contrary to the popular notion that antidumping is selling below cost, in both law and economic theory it is defined as international price discrimination or charging a higher price for sales in a foreign producer's home country than for export to the United States.[16]

COUNTERVAILING

The best domestic analogue to subsidized products in international trade is the subsidies granted by state and local governments (often as tax breaks) in exchange for firms' locating in the state or locality. Products the firm then produces in this location and exports to other states are subsidized in like fashion as the subsidized foreign exports on which the United States imposes CVDs.

However, since its inception, U.S. policy on subsidies has been to countervail foreign subsidies but to neither prohibit nor countervail their domestic analogues. The United States has no restrictions on internal state and local subsidies, and states are not allowed to countervail the subsidies of other states.[17] U.S. countervailing law as set forth in Section 303 and Title VII of the Tariff Act of 1930 provides for the levying of special additional duties to offset foreign subsidies on products imported into the United States. Before a countervailing duty can be issued, the Department of Commerce must find a countervailable subsidy. The Department of Commerce determines the existence and amount of any countervailable subsidy. The International Trade Commission decides if a U.S. industry is materially injured or threatened with material injury by such imports.

Countervailing duty petitions must identify alleged subsidies and provide factual information concerning the nature and amount of any subsidy provided with respect to the subject merchandise granted. If an upstream subsidy (covering input material or a component part of a finished product) is alleged, the petition must include information on domestic subsidies that the government of the affected country provides to the upstream supplier, the competitive benefits of subsidies bestowed on the merchandise and the significant effects the subsidies have on the cost of producing the merchandise.[18]

The United States does not countervail subsidies generally available to all industries but rather only those that, according to economic theory, affect trade. The U.S. Department of Commerce has had some questionable policies for determining what is a specific subsidy and what is a generally available subsidy.[19]

Countervailable subsidies include direct export subsidies, production subsidies and subsidies to factors of production when they distort international trade. U.S. law has interpreted this to countervail domestic subsidies that effectively *de jure* or *de facto* benefit specific industries as opposed to generalized subsidies that benefit many or all industries in the economy.

In particular the Department of Commerce has considered regional subsidies, such as, regional development programs, urban block grants and regional job training programs, to be specific subsidies regardless of how widely available they are to industries in a region, and it considers general agricultural subsidies to be nonspecific. "Those classifications are wrong, and they conveniently exempt the largest U.S. subsidy programs affecting trade—those in agriculture—from countervailing duties while allowing the United States to impose duties against subsidies that are more commonly used by other countries."[20]

Despite the Commerce Department's opposition to regional development programs, the United States as a member of WTO accepted the Agreement on Subsidies and Countervailing Measures, with its special treatment for regional subsidies. There have been proponents of the efforts to exclude regional development from countervailing duties.[21]

The distortion argument does not apply to measures undertaken to promote regional development when a duly elected government in any

democratic sovereign nation as a right determines its own incomes policy and redistributes income from one group of citizens to another as its
electorate sees fit. Such deliberate transfers cannot be regarded as subsidies resulting in distortion that injures people in other countries. In some
situations subsidies can improve the functioning of the market. Where
monopoly exists, subsidy per unit of output just equal to price minus
marginal cost at level of output that would prevail under pure competition will induce profit-maximizing entrepreneurs to move to that level of
output.[22]

A requirement in countervailing duty law is that a subsidy be shown
analytically to have some cross-border effect. Where such a showing is
not made, the international community has little cause to recognize the
subsidy and it should not be actionable. This is because if a sovereign
nation for its own good reasons desires to take an action that reduces its
own welfare, but does not affect other societies, that should be made
within the discretion of that national government. Regional aids offer a
critical example.[23]

To illustrate, assume the Italian government desires that a particular
glass factory be located in a depressed mountain region and investors
would invest in such a factory, but want it located at a port. Should the
Italian government grant a subsidy merely adequate to balance the added
costs of the less desirable location, presumably the only economy that suffers overall reduced welfare is the Italian. It is unlikely that there would be
any impact on the price of exports. In this type of situation no countervailing duty should be applied by the foreign importing country.[24]

Section 220(c), PL 103–465, December 6, 1994, in accordance with the
WTO agreement calls for a national review of antidumping and countervailing duty orders in place for five years. Unless there is likely to be a
continuation or recurrence of the dumping or subsidy, the order is
revoked. Since the sunset provision is implemented by national authorities rather than the WTO, enforcement is not likely to be as stringent.

NOTES

1. Andrew Hughes Hallett and Carlos A. Primo Braga, *The New Regulation
and the Threat of Protectionism*, Policy Research Working Paper 1349 (Washington:
The   World Bank, International Trade Division, International Economic
Department, August 1994).

2. Statement, Hon. Roy MacLaren, Minister for International Trade, Canada,
to the Centre for International Studies and the Centre for International Business,
University of Toronto, "Canada's Trade Policy for the 21st Century: The Walls of
Jericho Fall Down," January 18, 1995.

3. Thomas J. Courchene, *Celebrating Flexibility: An Interpretative Essay on the Evolution of Canadian Federalism* (Toronto: C. D. Howe Institute, 1995), p. 21.

4. Ibid., pp. 21–22.

5. Conrad Weiler, "GATT, NAFTA and State and Local Powers," *Intergovernmental Perspective* 20 (Fall 1993–Winter 1994), p. 38.

6. Peter Morici, *Trade Talks With Mexico: A Time for Realism* (Washington: National Planning Association, 1991), p. 89.

7. European Union, Commission, *Europe and the U.S.: The Way Forward*, COM (95) 411 final, July 26, 1995, p. 2.

8. Youri Devuyst, "Transatlantic Trade Policy: U.S. Market Opening Strategies" (Pittsburgh: Center for West European Studies, University of Pittsburgh, 1995), p. 17.

9. EU Commission, *Europe and the U.S.*, p. 12.

10. "All Free Traders Now," *The Economist* 341 (December 7, 1996), p. 23.

11. "Customs Unions and Free Trade Areas Since 1948," *FOCUS (WTO)* 3 (May–June 1995), pp. 7, 9.

12. U.S. General Accounting Office, *Government Reorganization Observations About Creating a U.S. Trade Administration*, GAO/T-GGD-95-234, September 6, 1995, p. 2.

13. Ibid.

14. Ibid.

15. U.S. Congress, Congressional Budget Office, *How the GATT Affects U.S. Antidumping and Countervailing Duty Policy* (September 1994), p. 22.

16. Richard Boltuck and Robert E. Litan, "America's Unfair Trade Laws," in Richard Boltuck and Robert E. Litan, eds., *Down in the Dumps: Administration of the Unfair Trade Laws*, (Washington: Brookings Institution, 1991), p. 8.

17. Congressional Budget Office, *How The GATT Affects*, p. 46.

18. U.S. International Trade Commission, *The Economic Effects of Antidumping and Countervailing Duty Orders and Suspension Agreements*, Investigation No. 332–344, Publication 2900, June 1995, pp. 2–4.

19. Congressional Budget Office, *How The GATT Affects*, p. 46.

20. Ibid., p. 46.

21. Boltuck and Litan, "America's Unfair Trade Laws," p. 8.

22. Benjamin Higgins, "Subsidies, Regional Development and the Canada-U.S. Free Trade Agreement," *Canadian Journal of Regional Science* 13 (Summer–Autumn 1990), p. 269.

23. John H. Jackson, "Perspectives on Countervailing Duties," *Law and Policy in International Business* 21 (1990), p. 751.

24. Ibid.

Chapter 4

World Trade Organization

BACKGROUND

The World Trade Organization (WTO) has broad significance for national sovereignty, which extends to internal regional economic development. The significance of the WTO is based on the specific inclusion of assistance to disadvantaged regions in the Subsidies Code. With the conclusion on December 25, 1993, after seven years of multilateral trade negotiations in the Uruguay Round, the General Agreement on Trade and Tariffs (GATT) contracting parties representing 117 countries in 1994 created the WTO. Its aim is to have members resolve their trade disputes multilaterally instead of bilaterally or unilaterally. It was given greater authority than the predecessor GATT to strengthen international trade by reducing barriers. GATT coexisted with WTO until December 31, 1995. The WTO was ratified by the United States with PL 103-465, December 8, 1994. The dispute settlement procedures were the biggest area of debate prior to congressional approval. The complexity of the legislation is indicated by the magnitude of the Agreements. The text, implementing bill statement of administrative action and supporting statements, and the President's message cover 4,004 pages.[1]

Following World War II, the major economic powers recognized that world trade barriers hindered economic development and growth. In 1947 they created GATT, a set of global rules for international trade. GATT became the primary multilateral agreement covering international trade, founded in the belief that liberalizing trade would help all national economies grow. Along with the International Monetary Fund and the World Bank, it was one of the postwar institutions designed to help regulate the international economy by preventing a recurrence of disastrous policies undertaken during the 1930s. GATT was charged with overseeing international trade in goods, in particular, the liberalization of this trade by means of a negotiated reduction in tariff barriers.

GATT was created in a global environment where firms competed internationally largely by exporting goods produced within a particular country. International trade issues focused primarily on border measures such as tariffs and quotas. Subsequently, factors such as trade in services and international investment became increasingly important and complex. The GATT system depended on the notion of an exchange of rights and obligations and an avoidance of the punitive approach. The original subsidy code was not considered completely adequate to the new global environment. The 1986 meeting in Uruguay of over 100 countries' trade ministers set in motion the Uruguay Round to expand substantially and change the GATT rules and strengthen the organization. The formation of a new organization, the World Trade Organization, was proposed. From a strictly legal standpoint, the WTO is not the successor to GATT but in practice WTO is GATT's successor. In respect to principles, personnel and procedures there is continuity. The fundamental GATT principles have not been materially changed except for greater detail and a more current interpretation. To correct the fragmentation that developed under GATT, acceptance had to be total rather than acceptance of side agreements being limited to a few countries.

There are differences between GATT and WTO's Antidumping Agreement and Subsidies and Countervailing Measures Agreement. The WTO establishes more detailed procedures and obligations regarding the imposition of antidumping and countervailing duties by national authorities than previously existed. The WTO Dispute Settlement Understanding establishes a faster timetable and stricter procedures for dispute settlement proceedings, which include the ability of governments to unilaterally block adverse panel reports.

WTO is a trade governing body with sizeable power, whereas GATT was considered a halfway agreement among member nations that could ignore any GATT rulings they did not like. WTO, by contrast, is an institution, not an agreement. It can set rules governing trade among its members and unlike GATT, its decisions are binding and can be rejected only by a unanimous vote.

WTO was designed to reduce obstacles blocking exports in world markets, to extend coverage and enhance discipline on critical areas of trade and to create a fairer, more comprehensive, more effective and more enforceable set of world trade rules. A major achievement was the strengthening of the multilateral dispute settlement and the related removal of the scope for unilateral action. Most relevant to this study is the provision on regional subsidies.

The agreement has far-reaching implications. It could have an even greater impact on non-tariff barriers than on direct tariffs. Though less obvious than tariffs, the barriers allow for greater discretionary activity by governments and thus are more likely to be the subject of controversy. Export subsidies are prohibited except for those that support disadvantaged regions, environmental and research activities. There are various conciliation mechanisms designed to arrive at amicable solutions. Those trade disputes that cannot be resolved through bilateral talks are adjudicated by the dispute settlement court. Panels of independent experts are set up to examine disputes in accord with WTO rules and to provide findings.

WTO AND NAFTA

There are differences between WTO and NAFTA. NAFTA completely eliminates tariff and non-tariff barriers among the United States, Canada and Mexico over a fifteen-year period. WTO will lower trade barriers and eliminate some tariffs among some 125 countries, including the major U.S. trading partners, such as EU and Japan. Unlike NAFTA, it will not completely eliminate all trade barriers. With so many countries involved, WTO is more complex than NAFTA. There is the matter of coexistence of NAFTA and WTO. While regional pacts can coexist within the WTO framework, they cannot initiate more restrictive trade policies than are allowed under WTO. Yet, over the past ten years international trade has grown faster inside regional trade areas than between them.[2]

The WTO agreements and streamlined dispute settlement procedures may make a WTO challenge more appealing. A contention is that the existence of these more detailed WTO obligations covering the imposition of AD and CVD and more effective dispute settlement procedures has rendered NAFTA's Chapter 19 unnecessary. In fact the role and type of review performed by NAFTA Chapter 19 panels and WTO panels are quite different and there is no redundancy between them.

The function of a WTO panel (in the context of an AD and CVD proceeding) is to determine whether a WTO member's law or particular administrative determination is consistent with the WTO Antidumping Agreement or Subsidies and Countervailing Measures Agreement. In contrast, the role of a Chapter 19 panel is to determine in applying the appropriate standard of review whether the agency's decision is consistent with the importing country's domestic law.

WTO panels and Chapter 19 panels are also very different in terms of procedure. WTO dispute settlement is limited to government disputes. The Chapter 19 binational panel review system is intended for use of private parties directly affected by national agency determinations, and the participants in binational panels reviews are private litigants. With the exception of the agency whose decision is under review, only in CVD cases do governments and subnational governments of the involved countries take an active part in Chapter 19 proceedings.[3]

A somewhat different view is that a problem with the WTO may be its inability to take too strong a stand on anything that could cost the WTO its leading role in global commerce. The result is that responsibility could fall to regional agreements such as NAFTA.[4]

STRUCTURE

The WTO is a single institutional framework, headed by a Ministerial Conference, which meets at least once every two years. Signers of the agreement have to accept it in its entirety. It contains a binding clause that requires members to bring their national legislation in line with the agreement. The Ministerial Conference has overall responsibility for the WTO and the authority to take decisions on all matters under the Multilateral Trade Agreements. The General Council, representatives of all the members, is responsible for performing the functions of the WTO between meetings of the Ministerial Conference. One of its three major duties is to act as the Dispute Settlement Body (DSB) when such a body is called for by the Dispute Settlement Mechanism. The WTO Secretariat is headed by a director general and has responsibility for administration. Most decisions are made on the basis of consensus, which is defined as no member making a formal objection. When there is no consensus, voting follows.

TRADE POLICY REVIEW MECHANISM (TPRM)

The Trade Policy Review Body (TPRB) has a broad mandate to review periodically trade policies of the member countries. It is not intended to carry out enforcement of obligations or for dispute settlement procedures. Its purpose is to examine the impact of a member's trade policies and practices on the multilateral trading system.

Subsidies

Subsidies are recognized as a legitimate tool of social and economic policy but with stricter control when they have an effect upon trade. If a country is found to be breaking the rules or if the subsidies it uses have adverse effects on its trading partners, there is a price to be paid.

In defining a subsidy there are two elements: the financial contribution by a government or any public body within that government's territory, and consequent control and conferral of a benefit.[5] The new code defines subsidies by incorporating a traffic-light approach, with red-light subsidies, which are prohibited in almost all circumstances; actionable yellow-light subsidies, which are prohibited if their effects on trade would cause injury to another country's industries (remedies may be sought against domestic subsidies if they are shown to distort trade); and green-light subsidies, which are nonactionable under certain conditions and criteria and against which other countries cannot freely retaliate.[6]

Green-light subsidies. These subsidies are nonactionable in almost all cases, meaning that countries are free to initiate them without being retaliated against and that countervailing duties cannot be imposed against them (Article 8 of the Subsidies Code). The following subsidies are nonactionable:

- Assistance to disadvantaged regions that is otherwise nonspecific, subject to certain restrictions
- Nonspecific subsidies
- Assistance for research
- Assistance for adapting facilities to new environmental requirements, subject to certain restrictions

Under Article 9 of the Subsidies Code, although green-light subsidies are generally nonactionable, a safeguard provision does exist. If a member thinks any of its domestic industries have suffered because of the subsidy, it may request consultation with the subsidizing member. If no mutually acceptable solution is reached within sixty days, the requesting member can refer the matter to the Committee on Subsidies and Countervailing Measures. If the recommendation is not followed, the committee must authorize by consensus appropriate countermeasures.

The United States was virtually alone in trying to extend restrictions against dumping and subsidies. With regard to the nonactionable category of regional development, some of the U.S. industry advisory committees expressed concern that in many countries, including Canada and the EU, most heavy industries such as steel have plants in regions that would meet the criteria for a disadvantaged region. Although some members of the advisory committees acknowledged that the "specificity" provision of the agreement (the provision that government subsidies limited to a specific firm or industry are actionable) may be of use in controlling these types of subsidies, they maintained that in many cases these subsidies are generally available in a particular region, which would make them nonspecific and thus not actionable. Some trade analysts believed that the agreement should have placed a cap on the amount of regional assistance that would be nonactionable.[7]

Senate Republicans were highly critical of the new world agreement for allowing certain government subsidies. They were basically opposed to terms that allowed subsidies for research and development, regional development and environmental compliance. They complained that such subsidies represented a major shift in U.S. trade policy from one promoting free market competition to one promoting government subsidies and industrial policy.[8]

The Subsidies Code stipulates that only specific subsidies are subject to being prohibited, retaliated against or countervailed. Among the principles determining whether a subsidy is specific are:[9]

- If a subsidy goes to a limited number of enterprises or goes disproportionately to particular enterprises, it is specific.
- Subsidies limited to enterprises in regions smaller than the jurisdiction of the government granting the subsidy are specific.

In the green-light category, subsidies are nonactionable subject to specific restrictions and include:

- Assistance for research up to 75% of the cost of industrial research and up to 50% of the cost of precompetitive development activity.
- Assistance for adapting facilities to new environmental requirements.
- Assistance to disadvantaged regions that is otherwise nonspecific.

On conditions for nonactionable or noncountervailable subsidies in terms of regional development, each such region is defined as:[10]

- Disadvantaged within a country and is a clearly designated contiguous geographical area with a definable economic and administrative identity.
- Disadvantaged on the basis of neutral and objective criteria indicating that the region is disadvantaged because of more than temporary circumstances. Such criteria include a measurement of economic development and are clearly stated.
- These criteria include a measure of economic development, based on one or more of the following factors:
  • Per capita income, household per capita income or per capita GDP not exceeding 85% of the average for the country subject to investigation or review;
  • An unemployment rate that is at least 110% of the average unemployment rate for the country subject to investigation or review;

• Programs provided within a general framework of regional development include ceilings on the amount of assistance that can be granted to a subsidized project. Such ceilings are differentiated according to the varied development levels of assisted regions, expressed in terms of investment costs or costs of job creation. Within such ceilings the distribution of assistance is sufficiently broad to avoid predominant use of a subsidy or the provision of a disproportionately large subsidy to an enterprise or industry.

The phrase "general framework of regional development" means that the regional subsidy programs are part of an internally consistent and generally applicable regional development policy, and that regional development subsidies are not granted in isolated geographical points having no, or virtually no, influence on the development of a region. The phrase "neutral and objective criteria" means criteria that do not favor certain regions beyond what is appropriate for the elimination or reduction of regional disparities within the framework of the regional development policy. Even if a subsidy program meets the criteria it may be actionable if it causes "serious adverse effects" to the domestic industry of another member, "causing damage which would be difficult to repair."

DISPUTE SETTLEMENT MECHANISM

Negotiations on subsidies have historically been a troublesome area because of the need to balance a national government's traditional rights to advance internal economic and social policies and the potential trade distortions they could cause for the other signatories. There are also the differing interests within a particular country of companies that are primarily domestically or export-oriented.

Subsequently, subsidies were recognized as a legitimate tool of social and economic policy, but with a stricter control over their use in cases where they have an effect upon trade. Recourse to the dispute settlement procedure was made available when a party considers the rules to have been violated.

The GATT dispute settlement procedure was fundamentally weak in that a consensus was required to establish a panel to examine a case, and then the findings or ruling of the panel had to be adopted. Thus, the country against which the original complaint was directed had the power to veto the start of proceedings. Subsequently, either party to the proceedings could veto adoption of the panel's findings. Thus, there was no assurance that either party would accept rulings contrary to their interests. Subsequent to the incomplete conclusion of the Tokyo Round in 1979, a number of agreements concerned with antidumping, subsidies and other non-tariff barriers were signed outside the main GATT framework, resulting in a fragmentation of the GATT system.[11]

Probably the most crucial component of the WTO is the Dispute Settlement Mechanism (DSM). The new DSM is much more detailed than that of the GATT, running to twenty-seven articles as compared with two for GATT. WTO has broad enforcement powers to police subsidy activities. Regarding settlement of disputes, under the old system, countries could ignore adverse rulings whereas WTO's decisions are binding. Each country has one vote and there is no veto.

The DSM sets deadlines for panel decisions and appeals. To combat unfair trading practices, it allows "cross retaliation" when a country fails to modify its laws or regulations in response to a dispute settlement. "Cross retaliation" means that if a country is found guilty of committing an unfair practice in a certain sector, another country can respond with a measure in another sector, allowing use of strongest means available to ensure that a country will implement its WTO obligations.

The dispute settlement understanding establishes time limits for each of the four stages of a dispute: consultation, panel, appeal and implementation. Unless there is unanimous opposition in the Dispute Settlement Body, the panel or appellate report is adopted. The recommendations and rulings of the Dispute Settlement Body cannot add to or diminish rights and obligations provided in the WTO agreements. Neither can they directly force countries to change their laws or regulations. However, if countries choose not to implement the recommendations and rulings, the Dispute Settlement Body may authorize the trade retaliation.

DSM is a process with fixed time limits[12]:

1. The first stage involves consultations among the concerned members. If there is no agreement as a result of the consultations, parties may refer the dispute to the director general for conciliation.
2. The complainant can ask for a panel to examine the case. If the other party does not respond, establishment of a panel is almost automatic. Parties have limited time in which to agree on the three panelists. Otherwise, the director general appoints the panelists, who act independently.
3. The panel has six months to produce a final report. After both parties make their cases, the panel produces an interim report that is given to the parties, who may request a review following which the panel submits its final report.
4. The DSB adopts the final panel report within sixty days unless a party appeals or there is consensus against adoption of the report.
5. Prompt compliance with the findings of the DSB is expected. Otherwise penalties are imposed. The final means against non-compliance with the DSB rulings are retaliation instead of any form of real enforcement, which would have consequences for its legal order.

The code provides for two basic sets of dispute settlement rules, one for prohibited subsidies and one for actionable subsidies.[13]

A separate dispute settlement process for nonactionable cases that are judged actionable involves referral to the Committee on Subsidies and Countervailing Measures (CCM), which includes all members of the WTO. CCM has up to 120 days to make its recommendation as to whether the subsidy needs to be changed. If the offending member does not comply, countermeasures may be taken.[14]

Under the new code, governments must amend their domestic trade legislation to require that a clearer link be established between a subsidized import and the alleged injury to domestic industry before a countervailing action is taken.[15]

From January 1, 1995, through August 30, 1996, the formal WTO dispute settlement procedure was utilized in fifty-three instances. Most of these cases were in progress by September 1996; thirty-five were in the consultation phase, under panel review or on appeal. Of the eighteen closed cases, sixteen have been settled or abandoned and two have been closed after a final appeal. The United States has availed itself of the dispute settlement mechanism more than any other member, which could be explained by the size of the United States and its volume of trade.[16]

STATE AND LOCAL GOVERNMENTS

Under Article 24:12, each member is fully responsible for the observance of all provisions and "shall take such reasonable measures as may be available to it to ensure such observance by regional and local governments and authorities within its territory."

State and local officials in the United States were concerned about sovereignty. Could their laws be challenged on the grounds that they posed a barrier to free trade and unfairly discriminate against foreign-based businesses? There is the view that WTO represents a significant change in the power alignment between states and the federal government, that many existing state laws are likely to conflict with WTO and NAFTA and that both trade agreements will constrain the traditional flexibility of Congress and state legislatures to respond to future problems.[17]

The Intergovernmental Policy Advisory Committee (IGPAC) in Congress, consisting of state and local officials, recognized that the agreement may affect many state and local government programs by making it explicit that they may be subject to international discipline or may require changes to bring them into conformance with the permissible category. Establishment of a "nonactionable subsidies" category recognized the legitimate roles of state and local governments in assisting the economic development of their areas, and does no serious damage to the interests of the United States since it is tightly defined and contains a mechanism for addressing serious problems that may result. Language of the agreement should provide adequate guidance to state and local governments about how to bring their programs into compliance with the rules.[18]

The requirement that there be notification of programs for eligibility as nonactionable subsidies presents state and local governments with an administrative burden. Notification procedures can be workable only if the federal government establishes and funds a clearinghouse process that all state and local governments may use to meet their obligations under the agreement. The notification process also implies that challenges to programs may be lodged by other countries.[19]

In response to the concerns about WTO undercutting the power of state and local governments, the Clinton administration included several clauses in Section 101 of the implementation bill, PL 103-465, to protect local and state sovereignty. Foreign companies are unable to challenge existing state and local laws in U.S. courts and the federal government would be required to consult state and local governments before proceeding in legal action against them. A foreign government can still mount a challenge on behalf of its companies, and the president can attempt to nullify a state or local law considered contrary to the agreement.[20]

Section 102 of PL 103-465 states that U.S. law prevails in the event of any inconsistency with U.S. law and that the U.S. Trade Representative will consult with states before accepting any adverse dispute settlement affecting them: "(A) In general—No State law, or the application of such a State law may be declared invalid as to any person or circumstance on the ground that the provision or application is inconsistent with any of the Uruguay Round Agreements, except in an action brought about the United States for the purpose of declaring such law or application invalid."

Despite administration claims to the contrary, critics question whether the United States would go so far as to accept trade sanctions for defending an individual state's law. In practice, many economists expect that such situations generally can be avoided.[21]

Another problem is that trade disputes can involve competing interests within a particular country and it would be difficult for the United States to speak with one voice and act in the national interest rather than in the interests of a single state or company. The opposite situation is that the U.S. government can take steps against actions of state and local governments in foreign countries that affect international trade.

THE UNITED STATES

Section 201 of the Trade Act of 1974 as amended has an escape clause authorizing the president to impose temporary import restrictions if a good is being imported in such increased quantities as to be a substantial threat or injury to the domestic industry producing a like or directly competing good. General subsidies are equally available to all industries and specific subsidies are available only to (or preferentially available to) individual industries or groups of industries.[22] The Subsidies Code requires WTO members to amend their domestic countervailing duty legislation in a way that on balance will require collection of more solid evidence before countervailing duties can be imposed.[23]

Section 301 of the Trade Act of 1974 allows the United States to retaliate against "unjustifiable" or "unreasonable " foreign practices that hinder U.S. commerce. The WTO dispute settlement mechanism alters the sequence in which Section 301 is used but does little else to limit its use. "Section 301 requires that, if a case involves an existing trade agreement, the United States must use the dispute settlement provisions of that agreement. If the United States wins a WTO case, and if the losing party does not change its practice or offer suitable compensation, Sec 301 retaliation is authorized by the WTO."[24]

The fundamental reason U.S. sovereignty is not limited by the WTO is that WTO agreements and dispute panel decisions have no legal force in the United States (or other member countries); they are not "self-actuating." Where existing U.S. legislation is contravened or new legislation is required, Congress must decide on action. "If the United States were to lose a dispute panel decision on a matter of fundamental national interest, it need not bring U.S. law or practice into conformity. The United States could instead offer compensation through liberalization in other areas, or accept equivalent foreign retaliation through increased barriers to U.S. exports." Panels decide on disputes that arise on rules and disciplines that WTO members have agreed to; they do not create new obligations. Furthermore, U.S. negotiators were especially careful to limit the scope of panel review in cases concerned with national health and safety standards.[25]

NOTES

1. U.S. Congress, *Uruguay Round Trade Agreements*, House Document 103-316, 103rd Congress, 2d Session, 1994.

2. European Union Commission, *An Industrial Competitiveness Policy for the European Union*, COM (94) 319 final, September 14, 1994, p. 32.

3. Guillermo Aguilart Alvarez et al., "NAFTA Chapter 19: Binational Panel Review of Antidumping and Countervailing Duty Determinations," Chapter 1 in *Trading Punches: Trade Remedy Law and Disputes under NAFTA*, Beatriz Leycegui et al., eds., Report No. 279 (Washington: National Planning Association, 1995), p. 36.

4. Helene Cooper and Shushan Bahree, "No Gattzilla World's Best Hope for

Global Trade Topples Few Barriers," *Wall Street Journal*, December 3, 1996, p. 1.

5. U.S. Congress, House Document 103-316, Vol. 1, p. 912.

6. U.S. Congress, Congressional Budget Office, *How the GATT Affects U.S. Antidumping and Countervailing Duty Policy*, September 1994, p. xii.

7. Ibid., p. 65.

8. Asra Q. Nomani, "Republicans Blast a GATT Provision That Allows Some Government Subsidies," *Wall Street Journal*, February 1, 1994, p. 2.

9. U.S. Congress, Congressional Budget Office, September 1994, pp. 62.–63.

10. U.S. Congress, House Document 103-316, Vol. 1, pp. 918–920.

11. European Union, Parliament, Directorate General for Research, *The World Trade Organization and the European Community*, External Economic Relations Series, Working Paper 8, 1995, p. 15.

12. Ibid., pp. 23–24.

13. European Union Commission, *The Uruguay Round Global Agreement—Global Benefits*, 1994, p. 5.

14. Charles Bram Cadsby and Kenneth Woodside, *Canada and the New Subsidies Code* (Toronto: C. D. Howe Institute, 1996), p. 5.

15. European Union, *The Uruguay Round Global Agreement*, p. 2.

16. U.S. General Accounting Office, *World Trade Organization Status of Issues to be Considered at the Singapore Ministerial Meeting*, GAO/T-NSIAD-96-243, September 27, 1996, p. 5.

17. Robert Stumberg et al., *GATT Impact on State Law California* (Washington: Center for Policy Alternatives, 1994), p. 2.

18. Intergovernmental Policy Advisory Committee (IGPAC), Report to the U.S. Congress, *The Uruguay Round of Multilateral Trade Negotiations*, January 1994, p. 21.

19. Ibid., p. 22.

20. Michael H. Shuman, "With GATT, We Must Guard Our Cities," *New York Times*, November 20, 1994, p. F13.

21. Helene Cooper, "World Trade Organization Created by GATT Isn't the Lion of Its Foes or the Lamb of Its Backers," *Wall Street Journal*, July 14, 1994, p. A12.

22. U.S. Congress, Congressional Budget Office, September 1994, p. 12.

23. Cadsby and Woodside, *Canada*, p. 1.

24. U.S. President, *Economic Report with The Annual Report of the Council of Economic Advisers*, transmitted to Congress, 1995, pp. 211–212.

25. Ibid., p. 213.

Chapter 5

North American Free Trade Agreement

CANADA-U.S. FREE TRADE AGREEMENT

A free trade agreement (FTA) can be defined as a form of preferential trade liberalization in which two or more nations within the world trading community eliminate or substantially reduce barriers to trade among themselves. They do not adopt a common tariff for non-members as they would in a customs union. Subnational or regional concerns are factors in the adoption of an FTA. An economic community would require stronger commitments for the harmonization of policies than does an FTA. It would necessitate creating a central administration which under present circumstances would not be favorably received by the United States, Canada or Mexico.

"The process of creating a free trade area, when foreign investment and many elements of domestic policy and regulation are on the table in addition to tariffs, takes negotiators a very long way toward creating a formal economic community."[1] The Canada-U.S. Free Trade Agreement (CUFTA) served as the foundation and model for NAFTA. Earlier steps were the reciprocal tariff reduction agreements in 1935 and 1938, the defense production sharing agreement in 1959 and automotive agreement in 1965.

A concurrence of political and economic events led to the Canada-U.S. Free Trade Agreement, including Canada's abandonment of its traditional policies. When Great Britain joined the EU in 1972, it abandoned all Commonwealth trade preferences. The British decision strengthened the efforts of those Canadians who wanted to draw closer to the United States and reduce the trade barriers between the two nations.[2] CUFTA went into effect on January 1, 1989.

CUFTA, in contrast to the EU, did not have integration as a goal but rather closer binational cooperation and elimination of tariff barriers. CUFTA made a start toward establishing fully integrated markets for goods, services and capital by reducing trade barriers, ensuring that there will not be more restrictive practices and establishing processes for reducing still others. Over a ten-year phase-in period, CUFTA would eliminate tariffs, duty drawbacks and most import restrictions. Over the next five to seven years, the two countries agreed to "develop more effective rules and disciplines, concerning the use of government subsidies" and to "develop a substitute system of rules dealing with unfair pricing and subsidization" (Article 1907.1). In the interim the two governments would apply existing national laws; however, judicial review of administrative agency findings would be replaced by a binding review from binational panels.

The CUFTA agenda included issues for which the EU had well-established procedures, such as rules for subsidies, including state aids. It appeared that if Canada and the United States were successful in forming an economic community it would be a trade area but without a common external barrier.[3]

The objectives of CUFTA were to maintain separate political entities— two markets, each with preferential access to the other, with separate currencies and passports. Canada and the United States did not seek to set up strong central institutions to administer the agreement. Little surrender of national sovereignty was involved. The effectiveness of the agreement relied more on cooperation rather than a shift of legislative power to central institutions. Binational panels would ensure joint resolution of trade disputes.

Subsidies

There is a divergence in Canadian and U.S. views of the degree to which each subsidizes its industries. Canada has typically been more willing to accept government involvement in the economy, while the United States has preferred to let market mechanisms operate more freely. The result has been that Canadian subsidies are more transparent, making them easy to identify, while U.S. subsidies are more covert. For example, most Canadian subsidies are provided through direct grants, equity infusions or government participation, whereas the U.S. subsidies more frequently are in the form of tax exemptions, low-interest loans, loan guarantees. "This can lead to conflict, particularly when the United States attacks subsidy practices, such as programs to alleviate regional disparities, that Canada considers central to its social policies."[4]

Locating government assistance in the United States is complicated by the large number of jurisdictions, its preference for ad hoc rather than direct legislative or program funding and the belief that U.S. governments do not subsidize business to any great extent.

Negotiations

The most contentious issue during the negotiations, which almost torpedoed the negotiations, was the effort to develop common rules on subsidies. The U.S. view in the negotiations was that Canada needed to be "disciplined" with regard to its developmental policies in spite of the fact that many of Canada's policies were similar to those being propounded by industrial strategy advocates in the United States.[5]

Throughout much of the negotiation process, the United States was reluctant even to discuss U.S. subsidies. The United States displayed no willingness to budge from its hard-line position: Subsidies to enterprises that are limited to a specific region—even a region as big as Atlantic Canada, the West, or Quebec—are just cause for countervail.[6]

In every list of "off the table" items presented by the Conservative Canadian government at the start of the trade negotiations, regional assistance programs received prominent mention. Yet these included precisely those social and industrial items most often identified as "subsidies" by the United States in countervail actions.[7]

STATES AND PROVINCES

Most provincial governments took positions on CUFTA. The three westernmost provinces and Quebec were strongly supportive; governments of the Atlantic provinces (except Prince Edward Island) gave more cautious approval, applauding expansion of their markets but fearing the potential constraints on their ability to pursue regional development policies. Manitoba (which changed position after a new political party took office), Ontario and Prince Edward Island were strongly opposed.[8] Ontario set up a number of conditions that had to be met before it would support the agreement, including one that regional development powers were to continue untouched.[9]

For the poorer Atlantic provinces, there was a very real risk associated with CUFTA. Regional development policies and government subsidies, which had been very important to these provinces, could have been at risk if they were interpreted as trade subsidies and hence subject to countervailing duties or other retaliatory actions. They would have covered both industry-specific (e.g., fisheries) or firm-specific (e.g., bailouts of specific firms) policies and subsidies. Even if such policies were not prohibited directly by the CUFTA, they could have been indirectly deterred in the new free trade environment, which placed greater importance on competitive market forces.[10]

The adjustment problems faced by Ontario as a result of CUFTA were considered significantly greater in scope and severity than those faced by any other region in North America. Ontario's particular vulnerability stemmed from the structure of its manufacturing sector. Its most distinctive characteristic was the excessively high proportion of branch plants. Branch plants engage in virtually no product development and usually have no export market mandate. With few exceptions branch plants operated at a suboptimal scale. When CUFTA was negotiated, branch plants had operating costs 10% to 15% higher than those in the larger and more modern U.S. plants. The average rate of effective tariff protection in Canada was roughly equal to the cost disadvantage of branch plants, accounting for roughly one-third of the manufacturing value added. Adjustment problems of branch plants came at the same time as other manufacturing sectors were also losing their comparative advantage as well as the competitive advantage in resource-based industries.[11]

Constitutional ambiguity gave provincial governments some legitimacy but not necessarily formal authority in the free trade debate. Authority of the federal government to enter into international treaties was unquestionable but authority to pass legislation implementing the agreement depended on whether the matters dealt with fell under federal or provincial jurisdiction. Provincial governments were not directly involved in the negotiations, although they were consistently briefed and consulted by the federal negotiators; and the agreement was carefully crafted to deal as much as possible with matters under federal jurisdiction. But some matters, such as energy supply and wine and beer pricing in local (provincial) markets, entailed provincial powers. Furthermore, Article 103 of the agreement specifically required that Canadian and U.S. federal governments "ensure that all necessary measures are taken in order to give effect to its provisions, including their observance...by state, provincial and local governments."[12]

The states had considerably less interest in the negotiations than did the provinces and did not seek major participation into either CUFTA or NAFTA. Congress represented the subnational interests. Even prior to

CUFTA, provincial governments have had a major role in Canada's exter-nal trade policy. In the early stages of the Tokyo Roundof GATT negotia-tions (1973–1979) the provincial governments demanded and obtained greater access to the negotiation process and decisions.

As Canada prepared for the CUFTA negotiations, it became clear that bilateral negotiations would touch more Canadian interests than pre-vious multilateral negotiations had done. Therefore consultations with provincial governments were a political necessity for the federal govern-ment. Prior to Canada's formal announcement of its intention to seek bilateral negotiations, meetings were held to assess provincial concerns. These meetings revealed some substantive differences. For example, Ontario and Manitoba were less enthusiastic about freer trade than the remaining provinces but all provinces agreed on the procedural point that provincial involvement in the negotiation should be maximized.

Provincial governments devised a plan for provincial participation that would have included participation at the negotiation sessions, veto power over any matter that involved provincial jurisdiction and partici-pation in sessions that dealt with negotiating mandates or strategy. The federal government firmly resisted these and similar demands and instead laid out a position that provided maximum consultation and exchange of information but no seat at the negotiating table or involve-ment in establishing mandates or strategies for negotiators.

In the end, the federal position carried the day but it created an obligation for the federal government to make good on the promise of full provincial participation. It was never clear what "full provincial par-ticipation" meant. Full consultation did not end provincial demands for participation and tensions between federal and provincial governments continued into the negotiations. The CUFTA negotiations fell within the legal jurisdiction of the federal government. The power of provincial gov-ernments was largely political and not legal, although the prospect that some issues involving provincial jurisdiction might be raised justified their political concern.[13]

Though the FTA was signed by the two national governments, it is the industrial policies of the states and provinces that determine the investment climate. The potential investor is concerned with their policies, programs and practices. The desirability of a site is set by a state, county or municipality. Subsidies, taxes, enforcement of environmental laws, training, labor laws, health care and workmen's compensation, training programs and the quality of life in the community are more dependent on state policies and attitudes than they are on the national agenda.[14]

Public Law 100-449, Sept 28, 1988, the U.S. act to implement the U.S.-Canada FTA, reflected the dominance of national law over state law and the concern with Canadian subsidies that affect U.S. industries. U.S.

trade officials had to determine which policies and practices would be acceptable within the context of the CUFTA. Yet, according to Article 1907 of the agreement, Canada's capabilities for pursuing regional development and social welfare programs remained unchanged and in fact had been strengthened.[15] Thus, nothing respecting regional support programs was given up by Canada in the FTA.

NORTH AMERICAN FREE TRADE AGREEMENT

Background

The United States, Canada and Mexico commenced formal negotiations in June 1991 on the North American Free Trade Agreement (NAFTA), building on CUFTA. Regional interests were both opponents and influential supporters of NAFTA. Passage of NAFTA in the United States owed much to the support emanating from a particular region. From its inception, NAFTA was a high economic and foreign policy priority for then-President George Bush and Secretary of State James Baker. Another strong supporter was then-Secretary of Commerce Robert Mosbacher, also a Texan. When Democratic support was vital, two Texans, then-Governor Ann Richards and Treasury Secretary Lloyd Bentsen, were crucial. Mexico was important to Texas, because it accounted for about a third of total sales by Texas companies outside the United States. Texas provided virtually half of all U.S. exports to Mexico, surpassing all the other states and regions, and receives by far the biggest slice of the NAFTA "pie." More than any other state, it has a larger stake in the prosperity of Mexico.[16]

Within a wider North American framework, the Canadian government reacted with caution. Mexico was a potential threat to its share of the U.S. market, especially so with Mexico's fast expanding automotive industry, which U.S. manufacturers were using increasingly to supply low-cost, reliable parts and vehicles.[17] Canadian trade with Mexico was modest; about 2% of Mexico's merchandise imports came from Canada. Thus, Canada entered the agreement more for defensive reasons than for direct economic benefits. Canadian administrations wanted to maintain the perceived benefits of CUFTA.[18]

During the 1987–1988 electoral campaign, Mexican President Carlos Salinas de Gortari initially rejected the concept of a free trade area with the United States. He is understood to have decided upon closer integration with Mexico's northern neighbors following his January 1989 visit to Western Europe, when he was disappointed by the response to his plans for closer ties with the post-1992 EU. Salinas and his colleagues observed how Spain and Portugal benefited.[19] NAFTA set a precedent, with a First World economy integrating with one from the Third World. The Mexican economy is one-twentieth the size of the United States'. Under terms of the treaty, Mexico will have to integrate with its First World neighbors more quickly (though less fully) than Spain, Portugal or Greece did in joining the EU.[20] The EU, when incorporating Spain, Portugal and Greece, recognized that if economic integration were not to pull its prosperous members down to the level of its poorer members, development aid had to be granted to the less developed regions. The Treaty of Rome commits its members to "reducing disparities between the various regions and backwardness of the least favored regions." Mexico receives nothing like the regional development funds received by these members. Spain has per capita income close to half that of the United States while Mexico's is a tenth as high. Portugal and Greece are poorer than Spain but still have per capita income twice Mexico's, and they contain only 6% of the total EU population. Mexico contains almost a quarter of North America's population. EU economic and political union will allow its economic policies to effect a high degree of consistency among members. By contrast, under NAFTA the United States and Canada accepted Mexico as it was.[21]

Compared with the EU, NAFTA does not have similar goals such as economic and monetary union, political union or a common external tariff. NAFTA is not a supranational institution with the power to override national laws. NAFTA, unlike the EU, has no parliament, court of justice, or commission. Institutionally, NAFTA has a secretariat with limited authority.

The EU has not only made much progress in eliminating internal trade barriers but has also established a common external tariff and is moving toward common internal regulations covering goods, services, capital and people. Within the NAFTA countries there is no comprehensive harmonization of internal regulations or policies, economic, social, cultural or otherwise. Yet NAFTA is more than a trade agreement; it encompasses a range of economic relations. After considerable controversy in the United States and Canada, NAFTA, PL 103-182, came into effect January 1, 1994. There were expectations that NAFTA could serve as the basis for the creation of a new trade bloc, with similar agreements with other Latin American and Caribbean countries.

NAFTA would create within fifteen years a free trade area extending from the Yukon to the Yucatan with a population base of 370 million people, a combined annual GDP of US $6.7 trillion and three-way merchandise trade exceeding US $270 billion annually. Three federal systems are involved in which authority is divided in different ways among national, state, provincial and local governments. Within the three national governments there are ninety-one state and provincial governments, two federal districts, six major territorial governments and innumerable county and local governments.[22]

Of the three governments, the U.S. system is the most stable. The demands for separatism in Quebec could lead to an unravelling of the Canadian system. The existence of a federal government in Mexico to date has been largely illusory. Power has been centralized in the federal government but the tight centralized control is showing strains. The extent of consultation with the subnational governments during the negotiations varied. In Canada the national government consulted regularly with the provincial governments during the CUFTA and NAFTA negotiations. In Washington meetings were held irregularly with representatives of the governors. In Mexico, as expected, there was little contact between the federal and state governments.[23]

The U.S. Constitution explicitly makes it clear that only Congress has the authority to regulate commerce between states or states and foreign government or to sign agreements with them. Section 8(3), Article I states Congress shall have power "to regulate commerce with foreign nations, and among the several States, and with the Indian tribes." In Canada the provincial governments have authority over natural resources and intraprovincial trade and commerce and the federal government does not have power unilaterally to implement agreements with other nations on matters involving provincial competence. This a matter subject to differing views.[24]

What Is NAFTA?

NAFTA provides rules and guidelines for dismantling trade barriers in goods and services and creating a trilateral free trade area encompassing the United States, Mexico and Canada. The free trade area eliminates barriers to trade but does not create full economic integration or a common external policy similar to the EU. NAFTA does, however, provide for substantially free flow of capital among the three parties to the agreement. Under NAFTA the definition of investment was broadened from that of CUFTA and covers virtually any investment, not just direct. CUFTA's institutional provisions were extended in NAFTA to include introduction of arbitration and dispute settlement procedures for investment.

NAFTA provides that investors from one member country should be treated no less favorably by federal, state or provincial governments than are the investors or investments of the domestic country or those of any other country. NAFTA has a Free Trade Commission to supervise implementation of the agreement. It consists of Cabinet-level representatives of the members. The Secretariat assists the commission in its work. NAFTA has no strong commission with an expert secretariat able to analyze issues, call attention to shortcomings of member countries in complying with obligations of the treaty or make proposals about new initiatives. Yet NAFTA has a variety of commissions, committees, working groups, panels, ad hoc advisory groups that is "mind boggling."[25]

Disputes

NAFTA permits each country to retain its laws, but it allows each to seek review of the others' rulings on trade through binational panels that will make binding judgments. A country has the option of trying to reverse these decisions by requesting a three-person challenge committee. The role of states and local governments in resolving disputes under NAFTA is limited. Only the federal government or in some cases individual investors have formal standing to utilize the NAFTA dispute resolution mechanisms. NAFTA does have a consultative process with states under a NAFTA Coordinator for State Matters.[26] Under Article 105, "The Parties shall ensure that all necessary measures are taken in order to give effect to the provisions of this Agreement, including the observance, except as otherwise provided in this Agreement, by state and provincial governments."

Subsidies

In the NAFTA negotiations the matter of subsidies was controversial and not easily resolved. In Canada and the United States, all levels of government are involved. In Mexico, most major subsidies have been given by the federal government.[27] There is no definition of a trade subsidy in the final text. Prime Minister Chretien of Canada obtained a commitment from the U.S. and Mexican presidents to address the definition of subsidies within two years. But the problem of defining subsidies has continued. A proposed solution is to use the WTO Agreement on Subsidies and Dumping as a basis for a precise definition of concepts such as "subsidies," "dumping," and "material injury."[28]

Many quarrels have arisen from the failure of CUFTA and NAFTA to prevent the use of domestic trade laws to settle international disputes. According to Roy MacLaren, Canadian minister for international trade, member countries' ability to apply their own national trade remedies, especially anti-dumping, is incompatible with the free trade area and remains NAFTA's unfinished business.[29]

Conditions for investment were more carefully spelled out. Article

1106:4 explicitly allows any advantages granted to an investor to be conditioned "on compliance with a requirement to locate production, provide a service, train or employ workers, construct or expand particular facilities, or carry out research and development, in its territory."

On the other hand, the receipt of an advantage in conjunction with an investment may not be conditioned with any of the following (Article 1106:3):

- to achieve a given level or percentage of domestic content
- to purchase, use or accord a preference to goods produced in its territory, or to purchase goods for producers in its territory
- to relate in any way the volume or value of imports to the volume or value of exports or to the amount of foreign exchange inflows associated with such investment
- to restrict sales of goods or services in its territory that such investment produces or provides by relating such sales in any way to the volume or value of its exports or foreign exchange earnings.

Chapter 19

Chapter 19 of NAFTA contains the review and dispute settlement procedure that specifically applies to antidumping and countervailing duties. Chapter 20 contains the institutional arrangements for implementation of the agreement and resolution of disputes other than those for antidumping and countervailing. Chapter 19 procedures provide for independent binational panels to review final antidumping and countervailing duty determinations made in each country. Panel decisions substitute for judicial review and are binding. Section 1902 gives each party the right to apply its AD and CVD to goods imported from the territory of any other party, including states and provinces. The same section states that if AD or CVD laws are amended, the amendment should not be inconsistent with GATT or successor agreements.

Chapter 20

Chapter 20 provides for rulings on the meaning of NAFTA. Under Chapter 20 the trilateral Trade Commission composed of cabinet-level officers, administers the agreement and assesses complaints from each country concerning violations of the agreement. If normal consultation fails to resolve a problem within forty-five days, a country could call a meeting of the Trade Commission for resolution. If that fails, a country could call for convening of an Arbitral Panel of experts from GATT or NAFTA, which issues a report with recommendations. If the parties do not accept recommendations, the country with the complaint can suspend application of equivalent benefits, for example, raising tariffs, until the issue is resolved. If the other country considers the retaliation excessive, it can seek another panel's recommendations.[30]

Adjustment Assistance

NAFTA contains no provision for adjustment assistance to displaced workers and affected communities. In the United States, two major federal dislocated-worker programs were in existence. Trade Adjustment Assistance (TAA) and Economic Dislocation and Worker Adjustment Assistance (EDWAA) were created to assist those who lose their jobs due to business closures and permanent layoffs. TAA is an entitlement program to help workers who lose their jobs because of increased imports. EDWAA gives assistance to all dislocated workers regardless of the reason for their dislocation.[31]

The movement of U.S. plants to Mexico and rising imports from Mexico were occurring prior to passage. NAFTA's implementing legislation set up special Trade Adjustment Assistance (NTAA) in January 1994 for U.S. workers who lost their jobs because production moved to or imports rose from Mexico and Canada. No requirement was included that a relationship with NAFTA be demonstrated.[32] It provides benefits in addition to those available under the EDWAA program. Certification process begins when a petition is filed with the governor of the state in which the affected workers' firm is located. Since NAFTA took effect, to 1997, 116,950 workers received special unemployment benefits under NTAA.[33]

In addition assistance is provided to secondary workers adversely affected by NAFTA. Secondary workers include those who supply or assemble products produced by directly affected firms certified under NAFTA-TAA. There are questions about dislocations extending beyond an individual state and coordinating the various states' petitions.[34] Nothing has been done about the adverse impact on communities. Assistance for workers should be supported by a program for communities since a viable community would facilitate the adjustment of workers.

An alternative trigger in the form of a regional determination has been suggested. This method could address two important elements of trader-related dislocation: First, trade-related dislocation tends to be highly concentrated by region; second, it is more difficult to find a new job in an area of high unemployment.[35]

NADBANK

Background

The North American Development Bank (NADBank) was created as an adjunct to NAFTA and opened in January 1995. Regional interests were involved in supporting formation of the bank. To facilitate its entry into NAFTA, Mexico wanted special economic support from the Clinton administration, such as a fund supported by the United States and Canada that would provide Mexico with capital to bolster areas such as infrastructure and environmental protection. It would be similar to the EU structural funds whereby poorer countries were rewarded for linking their economies with those of wealthier countries.

President Salinas said, "This is the first time in which there's going to be an agreement between economies so unequal in which there are no financial resources to support the less developed economy." The nations of North America should learn from the experience of Europe, he believed, in which "the channeling of resources" allowed the poorer countries "to rapidly advance toward a similar level of development as the other countries." Salinas pointed to disparities between the economies of the two countries. Since Mexico's GDP is just 3% that of the United States, some funding ought to be made available to Mexico.[36] The Canadian trade minister was quoted as saying that this was not a common market but rather a free trade zone, with a different relationship, and saw no basis for such help.[37] Canada did not become a member of the bank. President Clinton was more in accord with allocating financial resources for development that would be mutually beneficial. Any aid should go toward solving Mexico's environmental problems and building infrastructure.

A group of Mexican and U.S. economists proposed establishment of a Regional North American Development Bank and Adjustment Fund that would work on projects that included cleaning up the polluted U.S.-Mexico border and promoting development in rural Mexico. Such a bank would also provide funding for some programs in the United States and Canada, such as retraining workers who lose jobs because of plant transfers to Mexico. Professor Raul Hinojosa Ojeda of the University of California Los Angeles estimated that to get started, the bank would need a capital base of $5 billion, largely to be raised from member countries. With government guarantees, Hinojosa said, the bank could sell bonds that could raise its capital base to $20 billion.[38]

The U.S. Council of Mexico-U.S. Business Committee estimated that the two countries would need $6.5 billion over the next ten years to bring water supply, waste water treatment and waste disposal at the border to internationally acceptable levels. Billions of dollars more would be needed for roads, retraining programs and compensation for lost tariff revenue.[39]

The bilateral agreement between the United States and Mexico set up two new international organizations, the Border Environment Cooperation Commission (BECC) and the North American Development Bank (NADBank). BECC, which has its headquarters in Juarez, Chihuahua, assists border states in both countries to design and finance environmental infrastructure projects in the 2,000-mile border region. NADBank, based in San Antonio, finances environmental projects certified by BECC and provides support for community adjustment and investment projects. Paradoxically, there is no equivalent organization in the United States. NADBank is managed by a board that sets policies, oversees operations and approves its budget and all financial operations. The members are the U.S. secretaries of the Treasury and State and the administrator of the Environmental Protection Agency and Mexico's secretaries of Finance, Trade and Industrial Development and Social Development. The bank's decisions are subject to approval by both governments.

In addition to the environmental component NADBank has a second component called the Community Adjustment and Investment Program (CAIP). It utilizes up to 10% of NADBank capital to provide services in both countries, which need not be in the border region. The office for the program is in Los Angeles. The United States and Mexico each contribute $225 million for a total of $450 million over a four-year period to leverage additional funding. Earnings from this capital fund cover staff and office expenses.[40] Thus, capitalization was set at $3 billion: the $450 million of paid-in capital plus $2.55 billion in callable capital. While NADBank financing will concentrate on the area 100 kilometers on either side of the border, the international agreement also allows each country to use CAIP, 10% of paid-in capital contribution to NADBank, to finance domestic economic adjustment experienced by both communities and firms resulting from NAFTA in communities in both countries. NADBank will act as the lead bank in the financial packaging of border projects that have been environmentally certified by the Border Environment Cooperation Common (BECC). NADBank domestic financing will be coordinated with other programs and financial mechanisms available to national governments and to leverage NADBank capital to the maximum extent. It has been conservatively estimated that NADBank funds can leverage project financing of more than $29 billion for border investments.[41]

The NADBank U.S. domestic window has been constructed so as to make available up to $1 billion in federal financing for economic development, making NADBank the largest community development banking resource yet established.[42] Through the NADBank and BECC advisory committee structures, both institutions will rely on a continuous flow of information and advice from local governments, community groups and the private sector in regions where there is NADBank financing.

NADBank establishes a forum for a three-way dialogue: (1) non-governmental organizations (NGOs) representing the community constituent of the projects; (2) the private sector institutions that are potential investors to be leveraged by NADBank; and (3) the national and local governments on both sides of the border which must now learn how to combine and leverage their resources with NADBank funds.[43]

Transborder economic development projects differ from those within national boundaries in that government is a crucial participant in reconciling differing restrictions, inspections, import duties, safety and environmental requirements. Another difference in starting projects is that U.S. states close to the border have had much greater power to make decisions while Mexico has largely been tied to centralized decision-making. The multiplicity of funding sources for the U.S. projects indicates the complexity of obtaining financing.

BINATIONAL REGIONS

A byproduct of regional agreements such as CUFTA and NAFTA is a potential reduction in the importance of national borders and a stimulus to the advancement or formation of binational regional economies. The trade agreements contribute further to a diminution in the importance of national borders and the emergence of regional groupings. The existence of national borders is not conducive to optimum economic efficiency. The natural flow of goods, services, capital and labor between border areas is circumscribed. The future is likely to bring even closer economic, cultural, regional identities in which two cross-border cities have more in common with each other than with cities in their own countries. Should NAFTA stimulate economic integration in the natural regions that cross national boundaries, new subregional economic connections transcending national boundaries would arise. The direction of change is not toward a borderless world but toward more complex political organizations. Efforts to heighten competitive advantage are more likely to be undertaken successfully for many sectors at local and regional levels than at national levels.[44]

How will these areas evolve with overlapping boundaries? Will a border area become one entity? Will greater economic interdependence bring greater political interdependence? How will the economic inequality of the partners affect integration? Will both sides adopt the values of the stronger region or a new set of values or greater political friction? The border represents a region where problems of a new sort are generated. Municipalities in border cities bear the brunt of actions with state, national and international implications. An example of the lack of an action that delays integration, creation of a single trading market and more immediately affects border communities is the failure of NAFTA to have a common currency. Because of the weak Canadian and Mexican currencies, U.S. labor costs are increased and purchases in U.S. border communities deterred.[45]

Southwest

The Southwest border regions of the United States are already closely linked geographically and economically to Mexico. Even without NAFTA, the cross-border interchange is creating a new regional economy. The Southwest U.S. border region is defined as the counties adjacent to the 2,000-mile-long U.S.-Mexico border between the Pacific coast and Gulf of Mexico in the states of California, Arizona, New Mexico and Texas. The area is not a region in any formal sense but is sometimes considered one because it is a contiguous territory close to the border.

This new region's industrial capital is Monterrey, the northeastern Mexican city where the country's strongest conglomerates are based. The central Tex-Mex trading axis connects Monterrey to San Antonio, within the broader arc of an expanding Dallas–Mexico City relationship.[46] Nearly 40% of Texas's exports outside the United States go to Mexico. The U.S. Treasury estimates that of the 770,000 jobs that depend on exports to Mexico, one in three is in Texas.[47] Maquiladoras are an important component of the economic base. Mexico is Texas's largest trading partner and shares four border states: Nuevo Leon, Tamaulipas, Coahuila and Chihuahua. In 1995, the Texas legislature mandated that the commerce agency close its overseas offices in Asia and Europe while increasing funding for ties with Mexico.[48]

The governors of Texas and the four Mexican states sharing a border with Texas have been putting together a regional development plan that commits them to a joint effort in marketing and infrastructure. They have been working on a commitment of resources and time to jointly promote their region of 27.1 million people and GDP of $475 billion. Backers of the regional plan have been confident that a new era of cooperation is being ushered in, partly because for the first time in modern Mexican history, the centralized government is handing real powers and decision-making authority to the states.[49]

Canada

More large firms already see Canada and the United States not only as one market for trade but as a single area with a number of regions, for purposes of production. "To put it bluntly the logic of a single North American market is leading us to a major harmonization of provincial public policy in a whole range of areas which up to now were considered as the exclusive jurisdiction of our own 'distinct' society."[50] Since 1990, total trade between the Canadian provinces and the rest of the world has increased much faster than trade within Canada; much of the growth is due to the increase in north-south trade, especially after the inception of CUFTA, and to the improved cost-competitiveness of Canadian products. It raises the question of the economic future of Canada in terms of outside links. Strong internal economic links are crucial to Canada's economy, and these links should be strengthened. If foreign markets were totally open, there would be less need to strengthen the Canadian economic union.[51]

CUFTA facilitated the removal of the artificial border barriers between the two countries. The result has been the creation of two cross-border regional economies, Seattle-Vancouver and the Great Lakes. In the Pacific Northwest, the cities of Vancouver and Seattle have an extensive array of joint projects and are creating a de facto cross-border regional economy. Simultaneously, the province of British Columbia and state of Washington are confronting each other over such issues as softwood lumber, water diversion, salmon fishery and hydroelectric exports. In one case the states and provinces differ on trade-related matters and FTA, and in another the cities are cooperating.[52] In the Pacific Northwest, the growing trade of Oregon, Washington and Alaska with British Columbia has made "Cascadia" a standard marketing and industrial planning concept.[53]

The Pacific Northwest Economic Region (PNWER) is an association of state and provincial legislators from Alberta, British Columbia, Alaska, Oregon, Washington, Montana and Idaho. A de facto region, one of the most porous and most constructively cooperative in North America, exists in Quebec, New York state and New England.

NOTES

1. Peter Morici, *Trade Talks With Mexico: A Time for Realism* (Washington: National Planning Association, 1991), p. 91.
2. James E. McConnell and Albert Michaels, *A North American Free Trade Area: An Overview of Issues and Opinions* (Buffalo: Canada- U.S. Trade Center, State University of New York, March 1991), Occasional Paper No. 9, pp. 2–3.
3. Peter Morici, "The Implications for the Future of U.S. Trade Policy," in Peter Morici, ed., *Making Free Trade Work* (New York: Council on Foreign Relations, 1990), p. 128.
4. Thomas M. Boddez and Michael J. Trebilcock, *Unfinished Business Reforming Trade Remedy Laws in North America*, Policy Study 17 (Toronto: C. D. Howe Institute, 1993) pp. 235–236.
5. Bruce W. Wilkerson, "The Canada-U.S. Free Trade Negotiations: An Assessment," in David L. McKee, ed., *Canadian American Economic Relations Conflict and Cooperation on a Continental Scale* (Westport, Conn.: Praeger

Publishers, 1988), p. 92.

6. Benjamin Higgins, "Subsidies, Regional Development and the Canada-U.S. Free Trade Agreement," *Canadian Journal of Regional Science* 13 (Summer–Autumn 1990), p. 260.

7. Glen Williams, "Canadian Sovereignty and the Free Trade Debate," in Alan M. Maslove and Stanley L. Winer, eds., *Canadian Perspective on the Political Economy of Freer Trade with the United States* (Halifax: Institute for Research in Public Policy, 1987), p. 113.

8. Carolyn J. Touhy, *Policy and Politics in Canada Institutionalized Ambivalence* (Philadelphia: Temple University Press, 1992), p. 223.

9. Barbara McDougall, "Political Perspectives" in Jeffrey J. Schott and Murray G. Smith, eds., *The Canada-U.S. Free Trade Agreement: The Global Impact* (Washington: Institute for International Economics, 1988), p. 181.

10. Morley Gunderson, "Regional Dimensions of the Impact of Free Trade on Labor," *Canadian Journal of Regional Science* 13 (Summer–Autumn 1990), p. 247.

11. John O'Grady, Ontario Federation of Labor, "Labor Market Policy and Industrial Strategy After the CUFTA: The Policy Debate in Ontario," proceedings of the Industrial Relations Research Association, 1990 Spring meeting, Buffalo, May 2–4, 1990, p. 472.

12. Touhy, *Policy and Politics,* pp. 323–324.

13. Judith H. Bello and Gilbert R. Winham, "The Canada-USA Free Trade Agreement," in Leonard Waverman, ed., *Negotiating and Implementing a North American Free Trade Agreement* (Vancouver: the Fraser Institute, 1992), pp. 50–53.

14. Reed Scowen, delegate general for Quebec in New York, "Sovereign Citizens of America the Quebec Economy and the Clinton Administration," speech at the Canadian Club of Montreal, February 8, 1993, p. 6.

15. Harold Crookell, *Canadian American Trade and Investment Under the FTA* (Westport, Conn.: Quorum Books, 1990), p. 201.

16. William Orme, *Continental Shift* (Washington: Washington Post, 1993), pp. 151–153.

17. Richard Johns and Robert Graham, "Hands Across the Border," *Financial Times,* June 11, 1990, p. 16.

18. Edelgard Mahant and Xavier DeVansssay, "The Origins of Customs Unions and Free Trade Areas," *Journal of European Integration* 17 (Winter–Spring 1994), p. 204.

19. Johns and Graham, "Hands," p. 16.

20. Tim Golden, "Under Free-Trade Pact, Mexico Is Envisioning an Economy in U.S. Image," *New York Times,* July 23, 1992, p. D8.

21. Jonathan Schlefer, "What Price Economic Growth?" *Atlantic Monthly,* December 1992, p. 113.

22. Earl Fry, "The Economic Policies of Subnational Governments in North America: The Potential Impact on NAFTA," in A. R. Riggs and Tom Velk, eds., *Beyond NAFTA: An Economic, Political and Sociological Perspective* (Vancouver: Fraser Institute, 1993), p. 124.

23. Ibid., pp. 130–131.

24. Bello and Winham, "Canada USA Free Trade Agreement," p. 52 and Touhy, *Policy and Politics,* pp. 323–324.

25. Sidney Weintraub, *NAFTA: What Comes Next,* Washington Papers 166

(Washington: Center for Strategic and International Studies, 1994), p. 65.

26. Conrad Weiler, "GATT, NAFTA and State and Local Powers," *Intergovernmental Perspective* 20 (Fall 1993–Winter 1994), p. 41.

27. R. Cecelia Siac, *Does Mexico Subsidize Too Much? Perceptions vs. Realities,* Commentary No.r 36 (Toronto: C. D. Howe Institute, February 1992), p. 2.

28. Lorraine Eden and Maureen Appel Molot, "The Challenge of NAFTA: Canada's Role in the North American Automobile Industry," in *NAFTA's Impact on the North American Automobile Industry,* 5 North American Outlook (Washington: National Planning Association, November 1994), p. 86, and Robert Howse, *Settling Trade Remedy Disputes: When the WTO Forum Is Better Than the NAFTA,* Commentary no. 111 (Toronto: C.D. Howe Institute, June 1998), p. 2.

29. "NAFTA's Progress Northern Rumblings," *The Economist* 334 (January 14, 1994), p. 6A.

30. Harry L. Clark and John R. Magnus, "Fix NAFTA's Dispute System," *Journal of Commerce* (September 8, 1995), p. 6A.

31. U.S. General Accounting Office, *Dislocated Workers Comparison of Programs,* GAO/T-HRD-92-57 (September 10, 1992), p. 2.; Morris L. Sweet, "Plant Closing Legislation: An Influence on Location in Industrial Location Policy," in *Industrial Location Policy for Economic Revitalization* (Westport, Conn.: Praeger Publishers, 1981), Chap. 8; and Sheldon Friedman and Jane McDonald Pines, "In Search of a New Covenant for America's Dislocated Workers," in *Adjusting to NAFTA: Strategies for Business and Labor,* 4 North American Outlook (Washington: National Planning Association, September 1993), pp. 67–100.

32. U.S. Department of Commerce, International Trade Administration, *The Case for NAFTA,* September 26, 1995.

33. John Maggs et al., "Political Plutonium," *Journal of Commerce* (May 2, 1997), p. 1A.

34. U.S. General Accounting Office, *Dislocated Workers An Early Look at the NAFTA Transitional Adjustment Assistance Program,* GTAO/HCHS-95-31 (November 1994), p. 2.

35. Howard Rosen, "Assisting U.S. Labor Market Adjustment to Freer Trade Under NAFTA" *North American Outlook* (National Planning Association), September 1993, p. 34.

36. Matt Moffett and Dianna Solis, "Mexico Will Ask U.S., Canada for Aid to Smooth Its Entry to Free Trade Pact," *Wall Street Journal,* December 8, 1992, p. A11.

37. *NAFTA Digest* 2 (January 1993), p. 2.

38. Moffett and Solis, "Mexico Will Ask," p. A11..

39. Nancy Dunne, "Special Bank May Help NAFTA Win Approval," *Financial Times,* July 16, 1993, p. 4, and "On the Mexican Border the Sewage War," *The Economist* 348 (August 8, 1998), p. 29

40. U.S. General Accounting Office, *North American Free Trade Agreement Structure and Status of Implementing Organizations,* GAO/GGD-95-10BR (October 1994).

41. Paul Hinojosa-Ojeda, "The North American Development Bank Forging New Directions in Regional Integration Policy," *Journal of the American Planning Association* 60 (Summer 1994), pp. 301–302.

42. Ibid., p. 303.

43. Ibid., p. 303.

44. Stephen Blank, "The Emerging Architecture of North America" in A. R. Riggs and Tom Velk, eds., *Beyond NAFTA: An Economic, Political and Sociological Perspective* (Vancouver: Fraser Institute, 1993), p. 33.

45. Michelle A. Saint Germain, "Public Sector Impacts of NAFTA on U.S. and Mexico Border Cities," paper presented at the 56th Annual Conference of the American Society of Public Administration, San Antonio, Texas, July 1995, p. 2.

46. "The Mexican Rescue Scenes From a Border," *The Economist* 334 (February 4, 1995), p. 25.

47. Ibid.

48. Kevin G. Hall, "Texas Shifts Mexico Strategy to Stress State Ties," *Journal of Commerce* (January 3, 1996), p. 3A.

49. "Texas, Four American States Sign Accord," *NAFTA Digest* 5 (March 1996), p. 3.

50. Scowen, "Sovereign Citizens," p. 8.

51. Daniel Schwanen, *Drawing on Our Inner Strength: Canada's Economic Citizenship in an Era of Evolving Federalism*, Commentary Number 82 (Toronto: C. D. Howe Institute, June 1996), p. 8.

52. Peter Karl Kresl, "Sub-national Governments and Regional Trade Liberalization in Europe and North America, *Journal of European Integration* 17 (Winter-Spring 1994), p. 333.

53. Stephen Blank in Riggs and Velk, *Beyond NAFTA*, p. 31.

PART II

EUROPEAN UNION

Chapter 6

Institutions

TERMINOLOGY

An understanding of the European Union's institutional framework helps to clarify the regional structure and operations. In view of the confusion in terminology engendered by the Treaty on European Union, which came into force April 1993, the public perception has been muddled on the differences between the European Union (EU) and European Community (EC) and the effect on the decision-making process. There are three pillars to the EU. The Union encompasses them all but does not yet enjoy its own legal personality. Only the EC has the legal personality and the power to conclude treaties with non-member countries. For example, the EC, not the EU, is a member of the WTO. The first pillar is the EC, under which most policy matters fall, such as regional policy, single market, common agricultural policy. The other two pillars are the common foreign and security policy and justice and home affairs, under the jurisdiction of the European Union. In view of the difficulties in delineating the terms "European Community" and "European Union," for purposes of clarity, unless specifically designated or where EC was used previously, the term "European Union" will be used. For consistency, EU, which incorporates all aspects of the Maastricht Treaty, generally takes precedence.[1]

HISTORY

The foundations were laid on May 9, 1950, when Robert Schuman, the French foreign minister, proposed a plan worked out with Jean Monnet, who had headed the French postwar planning effort for France and Germany, to pool their coal and steel production under a joint high authority within an organization open to any other country in Europe that wished to join. The European Coal and Steel Community (ECSC) was set up in 1951 under the Treaty of Paris and given responsibility for the broad regulation of the two key sectors of the MS economies, coal and steel. Six countries, Belgium, Germany, France, Italy, Luxembourg, Netherlands, signed the treaty, which it was hoped would be the nucleus from which further political integration of Europe would grow, culminating in a European constitution. It involved guaranteeing market supplies of coal and steel, regulating prices, improving workers' conditions, promoting trade and investment, and helping the industries to make vital structural adjustments to meet changing world economic conditions.[2] The ECSC is scheduled to expire at the end of its fifty-year term in 2002.

The European Community was created by the 1957 Treaty of Rome; it established the European Economic Community (EEC) and European Atomic Energy Community (Euratom). EEC was concerned with general economic integration. The objective was to transform the member states' (MSs) separate and disparate markets into a large common market where people and goods could move about as freely as in a domestic market. The EEC was largely conceived as a customs union, without a strong commitment to the coordination of economic and monetary policies. By the end of the 1960s, when the customs union had been successfully built, plans were being laid for an eventual economic and monetary union (EMU). Euratom aimed to promote the growth and development of nuclear industries and to secure their supplies of fissionable material. The nuclear research and training programs led to setting up the Joint Research Centre, consisting of four nuclear research establishments.

The regional or subnational level of Europe was not overly involved in the first phase of the restructuring of Europe. Regions were not mentioned in the Treaty of Rome since in the Community of that period only the Federal Republic of Germany and Belgium had states or regions as institutionalized components of the state or administrative structure.

Originally the Community consisted of the six European Steel and Coal Community members. In 1973, the United Kingdom, Ireland and Denmark joined; Greece joined in 1981 and Spain and Portugal in 1986. Austria, Finland and Sweden became members on January 1, 1995 for a total of fifteen countries.

Article 3(j) of the Treaty of Rome established the European Investment Bank (EIB) "to facilitate the economic expansion of the Community by opening up fresh resources," and the EIB became fully operational shortly after the treaty went into effect. It began operations in 1959 under Articles 129 and 130 (now Article 198). It has been a source of development finance for the balanced and integrated development of the common market.

On January 1, 1959, the first step was taken toward eliminating customs duties among the MSs and establishing a common external tariff. In January 1962, the Common Agricultural Policy (CAP) was adopted. Until July 1967, the three communities had separate councils and executive commissions (the high authority in the ECSC). By contrast, Parliament and the Court of Justice have been common to the three communities since 1958. Since 1967, a single commission and single council exercised all the powers and responsibilities vested in their respective predecessors, EEC, ECSC and Euratom. The official name was changed from EEC to EC. On July 1, 1968, all customs duties were eliminated in trade among MSs, and a common external tariff was established.

In March 1979, the European Council launched the European Monetary System. This system established an official currency basket (called European currency unit or ECU) that is used as means of settlement among monetary authorities of the EC. This system requires member countries to peg their currencies to the ECU, and permits only a small fluctuation in value around the peg. The ECU is scheduled to be replaced by the Euro, a common currency.

The Single European Act (SEA) was signed in February 1986 to create the Single European Market (SEM), which extended the Community's field of competence and brought about significant changes in relations between institutions and their operating rules. The first and most important benefit was the creation of a single, integrated European market. In addition to the benefits from economic integration there would be other economic benefits, reduction of costs and creation of new opportunities.

The Treaty on EU (Maastricht Treaty) was signed Feb 7, 1992, effective November 1, 1993. The three Communities, European Community Steel and Coal Community (ECSC), European Atomic Energy Community (Euratom) and European Economic Community (EEC), were changed to European Community. From the legal point of view the three communities constituting the EC continue to exist side by side. In terms of political reality they can be treated as a single unit and their creation can be regarded as marking the start of the European Community under the European Union.

THE LEGISLATIVE PROCESS

The Treaty on EU changed the role of the institutions and the legislative process. The main actors in the revised legislative process are the Council of Ministers, the Commission, the Parliament and two consultative committees, the Economic and Social Committee and the Committee of the Regions. The European Council consists of the heads of state and its name was not changed by the EU. The Council of Ministers of the EC was changed to the Council of the EU, the main decision-making body. The various MSs are deeply enmeshed in the Union's political system and dominate it by having their hands firmly on the principal levers of decision-making in the Council. Though the Commission has a key role in proposing courses of action, it is the Council that decides. Ministers, who vary according to the matter under consideration, make decisions after prolonged discussions and negotiations with other bodies. The foreign minister is considered the country's main representative. Parliament also has to be consulted though its powers are limited. The Council is sensitive to demands from national governments and electorates as well as to the Union as an institution. Voting power is not allocated equally among the MSs:

Member States	Votes
Germany, Britain, France, Italy	10
Spain	8
Netherlands, Greece, Belgium, Portugal	5
Sweden, Austria	4
Denmark, Finland, Ireland	3
Luxembourg	2
	87

Eight countries out of fifteen constitute a simple majority. A qualified majority is based on the addition of votes allocated to each MS, bringing total votes in Council to a qualified majority of sixty-two votes out of eighty-seven, where Council's deliberations are based on a proposal from the Commission. In other cases those sixty-two votes must also include votes in favor from at least ten MSs.

The following provisions in the Treaty require unanimity in the Council:

Article 93	State aid
Article 103a	Financial assistance for an MS in economic difficulty
Article 130	Industry and undertakings
Article 130b	Specific actions outside the Structural Funds
Article 130d	Structural Funds and Cohesion Fund;
Article 198a & b	Committee of the Regions, appointment of members and officers;

There are four categories of legislation:

Regulations, which must be imposed and are directly applicable in law to all MSs;
Directives, which are binding as to ends to be achieved, but leave it to national
    authorities as to the means of introduction;
Decisions, which are addressed to specific groups and which are binding in their
    entirety;
Recommendations and *opinions*, which have no binding legal force.

COMMISSION

Commission members are nominated by MSs in common accord after consultation with the Parliament. The Commission acts as guardian of the Treaties and has power to initiate and implement legislation. The twenty members' term of office is set at five years concurrent with the EP. Members are appointed by the MSs as follows: Germany, Britain, France, Italy, Spain: 2; Netherlands, Greece, Belgium, Portugal, Sweden, Austria, Denmark, Finland, Ireland, Luxembourg: 1.

In addition to the twenty senior members there is the Commission's structure or the "civil service," the major divisions, the twenty-six Directorates-General, with a staff of 15,000.

EUROPEAN PARLIAMENT

Parliament represents the 370 million population of the EU memberr states and provides a forum for democratic debate. Membership has been increased to 626; members are elected and have five-year terms. Representation originates in the member states on a proportional basis:

Austria	21	Italy	87
Belgium	25	Luxembourg	6
Denmark	16	Netherlands	31
Finland	16	Portugal	25
France	87	Spain	64
Germany	99	Sweden	22
Greece	25	United Kingdom	87
Ireland	15		

The February 1997 breakdown by political party shows the largest group to be the European Socialists:

Party of European Socialists	214	Europe Radical Alliance	20
European People's Party	181	Independents for the	
Union for Europe	56	Europe of Nations	18
Liberal, Democratic and		Nonattached	33
Reform Parties	43	European Political Alliance	19
European United Left/		Europe of Nations	19
Nordic Green Left	33	Non-affiliated	31

The powers of the Parliament can be divided into three categories, legislative, budgetary and supervisory.

Legislative

Initially under the 1957 Treaty of Rome, Parliament had only a consultative role, with the Commission proposing and the Council of Ministers deciding on legislation. However, its powers have been increased by the Single European Act and Maastricht Treaty and extended beyond consultation to a degree of power sharing auch that Parliament has the influence to amend and adopt legislation. But its powers are essentially negative. It can veto legislation in fifteen areas; it has a say in the choice of the new Commission; and its formal approval is necessary for such treaties as WTO. Of greatest importance is the measure of control over the allocation of the EU's ECU 80 billion annual budget (though not in tax policy).

The consultation role, which still exists, calls for an opinion from the Parliament prior to adoption by the Council of a proposal emanating from the Commission. The cooperation process allows the Parliament to amend both the Commission proposal and the Council's preliminary position. This procedure applies to such areas as the ERDF, research and the environment. Decision-making power is shared equally between the Parliament and the Council. A committee made up of equal numbers of Parliament members and the Council with the Commission present looks for a compromise on a text that both the Council and Parliament can both endorse. If there is no agreement the Parliament can reject the proposal outright. The assent of the Parliament is a requirement for major international agreements, the organization and objectives of the Structural and Cohesion Funds.

Budgetary

The annual budget of the Union has to be approved by the Parliament. As part of the process, the Parliament can propose modifications and amendments to the initial proposals of the Commission as well as the positions taken by the members states in the Council. On certain types of spending, the Council has the final word, but on such expenditures as regional funds, the Parliament decides in cooperation with the Council. The Parliament can vote to reject the budget. Monitoring of expenditures is also a continuing function of the Parliament.

Supervisory

Executive power is shared between the Commission and Council, which regularly report to the Parliament and respond to interrogation by it. The Parliament has a role every five years in the appointment of the president and members of the Commission. In the most drastic circumstances, the Parliament can censure the Commission and bring about its resignation. Though the Parliament has been slowly accruing power, it remains a predominantly consultative body with powers to block rather than initiate legislation.[3]

ECONOMIC AND SOCIAL COMMITTEE

This Committee provides institutional representation to workers, employers and various interest groups; it has 222 members appointed for four-year terms by the Council after consulting with the Commission. It must be consulted before decisions are made on certain subjects and can issue opinions on its own initiative.

COMMITTEE OF THE REGIONS

The Committee of the Regions must be consulted on matters involving education, culture, public health, trans-European networks and economic and social cohesion and may also issue opinions on its own initiative.

COURT OF JUSTICE

The Court of Justice judicially interprets EU law and ensures that it is uniformly observed. The fifteen judges and nine advocates-general are appointed for renewable six-year terms by agreement with the MSs. The Court of First Instance covers actions by individuals and companies against decisions of the EU institutions.

COURT OF AUDITORS

The Court of Auditors monitors financial management of the Union. The fifteen members are appointed for six-year terms in agreement with the MSs after consultation with Parliament.

EUROPEAN INVESTMENT BANK

This Bank facilitates financing of projects that contribute to balanced development of the Union.

FEDERALISM AND FUNCTIONALISM

Prior to the inception of the ECSC in 1951, two approaches were considered for European integration — federalist and functionalist. The federalist approach is that local, regional, national and European authorities should cooperate with and complement each other. The functionalist approach favors a gradual transfer of sovereignty from a national to the Union level. Today the two approaches have merged in the conviction that national and regional authorities need to be matched by independent democratic institutions with responsibility for areas in which joint action is more effective than action by individual states: single market, monetary policy, economic and social cohesion, foreign and security policy.[4]

The EU differs from other international organizations in its unique institutional structure. By accepting the Treaties of Paris, Rome and Maastricht, the MSs give up a measure of sovereignty to independent institutions representing national and shared interests with the goal of forming a cohesive, indissoluble organizational and political unit.[5] They have endowed the Union with sovereign powers of its own, independent of MSs, which it can exercise to adopt acts that have the force of national law. This novel approach of pooling national sovereignty and policies is commonly referred to as integration. Though the Union has extensive autonomy and law-making powers, it does not have the enforcement machinery found in a federal state.

NOTES

1. "Community or Union? Some Matters of Style," *Eurecom* New York 5 (December 1993), p. 2.

2. International Labor Office, *Income Security in Europe in the Light of Structural Change*, Report III, Geneva, January 1974, pp. 49–51.

3. "The Men Who Run Europe," *Financial Times*, March 1, 1995, p. 1.

4. Pascal Fontaine, *Europe in Ten Lessons* (Brussels: European Union, Commission, 1995) second edition, p. 5.

5. Ibid., p. 9.

Chapter 7

Committee of the Regions

INTRODUCTION

Though the United States has independent subnational organizations representing cities, counties and states, there is no equivalent to the Committee of the Regions (COR) which has an official role in the EU. The Commission recognized the existence of the growing interest of regions in Community policy and in 1988 established an Advisory Committee of Regional and Local Authorities. It was not an influential body but was the first formal venue for influencing Community policy.

Establishment of the Committee of the Regions was a major achievement for groups that sought to use negotiations surrounding the Maastricht Treaty on EU as an opportunity to strengthen the role of regional authorities in the governance of the EU. These forces consisted notably of the German Lander, Belgian and Spanish regions/communities, the Strasbourg-based Assembly of European Regions, and the Conference on a "Europe of the Regions" launched by Bavaria to accompany the Maastricht process. They saw in the Committee an opportunity to obtain greater input in those EU policies relevant to the regions and in the long run to start a movement in the direction of a third chamber, possibly a Senate based on the regions, that would have full legislative power alongside the Council of Ministers and the Parliament.[1]

The German Lander objected to the Treaty speaking of the Committee as composed of "representatives of regional and local bodies." They did not want local government representatives as members. They recognized that in some MSs there was no administrative or political structure, such as regions, between the national government and the local government, and they contended that the Committee should consist of representatives from the next lower level of government beneath the national level.[2]

In October 1991, the Commission proposed establishment of a Committee of the Regions to advise the Council and Commission on relevant issues. The Commission wanted to strengthen the voice of the regions, but some national governments were cool to the proposal. However, several MSs were insistent that regional and local authorities should be directly involved in deliberations at the Community level. In these countries the subnational authorities enjoyed wide-ranging powers either because of the federal structure of the country or by virtue of legislative or constitutional measures adopted over the last few decades.[3]

The MSs agreed and a provision for a Committee of Regions was included in the Maastricht Treaty. Article 198, effective November 1993, was the first legal recognition of the existence of local and regional governments and a legal obligation to consult representatives of local and regional authorities on a variety of matters. It was modeled after the Economic and Social Committee (ESC) which was of concern to the Committee of the Regions. The Treaty of Rome gave ESC equal status with Parliament; Parliament proceded to become a major player, a status ESC never attained.

The election of the first president in 1994 was a compromise. The president represented the regional association, the Assembly of the European Regions, and the vice president represented the local government association with the understanding that they would swap jobs midway through their four-year terms.[4]

MEMBERSHIP

Members of the Committee and alternate members are nominated by the MSs and officially appointed by the Council of Ministers unanimously for four-year renewable terms. The president and vice president are elected by the assembly for two-year terms. The 222 members of the body include regional presidents, mayors of large cities and leaders of county and city councils. The distribution of members does not relate directly to population as for example in Luxembourg.

Members

Austria	12	Italy	24
Belgium	12	Luxembourg	6
Denmark	9	Netherlands	12
Finland	9	Portugal	12
France	24	Spain	21
Germany	24	Sweden	12
Greece	12	United Kingdom	24
Ireland	9		

Policy-related work of the Committee is carried on by eight commissions and four subcommissions, balancing regional and local interests:

1. Regional development, economic development, local and regional finances subcommission-local and regional finances.
2. Spatial planning, agriculture, fisheries, forestry, marine environment and upland areas subcommission tourism, rural areas.
3. Transport and communications networks subcommission, telecommunications.
4. Urban policies.
5. Land-use planning, environment, energy.
6. Education, training.
7. Citizen's Europe, research, culture, youth and consumers subcommission, youth and sport.
8. Economic and social cohesion, social policy, public health.

ROLE

The Committee represents formal recognition of the legitimacy of regional representation at the supranational level. Although it need only be consulted on Commission proposals with a direct or indirect regional impact, the Committee may deliberate on any proposal sent to the ESC and may issue opinions on its own initiative. The Council and Commission may consult the Committee in other areas of interest to territorial authorities. The Committee can adopt opinions on other subjects on its own initiative and send them to the Commission, Council, and Parliament.

The Committee must be consulted by the Commission in five policy areas:

1. Economic and social cohesion (including the Structural Funds).
2. Trans-European transport, telecommunications and energy infrastructure networks.
3. Public health.
4. Education and youth.
5. Culture.

The Committee has advisory status. Essentially it is a consultative body but the Commission and Council are obliged to consult the Committee where provided for in the Treaties or where they deem it appropriate. Neither the Council nor the Commission is required to act on Committee opinions.

A common theme in most Committee opinions is that local and regional authorities should play an important part in the definition, management and evaluation of Union policies of concern to them. Although the Committee has few real powers, there is some hope that it could eventually form a second chamber in the EP. Already regions are cooperating with little concern for national boundaries.[5]

The Committee has sought to strengthen its position in the Union as it seeks to have the definition of the subsidiarity principle (i.e., that decisions should be taken by public authorities as close to the citizens as possible) be revised to contain an explicit reference to the role of regions and local authorities. It should be given the right of recourse before the Court of Justice to protect its prerogatives or in cases where the principle of subsidiarity is violated. This right could also be given to regions that have legislative powers in their own MSs. The Committee should be made a full EU institution with a reinforcement of its advisory status and full organizational and budgetary autonomy from the Economic and Social Committee. The consultative function of the Committee should be strengthened.[6]

Because the Committee lacks any real legislative power it is forced to rely on its ability to persuade rather than to compel others ito accept its position. The Committee has sought to do this by building a close working relationship with the other institutions; however, as it has been operating for a relatively short time, the results of such cooperation are unclear. Thus, it is uncertain as to what extent Committee will be able to influence regional legislation.[7]

On April 19, 1995, the Commission adopted a set of rules on communications with the Committee to strengthen and formalize relations with the Committee.[8] The Commission sought to improve cooperation with the Committee in the following three ways:

1. When it draws up its annual work program, it will identify the items that it will be referring to the Committee for an opinion and will endeavor to consult the Committee when it publishes white or green papers. A white paper is an official set of proposals in a specific policy area. A green paper offers a range of ideas as a basis for discussions prior to reaching a decision.
2. The Commission will strive to provide the Committee with all the assistance it needs to operate smoothly.
3. The Committee will take greatest possible account of the Committee's opinions and views in its proposals as well as in implementation of policies.

As for items on which the Committee will be consulted, the Commission will not restrict itself to the five fields in which consultation is

mandatory under the Treaty (economic and social cohesion, telecommunications and energy, education, health and culture) but will apply the
following three criteria:

1. The matter in question falls within the scope of the regulatory or imple-
    menting powers exercised by decentralized bodies.
2. The planned rules are likely to have a direct impact on the operation of
    regional or local administration.
3. The economic impact of Union action is likely to differ from one region to
    another.

EVALUATION

If MSs appoint members, how independent will the Committee be in
representing regional as opposed to national interests? Regional and local
authorities of several countries have stressed that it is for them to designate their representatives on the Committee even if formal appointment
will be by the Council on the MSs' recommendation.

The establishment of the Committee increases the potential avenues
of influence for regional and local governments in the policy process. A
structure such as the Committee of the Regions can provide a forum for
exchanging experiences and an avenue for concentrating regional interests, perhaps even strengthening regional authorities. Will the channeling
and concentration of regional interests in the policy process lead to a
strengthening of regions in terms of influencing policy decisions?

In its brief existence the Committee has struggled with a wide range
of issues, including guidelines for a trans-European airport network,
development of rural tourism, the right of European citizens to vote in
local elections in a member state of which they are not citizens or nation-
als, and a transition to a European information society. A constant theme
running through its opinions is the need to involve the regions and localities much more closely in the design and implementation of policies.
One viewpoint is that in issuing opinions on its own initiative, "it may be
running the risk of casting its net too wide."[9]

As to the future of such entities as the Committee, one approach is
that Europeans are more inclined to link their identities and allegiances
to cities and regions while national governments have less relevance to
their lives. As borders have become more porous across Europe, many
cities and regions have forged new transnational ties. They are slowly
building a new political structure for Europe based on city-states remi-
niscent of the Hanseatic League, the alliance of northern port cities whose
economic clout helped them become sovereign entities in the fifteenth
and sixteenth centuries.[10]

NOTES

1. Charles Jeffrey, "Whither the Committee of the Regions? Reflections on the Committee's Opinion on the Revision of the Treaty on European Union," *Regional and Federal Studies* 5 (Summer 1995), p. 27.

2. Guenther Schaefer, "Regions in the Policy Process of the EC—Reflections on the Innovations of the Maastricht Treaty," *EIPASCOPE* European Institute of Public Administration 3 (1993), p. 9.

3. Emile Noel, *Working Together The Institutions of the European Community* (European Union, Commission, European Documentation, 1994), p. 50.

4. Jeffrey, "Whither the Committee?"pp. 253–254.

5. Dana Milbank, "With European Union as a Safety Net, Many Regional Groups Seek Autonomy," *Wall Street Journal,* February 24, 1995, p. A6.

6. European Union, Committee of the Regions, *Institutional Reform,* May 1995, p. 27.

7. American Chamber of Commerce in Belgium, *EU Environment Guide* (The EC Committee, 1995), p. 123.

8. European Union, Commission, "Commission Communication on Relations with the Committee of the Regions," *Bulletin* 4 (1995), p. 94.

9. European Union, Commission, Intergovernmental Conference, Report for the Reflection Group, *Treaty on European Union* (Maastricht, 1995).

10. William Drozdiak, "Regions on the Rise," *Washington Post,* October 22, 1995, p. A22.

Chapter 8

Regional Policy

THE CASE FOR A REGIONAL POLICY

The aim of EU regional policy is to reduce and prevent regional disparities by allocating resources to less-favored regions without replacing national regional programs and taking account of integration, enlargement, globalization and technology. The need to reduce regional disparities has long been recognized by the principal MSs. In contrast the existence of a separate EU regional policy is a fairly recent phenomenon; the European Regional Development Fund (ERDF) was established only in 1975. With problem regions heavily concentrated in MSs unable to allocate adequate financial resources, the Union had to become involved in regional issues. Furthermore, the Union as a whole benefits from a high level of prosperity and the elimination of inequities. Fifteen MSs trying to resolve their own regional problems can produce chaos if local authorities, regional agencies and national governments all actively promote economic development at the expense of other Union entities. The Union has to ensure that regional development occurs where most needed and resources are channeled into the most severely disadvantaged regions. The Union regional policy has gone beyond traditional national government practices such as direct subsidies and tax incentives to restructure problem regions. Regional policy has been shaped by clearly defined goals deriving from the Single European Act (SEA) and Economic and Monetary Union (EMU).

EVOLUTION OF THE POLICY

Structural policy is the means by which the Union promotes cohesion (i.e., reduction of economic and social disparities between richer and poorer regions). It encompasses regional policy (to reduce spatial disparities, regenerate old industrial areas, assist rural development), aspects of social policy (to combat long term unemployment, foster vocational education and training), and a small part of the Common Agricultural Policy (CAP) (to assist rural development). The instruments of structural policy are the European Regional Development Fund, European Social Fund (ESF), Guidance Section of the European Agricultural Guidance and Guarantee Fund (EAGGF) and Financial Instrument for Fisheries Guidance (FIFG). Additional instruments are the European Investment Bank (EIB) and European Coal and Steel Community (ECSC).

There have been three phases in regional policy. The first, which lasted until 1975, was characterized by a lack of any common regional policy. The second was marked by the creation of new instruments, strengthening of the regional policy dimension and the amounts of money spent. The third phase is connected to the reform of the Structural Funds in 1988.

Regional policy was not a major consideration in the establishment of the Community. The Spaak Report, which predated the Treaty of Rome, did not anticipate that any long-run disruptions or imbalances would result from the creation of a customs union. The belief was that the "invisible hand" of market forces would correct any significant regional disparities in a homogeneous economic space. In drafting the Treaty the free market was emphasized, and only a secondary role was given to overcoming disparities, considered largely temporary and exceptional rather than endemic. They could be minimized by careful coordination of economic policies of MSs and opting for establishment of the EIB.[1]

The preamble to the 1957 Treaty of Rome mentioned the need to reduce regional disparities but contained few specific approaches. References to regional problems in Article 129 authorized the EIB to finance "projects for developing less-developed regions"; Article 392 (a), on the objectives of the Common Agricultural Policy (CAP), noted that account be taken of "the particular nature of agricultural activity, which results from the social structure of agriculture and natural disparities between the various agricultural regions"; and Article 123 referred to the task of the ESF to render "the employment of workers easier and of increasing their geographical and occupational mobility within the Community." Article 92(3) declared that state aids were compatible with the common market if they promoted "the development of areas where the standard of living is abnormally low or where there is serious under-employment." A specific category of regional problems had already been recognized in the 1951 Treaty of Paris. The ECSC High Authority was given power to authorize discriminatory aids to mitigate unemployment in regions suffering from rationalization of the coal and steel industries. The ECSC came about because of a culmination of sectoral and spatial problems since the target industries were concentrated geographically.

Apart from the aforementioned concessions, the prevailing attitude in 1957, enunciated in Article 2 of the Treaty of Rome, was that the common market would, of its own accord, "promote throughout the Community a harmonious development of economic activities" and thereby lessen disparities among regions. Economic integration was given a higher priority than regional development. The Treaty was a package deal to distribute losses and gains among MSs and not redistribute resources between rich and poor regions. The development of a common foreign trade policy deprived MSs of the trade instruments by which they protected industries within their borders from other MSs. Economies developed in different ways. Whereas in the north, the Federal Republic (Germany), the Netherlands, Belgium and France had extremely modern industrial firms and a highly intensive agriculture system; in the south and other less developed areas, there were many unproductive agricultural undertakings and outmoded service industries.[2]

The Commission recognized the existence of regional problems, leading in 1965 to its first regional policy memorandum. In 1968, the Directorate General for Regional Development was established.[3] Proposals for a common regional policy were issued in 1969, recommending coordination of national regional and Community policies with a regional impact, and the creation of ERDF. The proposal was not enthusiastically received by the Council of Ministers.

With the notable exception of Italy, regional disparities in the Community of Six were not as striking as in the Community of Nine, Ten or Twelve. Italy, with the most serious regional imbalance (the poorest regions, e.g., Mezzogiorno), was an outspoken proponent of regional assistance. Other MSs were not as prone to back increases in expenditures and have their sovereignty invaded. The wealthier states did not envision financial redistribution to poorer regions, though each MS had a regional policy to raise economic levels of less prosperous regions. West Germany was already concerned about the financial implications of the CAP and was not pleased about any further open-ended commitments.

France had both political and economic reasons for opposing a common regional policy. Progress on regional policy had to wait until the first enlargement.

The original Community regional policy was essentially based on individual national policy in which the Community participated by contributing to financing. It began to take on a community character in 1984.

IMPACT OF ENLARGEMENT

Successive enlargements increased the regional disparities with regard to income, employment, education and training, productivity and infrastructure. The Community's growing regional differences were revealed in a north-south divide, with Ireland included in the southern group. Thus, the Community built its structural policy largely on the assumption of a poor periphery (Scotland, Ireland, Portugal, central and southern Spain, Corsica, southern Italy, Greece and eastern Germany) and a rich core (southern England, northeastern France, Low Countries, northwestern Germany and northern Italy). Britain and Ireland, with serious regional problems, were less prosperous than the existing members except for Italy. A new coalition in favor of a regional policy emerged but the British position was probably crucial as both West Germany and France wanted Britain as a member.

THOMSON REPORT

The 1973 Thomson Report highlighted the large spatial variations in socioeconomic welfare in the Community and was the basis of the proposed Community regional policy.[4] The report pointed out that the Treaty of Rome states as an objective "a continuous and balanced expansion" in economic activity (Article 2), and the existence of regional imbalances works against this objective. There was an inefficient use of resources and no balanced expansion. The poverty of the weaker regions limited the size of the potential market for products of the stronger regions.

Second, the report argued that the commitment to EMU was jeopardized by the existence of such disparities. Regional weaknesses do not coincide exactly with national boundaries but there is a tendency for the weakest national economies to be composed predominantly of regions that have the most serious problems and for stronger national economies to contain fewer problem regions.[5]

Third, unresolved regional disparities might pose a threat to the common market and to the basis of the Community itself. No community could maintain itself or have meaning for its population and there were doubts about the common will to help each member improve conditions as long as there were different living standards.[6] The warning took on a new immediacy in the context of the 1970s recession; pressure grew for governments to take protectionist measures to alleviate unemployment.

The ERDF was established in 1975 with a budget of ECU 1.3 billion. The objective was "to correct the principal regional imbalances within the Community resulting in particular from agricultural preponderance, industrial change and structural underemployment." A factor in the establishment was the decision to compensate Britain for its poor return from the CAP. When Prime Minister Harold Wilson negotiated Britain's membership in 1975, he made certain that a regional fund was set up as a means of recycling Community aid to Britain. The Council's adoption of the regulation creating the ERDF was the culmination of a process leading to a Community regional policy. Paradoxically, this took place during a period of recession, which made regional problems even worse for regions already in crisis.

SINGLE EUROPEAN MARKET (SEM)

Completion of a large internal market would make a decisive contribution to the establishment of dynamic conditions, without which there was little prospect of restarting the convergence process. The June 1987 Single European Act (SEA) reaffirmed the need in terms of regional development to strengthen economic and social cohesion, and to enhance the Community's monetary capacity with a view to economic and monetary union, to reinforce the scientific and technological base, to harmonize working conditions with respect to health and safety standards, to promote dialogue between management and labor and to initiate action to protect the environment. The SEA was a catalyst in the development of regional policy; the concern that the single market would benefit wealthier regions, while the poor regions would become even more so and thus increase the disparities, brought about the inclusion of structural policy in the SEA. The contribution that regional policy could make to economic and social cohesion was recognized in the 1988 reform of the Structural Funds to rationalize and coordinate their operations.

Prior to the 1988 SEA reforms, no serious Community regional policy existed. Community expenditure was limited, and the failure to target resources for specific objectives and regions and the funds' impact on growth and investment in less-favored regions was dissipated. MSs often ignored the principle of additionality and used funding transfers from the Community to substitute for or to replenish national finances.

The single market contained risks. Structurally weak regions and countries would no longer be protected from new and stronger competition. There was the danger that problem regions would not be able to respond to the new challenge. Protected industries would have to adapt to a more competitive environment. The removal of barriers to the free movement of goods, services and capital would benefit first and foremost the stronger and more attractive regions. Peripheral or remote regions faced an additional challenge resulting from their uncompetitive locations. Their economic base to a disproportionate degree was based on agriculture and to a lesser degree on industry and the service sector. The level of unemployment in many of these areas was disproportionately high. The tendency of high-technology industries to avoid locating in backward and peripheral regions and old declining industrial regions had to be overcome. The preference for clustering in areas with major academic and research centers did not bode well for older industrial centers. With full freedom of capital movement and integrated financial markets, incompatible national policies would quickly translate into exchange rate tensions and put an increasing and undue burden on monetary policy and exchange rate arrangements. The 1988 reform set out to transform this situation into one in which structural funds would have a tangible effect on investment and growth in less-favored regions and lead to a substantial narrowing of income differentials. A complete overhaul of objectives, modes of financial assistance and management procedures was therefore required.[7]

The legal foundations for the reform of the Structural Funds in 1988 were contained in the SEA, which introduced Title V, Article 130, to the Treaty of Rome under the heading of economic and social cohesion. It was a formal recognition of the greater political importance of the redistributive function, while also constituting an integral part of the overall package deal behind the SEA and the relaunching of European integration. In return for the increased competition that would result from the internal market, the poorer members would be compensated.

Article 130a, which states, "In order to promote its overall harmonious development, the Community shall develop and pursue its actions leading to the strengthening of its economic and social cohesion," committed the Community to "reducing disparities between the levels of development of the various regions and the backwardness of the least-favored regions including rural areas." The previous version of Article 130a referred to "reducing disparities between the various regions and the backwardness of the least favored regions." With the adoption of the revised Article 130a, redistribution became a Treaty obligation.

The new Articles 130a to 130e were the first attempt to link the objective of "harmonious development" and the reduction of regional disparities, previously mentioned only in a very general way in the preamble and Article 2 of the original text of the Treaty, with specific Community instruments, ERDF, ESF, EAGGF-Guidance Section (referred to as the Structural Funds), and the EIB. It called for the effective coordination and rationalization of the activities of the Structural Funds and the Commission was invited to submit proposals in this direction. The Community ushered in a new phase in terms of regional policy. Article 130b revised by the 1992 Treaty on European Union calls on MSs to "conduct their economic policies, and coordinate them, in such a way as…to attain the objectives set out in Article 130a" and stipulated that "the formulation and implementation of the Community's policies and actions …of the internal market shall take into account the objectives set out in Article 130a."

The 1988 reform of Structural Funds called for a doubling in real terms of the three funds between 1987 and 1993. A link was established between forming the internal market and the doubling of resources through the Structural Funds. it was an implicit recognition of the danger that the weaker regions could end up as net losers from further market integration. The addition of new resources was a necessary side payment for political acceptance of the internal market program and a means of preparing the weaker regions for the new rigors of competition. Spending was to be directed to the poorest regions. There was to be closer coordination among these funds. Merely doubling the funding was not considered sufficient to redress the regional imbalances. Five objectives were introduced: 1, 2, and 5b with a specific regional dimension and 3, 4 and 5a, horizontal in nature. The Structural Funds were coordinated with the EIB and other financial instruments, and with competition policy. Emphasis was shifted from project to program financing.

MAASTRICHT TREATY

The Maastricht Treaty, signed February 7, 1992, defined economic and monetary union (EMU) and recognized the benefits of regional policy. The Treaty reaffirmed the need for economic and social cohesion and considerably strengthened the existing measures. The European Union was established, coexisting with the European Community. The Council agreed to almost double the Structural Funds in the 1993–1999 period. A special Cohesion Fund was agreed with an initial annual budget of ECU 1.5 billion rising to 2.5 billion by 1997 to be used specifically for four MSs with the lowest standards of living in the Union—Portugal, Greece, Ireland and Spain—to finance environmental improvements and trans-European transport links. Even with the additional resources there still would not be enough to meet the needs of EMU. The persistence of major regional imbalances would put a heavy economic and financial burdens on the governments least capable of carrying them. No union would be sustainable or justifiable if there were major disparities among members' standards of living.

REGIONS

The Maastricht Treaty formally recognized the existence of regions directly through the establishment of the Committee of the Regions (Article 198a–c), primarily from Belgian and German pressure. Since regional authorities were increasingly affected by Union policy, they understandably wanted to increase their voice in shaping it, and they gained a more institutionalized role through the Committee of the Regions.

However, the Community and successor Union were and are the creation of the MSs and the MSs in the Council have had for the most part the last word.[8]

SUBSIDIARITY

The principle of subsidiarity is embodied in Article 3b of the revised Treaty: "In areas which do not fall within its exclusive competence, the Community shall take action, in accordance with the principle of subsidiarity, only if and in so far as the objectives of the proposed action cannot be sufficiently achieved by the MSs and can therefore, by reason of the scale or effects of the proposed action, be better achieved by the Community." Subsidiarity places responsibility as close as possible to the level best tailored to the situation. The greater the degree of decentralization, supposedly the better the chances of success. Subsidiary extends beyond Union-MS relations; regions have an important role particularly with the Structural Funds. The future may involve a shift in accordance with the subsidiarity principle of functions from the national governments both upward to the Union level and downward to institutions at the subnational level.[9]

The principle of subsidiarity may have been oversold as an all-purpose remedy.[10] Most measures are taken at the behest of MSs, even though the Commission has the sole right to propose. But governments regularly pass the buck back to Brussels to avoid opprobrium for unpopular or misfired measures. The two areas in which the EU partly practices the "bottom-up" approach are regional and social policy. Union regional funding in backward and industrially stricken areas elicits initiatives by regional and municipal governments to put forward projects and help finance them. This has irked some national governments when the Commission bypasses them. Subsidiarity can have the unintended consequence of developing into an instrument for subnational actors to challenge the national center.[11]

Subsidiarity has dangers in that subnational entities often lack the capability for determining and delivering policy.[12] The process of economic integration inevitably raises the issue of transfer of sovereignty in political as well as economic terms. Economic integration develops its own momentum, and the logic of the process leads inexorably to transfer of important areas of policy responsibility to the Union level.[13]

In the area of economic management, a substantial transfer of responsibility has already taken place. Agricultural policy, trade policy, large parts of industrial and competition policy and regional policy, both in respect to rules of state aid and contributions from the Structural Funds, are determined at the European level. The scope for application of the principle of subsidiarity in these areas is therefore restricted primarily to means of delivery. National and local discretion continues to apply to the choice of particular instruments and institutions.

ECONOMIC AND MONETARY UNION

EMU implied far more than the single market program. In a broad context, the pursuit of EMU was most relevant to safeguarding the achievements of the common market and ensuring the continued progress of European integration toward the goal of European union. Components of EMU reflect complete freedom of movement for persons, goods, services and capital as well as irrevocably fixed exchange rates between national currencies, and finally, a single currency. This, in turn, implies a common monetary policy and a high degree of compatibility of economic policies and consistency in a number of other areas, particularly in fiscal policy. These policies should be geared to price stability, balanced growth, converging standards of living, high employment and external equilibrium. EMU would represent the final result of the process of progressive economic integration in Europe.

The Effect on Regions

EMU has strong implications for regional development. Before its approval, there was much concern about how EMU would affect regions. The national policy instruments available to benefit the poorer regions suffering from the effects of market integration could be restricted. Loss of the nominal exchange rate instrument, as well as stricter discipline imposed on national budgetary policies, would be crucial to economies undergoing deep structural change.

Thus, regional policy should incorporate the following principles[14]:

- need to eliminate locational disadvantages of the poorer regions in the production of goods and services
- large-scale movements of labor must not become a major adjustment factor
- regional transfers should be sufficiently large to effect the necessary reduction in disparities among MSs
- need for aid should be determined on the basis of regions, not of countries, and aid should be concentrated in the poorer regions
- composition of regional transfers should be weighted in favor of program financing rather than project financing; moreover, it should be designed, as far as possible, to catalyze private sector investment in the regions so that they become self-sustaining
- Union regional transfers should be financed from the resources of the Union and should be complemented by macroeconomic policies directed toward financial stability in the medium term
- a sizeable Union budget.

The principal objective of regional policies should not be to subsidize incomes and simply offset inequalities in standards of living, but to help to equalize production conditions through investment programs in such areas as physical infrastructure, communication, transportation and education so that large-scale movements of labor do not become a major adjustment factor. Success of these policies would hinge not only on the available financial resources but to a decisive extent also on their efficient use and private and social return on the investment programs. The Treaty on European Union (Maastricht) revised Article 2 of the Treaty of Rome to read: "The Community shall have as its tasks, by establishing a common market and an economic and monetary union..., to promote throughout the Community a harmonious and balanced development of economic activities, sustainable and non-inflationary growth respecting the environment, a high degree of convergence of economic performance, a high level of employment and of social protection, the raising of the standards of living and quality of life, and economic and social cohesion and solidarity among Member States."

Progress toward EMU imposes harsh conditions of convergence on MSs with problems of inflation, debt, internal and external imbalance, with consequences for the domestic ability of less-favored MSs to achieve structural change and to promote regional equality. Under the Maastricht Treaty (Article 109j and Protocol No. 6), as a prerequisite to joining EMU, each country must satisfy these nominal convergence criteria:

- inflation no more than 1.5 percentage points above the average of the three lowest MSs' inflation rates

- long-term interest rates must be no more than two percentage points higher than the average of the three lowest MSs
- exchange rate within the narrow band of the European Monetary Systems' exchange rate mechanism for two years without a realignment that would be devaluing against the currency of any other MS
- government's annual budget deficit must be no more than 3% of GDP
- total public debt must not exceed 60% of GDP

EMU was to be achieved in three stages. The first stage began July 1990, in which the MSs would draw up convergence programs directed at converging and improving economic performance, thus making it possible to establish fixed exchange rates. The 1992 Maastricht Treaty set the date for the beginning of the second stage, in January 1994. It is a transitional stage with the goal of attaining economic convergence. A European Monetary Institute (EMI) was established in 1994 to strengthen the coordination of national monetary policies, promote the use of the ECU as a single currency and prepare for the setting up of a European Central Bank in Stage 3.

Stage 3 starts January 1999 without the UK, Sweden, Greece and Denmark as members. At the inception of Stage 3, a European Central Bank will be established and exchange rates between the participating currencies will be fixed permanently. The bank will be independent of MSs and will manage the monetary policies of the participating MSs. After the exchange rates are fixed, the single currency, the Euro, would be introduced as an alternative to national currencies and placed in circulation in 2002. It is anticipated that by January 1, 2002 at the latest, notes and coins denominated in Euros will begin to circulate alongside notes and coins in national currencies. By July 1, 2002, national currencies will be completely replaced by the Euro.

Pending use of the Euro, the ECU plays a central role. It comprises a basket of currencies of the MSs, each currency accounting for a proportion determined on the basis of its economic strength. It has been used as a unit of account for the Union budget; all specific external duties, levies, refunds and other internal payments are expressed and settled in terms of ECUs. The exact value is fixed daily by the Commission; average value for June 1998 was US $1.101140.

CONVERGENCE-COHESION

The revised Article 2 calls for the promotion of "a high degree of economic convergence" and "economic and social cohesion." Though the terms appear similar, they represent different but related objectives. In general terms convergence can be defined as the narrowing of differences among countries in the development of certain economic and monetary variables. In a broad sense, real convergence relates to working conditions and living standards and the convergence of economic institutions or structures. Attention on preconditions for EMU has focused on the need to attain nominal convergence as opposed to real convergence. In the Union context, nominal convergence relates to rates of inflation, interest rates, exchange rate stability, government borrowing and debt and cohesion to regional equality. Nominal convergence programs are rigorous action plans to enable MSs to qualify for membership in EMU; within the Union context, cohesion refers to reducing regional disparities. Real convergence is closely allied with structural programs. It relates directly to cohesion since it is a measure of the relative well-being of different parts of the EMU.[15]

A matter of concern to many regions is that integration and the move toward EMU and the obligation to ensure convergence of nominal indicators will involve restrictions on macroeconomic policy that will be most burdensome for the poorer MSs. A number of the weaker MSs current ratios will require a combination of high rates of economic growth and substantial fiscal prudence if the convergence criteria are to be met over the medium term. Thus, achieving the Maastricht convergence criteria will not be painless and may lead to relatively unpopular economic policies being implemented. A danger is the use of EMU criteria as justification for a restrictive budgetary policy to reduce the debt. Measures to achieve real economic convergence would be endangered without associated action to improve economic and social cohesion. Thus, there are conflicts inherent in the convergence aims: the need to pursue deflationary convergence as well as to fight unemployment. A deep recession could make the convergence criteria unrealistic.[16]

To the extent that public expenditure is reduced, there could be an adverse impact upon support for regional economic development. Unless Union funds are available to substitute for a national programs (i.e., increased support for structural operations) it is difficult to see how a widening in the cohesion gap can be avoided. Within a monetary union, the inability to change exchange rates may impose a greater unemployment cost.

In response, the December 1996 summit adopted rules that give MSs more flexibility in meeting the convergence criteria. If their economies shrink by over 2% they can cite exceptional circumstances to postpone meeting the criteria.[17]

COHESION

The Treaty on EU makes the strengthening of economic and social cohesion a fundamental objective of union (Article B), alongside the completion of the internal market and the establishment of economic and monetary union. Without adequate cohesion, achievement of full EMU is endangered.

Yet the meaning of "economic and social cohesion" in the Treaties is still unclear. Despite being the underlying objective for a policy area that is allocated an increasing proportion of the Union budget, the concept of cohesion is nebulous and open to differing political and economic interpretations. It is common to equate cohesion with convergence in per capita real incomes.[18] Cohesion in the context of the Union has no easy definition. It is best explained as the degree to which disparities in social and economic welfare among different regions or groups are politically and socially tolerable. The question as to whether it has been attained is primarily political and the answer differs by region and by passage of time. Objective indicators can help to determine absolute gaps and to devise targets to meet them. Per capita GDP and the percentage of the labor force that is unemployed, though not entirely adequate, are the most widely used indicators.[19] Another distinction views economic and social cohesion in terms of relative levels of activity and output; similarly, development is conceived in terms of economic growth.[20]

In a narrow sense, cohesion concerns economic and social welfare. A simple definition is that it is the degree of disparity among different regions or groups within the Union that is politically and socially acceptable. In general terms, economic cohesion is meant to refer to a narrowing in regional economic disparities within the Union. One of the determining factors for economic and social cohesion is the principle of concentrating assistance on the countries and regions with the greatest problems in development and conversion and on certain priority sectors of the economy. A practical expression of economic and social cohesion was the institution in May 1994 of the Cohesion Fund in addition to aid from the Structural Funds. The Cohesion Fund may not realistically enable the four poorer countries to meet directly the convergence criteria; the funds designated for environmental projects and trans-European networks may be more politically symbolic than effective in terms of actual economic enhancement.[21]

The Economic and Social Committee (ESC) expressed concern over the long-term consequences of integration in that the Union economy would develop dualistic tendencies, with some regions enjoying a disproportionate share of the gains from integration and others a disproportionate loss. Completion of the internal market program, along with increasing globalization of production, was expected to result in a rationalization of production, with industrial activity being concentrated in fewer but larger operations. There could be an adverse effect on the less-advantaged regions, especially those that are also peripheral geographically to the advanced Union centers.[22]

In the absence of countervailing policies and left to purely market forces divergence among regions would widen rather than decline. Transport costs and economies of scale would tend to favor a shift in economic activity away from the less-developed regions, especially if they were at the periphery, to highly developed regions at its center.

To the extent this tendency occurs, the goal of securing economic and social cohesion would become more difficult and demands upon the development funds even greater. Unless steps were taken, economic disparities would widen. In this context cohesion thus could be defined as preventing regional disparities from becoming too wide. The risk could be neutralized only with the continued development of appropriate cohesion measures.[23]

COMMENTS

In light of the challenges EMU creates for cohesion, there is a strong case for increasing the financial resources available to the Structural Funds. The level of regional aid can be considered ameliorative rather than transformational. The budget is still dominated by agriculture.[24] Structural Funds account for less than one half of 1 percent of EU GDP.[25] This comparatively small amount in the context of these challenges can play only a small part in promoting economic and social cohesion. External economic shocks that may adversely affect a particular region can jeopardize economic development for many years. The Structural Funds cannot assist such regions, other than through the very constrained resources available under the Community Initiative programs. "Given the dynamic nature of the determinant of economic and social cohesion, the ESC considers that there are powerful arguments supporting an enhanced financial capacity for the Structural Funds and for greater flexibility and response in the configuration of Structural Fund assistance."[26]

New members, such as Central and Eastern European Countries (CEEC), when accepted are eligible for assistance from the Structural Funds. Without a significant increase in resources, the additional aid can be met only by switching funds from disadvantaged recipients. Moreover, it is questionable whether the Structural Funds as constituted are the appropriate instrument of assistance to meet the particular needs of the CEECs. Consequently, ESC suggests the possibility of devising temporary and (digressive) transition instruments aimed specifically at promoting the economic and social development of the CEECs as they approach membership and beyond.[27] Otherwise there is a risk that economic and social cohesion between the present MSs will decline as the territorial focus of the Structural Funds expands and progress toward cohesion among the new and current MSs is frustrated.

A high level of aggregate growth and activity in the Union can be helpful to the least-favored regions. As demand pressures rise, skilled labor resources become more fully utilized; increased costs of doing business, congestion and rising property prices are incentives to consider the least-favored regions for new facilities. Conversely, in periods of weak demand, least-favored regions are most vulnerable.

The relationship of sectoral and regional policies has to be explored. The emphasis on international competitiveness and technological advancement reveals the contradiction between sectoral and regional policy. If regional considerations are not taken into account, regional disparities will accelerate. Growth of technology in industry weakens the attractiveness of backward and peripheral regions as well as of declining regions. The tendency of high-technology industries to cluster, starting up and locating in areas characterized by a supply of skilled labor and proximity to major research and academic centers, makes these industries disinclined to move to the older industrial centers, especially those with less attractive environments. The Union has concentrated on improving competitiveness in technology but a successful sectoral policy in technology could also intensify regional disparities unless actions are taken to enhance the ability of the least-favored regions to attract technology-oriented firms.

The problems of structural change in terms of technology are particularly acute for older industrial areas with a concentration of industries suffering from overcapacity and obsolete facilities (steel, textiles, shipbuilding, etc.) and vulnerable to competition from Third World countries. An anomaly in terms of policy is the lack of any references in the Treaty of Rome and Maastricht Treaties to urban policy and development, despite the EU's being one of the world's most urbanized areas. Yet Union policies and programs do have a strong impact on urban areas, such as in regional, transport, environment, trade treaties. The Committee of the Regions has called for expanding and coordinating urban policy into a coherent framework.[28]

An accepted criticism of the various funding mechanisms is that too many are taking up a "disproportionate amount of administrative effort." There are four funds, seven Objectives, fourteen Community Initiatives and a "multiplicity of operational programs at central, regional and sectoral levels" within the MSs.[29]

Subsidiarity means that the Commission, by working closely with regional authorities, reduces the role of national governments. The Commission is also promoting the financing of new Euro-regions on both sides of national frontiers. This could lead to the recognition of new *de facto* regions with MSs ceding power to the Commission.

Will regions have an increasing voice in the policy process? A structure such as the Committee of the Regions can provide a voice for regional interests, and possibly strengthen regional authorities in MSs where they have only started to seek a stronger voice. Will there be a strengthening of regional influence on Union decisions?[30]

NOTES

1. Allan M. Williams, *The European Community: The Contradictions of Integration* (Oxford: Blackwell, 1991), p. 124.

2. European Union, Hans Van der Groeben, *The European Community, The Formative Years: The Struggle to Establish the Common Market and the Political Union (1958–1966)* (Brussels: European Perspectives Series, 1986), p. 81.

3. John Deeken, "Regional Policy and the European Commission: Policy Entrepreneur of the Brussels Bureacuracy?," paper, European Community Studies Association, May 1993, p. 10.

4. European Union, *Report on the Regional Problems in the Enlarged Community* (Thomson Report), COM (73) 50, 1973.

5. Stephen George, *Politics and Policy in the European Community* (Oxford: Clarendon Press, 1985), p. 144.

6. Ibid., p. 145.

7. Declan Costello, "Cohesion and the Structural Funds," in Peter Ludlow (Centre for European Policy Studies, Brussels), ed., *The Annual Review of European Community Affairs 1990* (London: Brassey's, 1990), p. 112.

8. Guenther Schaefer, "Regions in the Policy Process of the European Community—Reflections on the Innovations of the Maastricht Treaty," *EIPAS-COPE* (European Institute of Public Administration, 1993:3), p. 8.

9. Gavin McCrone, "Subsidiarity: Its Implications for Economic Policy," *Quarterly Review,* National Westminster Bank (November 1992), p. 46.

10. David Gardner, "Pandora's Box or a Panacea," *Financial Times,* October 12, 1992, p. 12.

11. Kees Versbergen and Bertian Verbeek, "The Politics of Subsidiarity in the European Union," *Journal of Common Market Studies* 32 (June 1994), p. 228.

12. Iain Begg and David Mayes, *A New Strategy for Social and Economic Cohesion After 1992,* European Union, Parliament, Directorate General for Research, Research and Documentation Papers, Regional Policy and Transport Series 19, 1991, p. 71.

13. McCrone, "Subsidiarity," p. 48.

14. European Union, Committee for the Study of Economic and Monetary Union, *Report on Monetary and Economic Union in the European Community and Collection of Papers* (1989), pp. 78–79.

15. Iain Begg and David Mayes, "Cohesion as a Precondition for Monetary Union in Europe," in Ray Barrell, ed., *Economic Convergence and Monetary Union in Europe* (London: Sage Publications, 1992), p. 221.

16. Jean-Luc Dehaene (prime minister of Belgium), "The Communications Challenge," *Round Table on the Euro,* European Union, Commission, 1996, p. 50.

17. "Bridging a Continental Gap," *The Economist* 341 (December 21, 1996), p. 61.

18. Begg and Mayes, *A New Strategy*, p. 13.

19. Ibid., p. 13.

20. Joanne Scott, *Development Dilemmas in the European Community Rethinking Regional Development Policy* (Buckingham, UK: Open University Press, 1995), p. 41.

21. Desmond Dinan, *Ever Closer Union? An Introduction to the European Union* (Boulder, Colo.: Lynne Reiner, 1994), p. 435.

22. European Union, Economic and Social Committee, *Opinion on the Future of Cohesion and the Long-Term Implications of the Structural Funds*, CES 246/96, February 20, 1996, p. 11.

23. Ibid., p. 12.

24. John Bachtler, "Policy Imperatives of the 1990s," *REGIONS: The Newsletter of the Regional Studies Association* 179 (June 1992), p. 11.

25. Economic and Social Committee, *Opinion on the Future*, p. 18.

26. Ibid.

27. Ibid., p. 17.

28. European Union, Committee of the Regions, *Two Years of Consultative Work 1994–1995*, 1996.

29. Padraig Flynn, commissioner for Employment and Social Affairs, "The European Social Fund: Starting a New Millennium," speech, Centre for European Policy Studies, Brussels, March 4, 1997, p. 2.

30. Schaefer, "Regions in the Policy Process," p. 10.

Chapter 9

European Regional Development Fund

The European Regional Development Fund (ERDF) is the main instrument of Union regional development policy, the only instrument whose specific and exclusive responsibility is to correct regional imbalances though other Union policies and programs that also affect regional development. Regional policy and the ERDF are not identical, and the ERDF does not completely reflect the totality of Union policy.

The ERDF is intended not only to help redress regional imbalances but also to strengthen the economic potential of the regions, support structural adjustment and growth, and create permanent employment. It contributes to financing of productive investment, infrastructure investment and measures designed to develop the indigenous potential of the regions.

How did regional policy in the form of the ERDF develop? What is the program? What lessons can be derived from the evolution of this program? ERDF funding was initially apportioned on the basis of a quota system in support of regional measures approved by MSs rather than within a meaningful Community context. The MSs determined allocations through the negotiation of fixed quotas. Subsequent reforms in 1979, 1984 and 1988 shifted power from the national governments to the Commission.

The 1975 regulations stipulated that applications by MSs for assistance fall within the framework of regional development programs. These multiannual programs were to be drawn up in accordance with a

common outline and were to provide an analysis of the economic and
social situation of the region in question, to specify development objectives and measures envisaged to achieve these objectives, the financial
resources to be committed and implementing instruments.

In 1979, the Community was given increased power; a major reform
was the establishment of the non-quota section under which specific
Community regional development measures could be financed. These
measures in the form of regulations were designed to cope with the
regional consequences of Community policies. The non-quota section
was limited to 5 percent of the ERDF allocation. For the first time, MSs
had to maintain files in Brussels that contained profiles of problem
regions, and listed projects and details of medium-term development targets. The non-quota section had three features:

- Implementation in the form of multiannual programs
- Assistance was no longer confined to physical investments but extended to
  non-physical investments to assist small and medium-size enterprises (SMEs)
- Geographical coverage was determined by reference to Community criteria,
  which could differ from that of nationally designated assisted areas.

After 1979, the program concept developed out of the non-quota section. The program contract was a multiannual coordinated package of
initiatives jointly agreed to by the Community and MSs. It was devised
and targeted to cover specific regional problems: "To contribute to the
correction of the principal regional imbalances within the Community by
participating in the development and structural adjustment of regions
whose development is lagging behind and in the conversion of declining
industrial regions."[1]

The 1984 reforms marked a limited move toward a Community
regional policy. ERDF objectives were further revised to take account of
the increased regional problems associated with industrial restructuring.
The new regulation made regional policy more Community-oriented.
The quotas were replaced by a system of ranges denoting upper and
lower limits of resources available to each MS over a three-year period.
The allocation of resources above the lower limit depended on the extent
to which grant applications satisfied priorities and criteria laid down by
Community regulations. Program financing, which made for greater
coherence of regional development measures, was extended to the entire
ERDF. The Community's ability to influence geographical distribution
and use of the fund's resources was expanded. To secure more than the
guaranteed share, MSs were obliged to submit grant applications without
any certainty of success solely on eligibility grounds. Response to the program approach was slow, which could indicate a reluctance on the part of

local and national authorities to invest resources on complicated proposals while risking not being selected because of the limited availability of funds. The greater bureaucratic effort involved in the program approach combined with the increased competition for scarce resources could work against the poorer administrations in that they are more unlikely to have the resources necessary to construct an effective application.[2]

The main driving force behind this shift toward program financing was the Commission's view that programs were a better means of coordinating use of its limited resources in a rational and cost-effective way. The Commission's workload was also reduced by cutting the number of applications and permitting a shift of much of the burdens of administration to MSs. The Commission was given greater power in deciding where and how ERDF monies were disbursed and in influencing more generally the pattern of regional policy initiatives and expenditures.

The 1984 reforms also reflected a new facet of regional policy, that of stimulating indigenous development that helped small firms and service industries as well as manufacturing. The program approach gradually developed into the main forms of assistance from the Structural Funds. This approach offers the following advantages:

- It allows for more broadly based consultation among regional, national and Community authorities on regional strategies and priority measures to be chosen under the program approach; commitments of various partners in respect to measures agreed to and put on a contractual basis.
- It makes provision for improved monitoring of operations by the authorities involved; such monitoring is to make it possible to implement various measures in a coordinated manner, to detect any blockages and propose necessary improvements.

1975–1988

In its first fourteen years, 1975–1988, the ERDF provided the least-developed regions with subsidies totaling ECU 24 billion. It took responsibility for the creation and continuation of almost a million jobs and a contribution to the realization of more than 40,000 projects.[3]

ERDF's share of the Community budget increased annually, with the exception of 1988, when the reform was instituted. During the first fourteen years, virtually all the appropriations available were committed while the amount appropriated increased annually. In 1975, the appropriation was ECU 0.3 billion, 4.8% of the Community budget; in 1988, it was ECU 3.7 billion, 8.1% of the budget.[4]

EVALUATION

While Community regional expenditures grew, there was limited evidence to indicate that prior to the 1988 reform the ERDF assistance was actually in addition to any regional aid given by MSs. MSs may have considered ERDF help a substitute for national expenditures. Indications were that for many years the overwhelming majority of ERDF-assisted projects had been started before the MSs had applied for Community funding.[5]

The ERDF was criticized for lacking a Community dimension and having a limited impact in that there was a failure to integrate a whole range of factors with the other Structural Funds. By the time the Community had grown to include Greece, Portugal, and Spain, it became evident that the scale and mechanisms of the ERDF were inadequate to reduce the much greater regional disparities in the twelve MSs. The fund was far too small to make a significant contribution to redressing the regional imbalances.

Related to other criticisms, the contention was made that the ERDF was essentially a cosmetic policy instrument camouflaging a lack of serious effort to reduce regional inequalities.[6] Other criticisms included:

- The Fund is too small.
- It has not provided resources truly additional to those already available from national budgets.
- These limited Community resources have not been sufficiently concentrated on the neediest regions in the poorest MSs.
- ERDF expenditures within regions were largely uncoordinated in nature, scattered around a variety of projects in a rather ineffectual way.

Farm price-support expenditures were overwhelming in comparison with those for the ERDF, 63% vs. 8.6% of the Community budget in 1986.[7] Both relatively and absolutely, the amount of Community regional development was extremely limited. Inflation eroded real growth in ERDF resources. In nominal terms, the fund's allocation in 1985 was up 7% from the previous year, but with average inflation at 5.1%, it was a real increase of only 1.8%.[8]

The averages or totals concealed large variations in the financial impact from country from country. The fund had been providing up to 20% of public infrastructure expenditures in Ireland and Greece. Despite the fact that the national expenditure on regional development overwhelmed that by the Community, there was no significant change in the spatial patterns of well-being. Thus, it was difficult to envision the relatively small ERDF resources accomplishing much.[9]

Another critical assessment of the fourteen-year expenditure of ECUs 24 billion found the results disappointing.[10]

- The assistance was too dispersed and scattered, and there was no planning.
- Most of the ECU 24 billion was used for small, isolated projects rather than real programs.
- Nearly all of this expenditure concerned infrastructure (half of which was used for roads, and only a small proportion for productive investments).
- The obvious lack of preparation, and sometimes the acquiescence to national and local authorities, meant that projects were often proposed for which the authorities already had prepared.
- Tthe lack of genuine control on the implementation of the programs.

Concomitant with the increase in the allocation of resources, there was growing apprehension about ensuring that there was a proportional return for the expenditure and that the ERDF allocations represented additional activity instead of replacing national expenditures.

Despite the shortcomings and criticisms of the ERDF, there were benefits. There was a clear redistributive bias in favor of countries with more severe regional problems and an increasing concentration of resources on least-developed regions.[11] Though returns from the program were not maximized, ERDF did represent a positive involvement in regional development. Taking into account the criticisms, the Community recognized the need for increasing the funding, and reform of the Structural Funds came into effect January 1, 1989.

NOTES

1. European Union, Commission, *Regions,* Third Periodic Report, 1987, p. 82.
2. Mark Wise and Gregory Croxford, "The ERDF: Community Ideals and National Realities," *Political Geography Quarterly* 7 (April 1988), p. 179.
3. European Union, Commission, *Working for the Regions,* 1991, p. 6.
4. European Union, Commission, *European Regional Development Fund,* 14th Annual Report (1988) COM (90) 136 final, May 10 1990, p. 68.
5. Loukas Tsoukalis, *The New European Economy: The Politics and Economics of Integration* (Oxford: Oxford University Press, 1991), p. 212.
6. Wise and Croxford, "The ERDF," p. 165.
7. Ibid.
8. Ibid., p. 164.
9. Ibid., p. 165.
10. European Trade Union Institute, *European Community Regional Policy: A Trade Union Perspective,* December 1990, pp. 40–41.
11. Tsoukalis, *The New European Economy,* p. 212.

Chapter 10

The Structural Funds

BACKGROUND

The United States has no program with the range or scope of the Structural Funds, which are the principal means whereby the Union supports the member states in their efforts to reach greater economic and social cohesion. This requires the reduction of disparities between the advantaged and disadvantaged regions in living standards, infrastructure provision and employment opportunities.

There are four components to the Structural Funds: European Agricultural Guidance and Guarantee Fund (EAGGF)-Guidance Section, European Social Fund (ESF), European Regional Development Fund (ERDF) and the latest, Financial Instrument for Fisheries Guidance (FIFG).

Other financial instruments are also utilized for structural purposes. The European Investment Bank (EIB), established under the Treaty of Paris, is intended under Article 198e to contribute "to the balanced and steady development of the common market in the interest of the Community" by granting loans and guarantees that facilitate the financing of projects "for developing less developed regions."

Another set of instruments for assistance is available through the European Coal and Steel Community (ECSC) and Euratom Treaty. Since

1975, resources for structural purposes have taken on significant proportions. The EIB and the ERDF, the two financing bodies were entrusted with the general task of assisting regional development. The operations differ; the EIB is a bank while the ERDF is a fund administered by the Commission. More recent related instruments are the Community Initiatives, Cohesion Fund and European Investment Fund. Also related are the Commission's competition criteria for assessing national regional aid under Article 92 (3) (a) and (c) of the Treaty of Rome.

By the mid-1980s, structural problems were considered so severe that they could not be attenuated, let alone solved without considerable financial support. They would have to be targeted as priorities on the hardest-hit areas or industrial sectors. Money should be used not only for workers' redeployment but also for environmental improvement and setting up new economic infrastructures. Reform of the funds was considered essential if they were to become true instruments for promoting economic and social development. All three funds (EAGGF-Guidance, ESF and ERDF) suffered from a lack of resources. The problems of unemployment, regional disparities and sectoral industrial and agricultural decline were accelerating, but resources available to the funds were not keeping pace. The expansion incorporating Greece, Spain and Portugal had caused increased financial strain, exacerbating the already considerable regional disparities.

Regulations regarding assistance from the funds were becoming more complex. There was concern about the bureaucratic demands in administering the funds. To make the best use of the limited funds available, each fund tried to establish priority objectives, and often these changed over a relatively short period of time. Coordination among funds was difficult because of the plethora of rules in effect. It became difficult to establish a direct connection between Structural Funds, spending and the desired results in regard to job creation, income generation or increases in regional competitiveness. The absorption of funding was not easy since national or regional authorities were unable to generate an adequate number of quality projects that conformed to fund requirements; some had been laggard or overly bureaucratic in implementation. Additionality had been difficult to enforce with MSs using Structural Funds to reduce domestic expenditures.

There was concern that more attention was placed on the symptoms than on the underlying causes of regional imbalances and growth differentials. In particular, there was an impression of an ongoing backward look in respect to policies concerning the decline in agriculture and traditional industries rather than concentrating on growth opportunities in new sectors and markets. This had been especially true in agriculture, which received very strong policy focus and support in the Structural Funds, despite Commission data revealing there were only seven regions in which agriculture was the predominant employer. In contrast, the service sector, the most important sector in every MS, received little attention in regional policy. Cofinancing rules restrained financially weak countries from full participation.

Since benefits from completion of the internal market would not automatically be evenly distributed spatially, the weakest economies would need assistance to improve their competitiveness and facilitate the move toward more modern and efficient structures. Thus, there was a need for resources to respond adequately.

REFORM

Reform of the funds was set in motion, effective, January 1, 1989. The pressure for greater integration and social cohesion in Article 130b of the Treaty required coordination of the Structural Funds and the Community's lending instruments, the EIB, and Article 130A, leading to "the strengthening of its economic and social cohesion" and "reducing disparities between levels of development of the various regions and the backwardness of the least favored regions, including rural areas."

Reform focused mainly on the three Structural Funds (ERDF, ESF, EAGGF) whose operational rules were amended. But reform of the Structural Funds was not the only means of reinforcing economic and social cohesion. MSs must contribute to achievement of this objective by bringing their economic policies closer together, and the Union must take account of this cohesion in formulating its common policies.

In February 1988, the Council decided to increase the budget for the Structural Funds from ECU 7.2 billion in the 1988 budget to ECU 14 billion (in 1988 figures) by 1993. This represented a major change in spending: In 1986 the funds took up 18% of the budget; by 1993, 25%.

Based mainly on Articles 130d and 130e of the Treaty of Rome, basic regulations governing reform of the funds were adopted. Regulation (EEC) No. 2052/88, June 24, 1988, the so-called Framework Regulation, outlined the tasks of the Structural Funds, their effectiveness, and coordination of their activities with operations of the EIB and other financial instruments. This Framework Regulation lays down the basic rules: objectives and tasks of the Funds, method of structural assistance, identification of the five priority objectives of the reform, financial provisions, and so on.

It sets out the broad principles underlying reform, which should facilitate attainment of the following Community priorities:

- completion of the internal market and correction of regional imbalances (development of backward regions and conversion of industrial areas)
- industrial modernization

- social progress in the Community
- reform of the CAP

According to then-Commissioner Grigoris Varfis, "In addition to the expansion and simplification of the structural funds it is hoped that reform will lead to a concentration of aid in a relatively low number of large projects rather than innumerable small interventions." Equally, Commissioner Varfis stressed that the combination of loans and subsidies will represent an important principle in the future management of the funds.[1]

Legislation was relatively general, setting out for the most part fairly broad criteria for establishing eligibility of individual regions for fund assistance. The main influence of MSs in the negotiations was the weakening of the more rigorous eligibility definitions proposed by the Commission to ensure potential inclusion of certain marginal areas with exceptional problems.

The Union tried to concentrate assistance in those regions and sectors experiencing the greatest difficulties, directing substantial flows of resources to the least prosperous MSs. An overall view of assistance would follow from the improved coordination of the structural instruments, and an integrated approach would enhance the impact of the structural instruments. By approaching problems as a whole an overall strategy would be formed and applied for a number of years to help the weaker regions.

The Commission proposed that resources be doubled and rules and techniques adopted to ensure improved use of the appropriations and presented to the Council with comprehensive proposals aimed at increasing the efficiency and coordination of the Structural Funds.

Table 10.1
Structural Funds Programming, 1994–1999 (in billions of ECUs)

Objective	ERDF	ESF	EAGGF	FIFG	Total
1 Lagging Regions	56.3	22.0	13.7	1.8	93.8
2 Declining Industrial Areas	5.4	1.6	—	—	7.0
3 and 4 Long-Term Unemployment and Youth Employment	—	14.0	—	—	14.0
5a Farm Modernization	—	—	4.6	0.8	5.4
5b Rural Development	2.6	0.9	2.6	=	6.1
Total	64.3	38.5	20.9	2.6	126.3
Percentage	50.9	30.5	16.5	2.1	100.0

Source: European Union, Commission, *Sixth Annual Report on the Structural Funds 1994,* COM (95) 583 final, December 14, 1995, p. 10.

By 1999, the appropriation for the Structural Funds will amount to 0.46% of the Union GDP. Taking this percentage as a reference point, there would be about ECU 260 billion available over the 2000–2006 programming period, an average of ECU 37 billion a year compared with the ECU 28 billion a year in the current 1994–1999 period.[2]

The reform proposals revolved around a number of basic principles: concentration, programming, partnership and additionality. These principles were reaffirmed by the Maastricht Treaty.

CONCENTRATION

Concentration involves focusing resources and actions on a limited number of objectives (five), geographical concentration on particular eligible areas experiencing the greatest hardship, and concentration of assistance on certain "thematic areas." It maximizes the impact and effectiveness of operations. Concentration is reinforced by demanding eligibility criteria. In some cases they are geographical and in others, functional. The principle of concentration prevents the dispersal of resources over too wide an area and among too many objectives.

Over the longer term the Commission has made it clear that it would prefer to see reductions in the total area covered by the funds and that the MSs be circumspect in the designation of assisted areas. Regional incentive policies of MSs should seek to support indigenous development rather than induce industry to relocate. In return for allowing more regions to be designated, the Commission insisted on more control in the implementation of the funds, with a view to ensuring a suitable concentration of assistance on comprehensive programs rather than individual projects. Activity in 1995 reflected confirmation of the concentration principle in practice. The largest share of the Commission's work was concentrated on Objective 1 (lagging regions), with 64% of appropriations committed and 70% of all payments implemented.[3]

PROGRAMS

Structural Funds are not normally used to finance individual projects or special measures proposed by the Commission but rather for development programs consisting of coordinated sets of multi-year measures managed by national or regional authorities, with budgets to finance resultant activities and projects. Programs are the culmination of a process involving a number of partners: MSs, regions, competent authorities and the Commission.

At the beginning of a programming period MSs draw up plans for the use of Structural Funds resources in their countries according to the regulations. The use of resources then is negotiated between the Commission and the MS on the basis of these plans and the MSs apply to the Commission for funding. Operations are spread over a number of years with joint action by the funds, the EIB and other financial instruments, enhancing the ability to respond to changing economic and social realities. From the viewpoint of management, recourse to programming and the gradual disappearance of assistance to small projects make it possible to have a better perspective of the objectives of funding.

Single Programming Documents

The acceleration and simplication of programming procedures was made possible by Single Programming Documents (SPDs) making it feasible to approve in a single document both priorities for assistance and the specific measures granted financial aid by the Commission. Previously these two elements were decided in two separate documents: first the priorities for assistance, then the specific forms of assistance. In the SPD the MS outlines its priorities for action and proposals for programs, and financing, whereupon the Commission adopts a single decision.

Programming, the way in which the Structural Funds resources are allocated to the MSs, has three basic components: the plan, Community Support Framework and Operational Programs. These can be submitted one after the other or, in order to speed up procedures, they can be submitted simultaneously in the form of a Single Programming Document.

The program approach emphasizes what are called "immaterial" investments, those that enhance indigenous entrepreneurial and management skills, especially SMEs, as distinct from infrastructure projects. Systematic approaches are made to evaluate the performance of individual programs. The Commission will be strengthened by this process, have a direct channel to the regions and challenge the MSs with respect to centralized decision-making.[4]

Overall it can be contended that the process of developing programs has stimulated the strategic planning and development at the regional level, buttressed by extensive consultation with regional institutions and other partners. Many Objective 2 (industrial decline) areas have taken advantage of the development planning process to start a serious and systematic evaluation of regional development needs and strategic priorities.[5]

PARTNERSHIP

The requirement for a partnership was the first time regional authorities had been given a formal role in Community decisionmaking. The Commission's operations were to complement or contribute to corresponding national operations to be established through close consultations among the Commission, the MS concerned and authorities designated by the latter at the national, regional, local or other levels, with each party acting as a partner in pursuit of a common goal. These consultations are referred to as the partnership. The partnership covers preparation, financing, monitoring and assessment of operations. The aim is to provide for decentralized administration of the funds' operations with the intention of establishing a true partnership among the various governmental entities. The constitutional structure of certain MSs (not to mention differences in political affiliation at national and regional levels) means that the three-cornered relationship has been difficult to establish.[6]

A number of MSs have remained reluctant to commit themselves to a full and open partnership with the regions, despite the experience and expertise achieved during the previous programming period. Partnership implies participation of all parties involved at the regional and national level at different stages of the process (preparation and implementation of measures). To this end the Commission has set up Monitoring Committees, made up of national and regional officials, to monitor the execution of projects and assess their impact.[7]

Monitoring Committees were established in 1995, by which time partnership had become a widespread and accepted practice and functioned "satisfactorily on the whole" for regional authorities. But partnership particularly at the local level is not as well developed. The situation in regard to involvement of the social and economic partners in the Monitoring Committees varies from no involvement in some MSs to to real involvement in others.[8]

FUNDS

ERDF

The ERDF, established in 1975, is the main instrument for ensuring the development and structural adjustment of regions whose development is lagging. It plays a central role in the conversion of regions, frontier regions and parts of regions (including employment areas and urban communities) seriously affected by industrial decline. The scope of assistance encompasses productive investment to permit creation or maintenance of permanent jobs; investment in infrastructure, including trans-European networks for regions eligible under Objective 1; investment in education and health in the regions eligible under Objective 1; development of indigenous potential; local and SME development; research and development measures; and investment linked to the environment.

Included are measures to exploit the potential for internally generated development of target regions. Support is also furnished for studies or pilot schemes for regional development at Union levels, especially where frontier regions are involved. The essential task of the ERDF is providing support for Objectives 1 and 2; however, it also participates in the operations of Objective 5b, development of rural areas.

ESF

The ESF, established in 1972, supports economic and social cohesion. It is an instrument of decisive importance in the promotion of consistent employment policies in the MSs and in the Union. Its priority mission is to provide support for vocational training measures, aids for employment, for creation of self-employed activities in order to combat long-term unemployment (Objective 3) and to integrate young people into working life (Objective 4). There is also support for measures under Objectives 1, 2 and 5b. ESF supports measures aimed at promoting stability and expansion of employment.

EAGGF-Guidance

The Guidance Section of the EAGGF is the main instrument for financing adjustment of agricultural structures and development or rural areas with a view to reform of the common agricultural policy. EAGFF was established in 1962 and comprises two parts. The first and much larger, the Guarantee Section, includes the price support and export refund schemes. The second, the Guidance Section, provides funds for restructuring in the agricultural industry. Both have significant regional implications but only the Guidance Section is included in the Structural Funds. Excluding FIFG, Guidance is the smallest of the Structural Funds.

This fund, according to Objectives 1, 5a and 5b, is geared to the following tasks:

- Strengthening and reorganizing agricultural structures, including those for the marketing and processing of agricultural, fishery and forestry products, especially with a view toward reform of the CAP
- Ensuring conversion of agricultural production and fostering development of supplementary activities for farmers
- Ensuring a fair standard of living for farmers
- Helping to develop the social fabric of rural areas, to safeguard the environment, to preserve the countryside (*inter alia* by securing conservation of natural agricultural resources) and to offset effects of natural handicaps on agriculture.

FIFG

In 1993, all the financial resources in the fisheries and aquaculture sector were integrated in the Financial Instrument for Fisheries Guidance (FIFG,) coordinated with the Structural Funds. The Treaty of Rome did not provide for a full-fledged fisheries policy.

FIFG now finances all structural action in the fisheries sector, in particular, the renewal and modernization of fishing fleets, the development and rationalization of aquaculture, equipment of coastal zones, facilities at fishing ports, and processing and marketing of fisheries and aquaculture products. Assistance comes through Objectives 1 and 5(a) as well as other Union instruments. The Structural Funds are used in the least-developed regions to support numerous programs that take particular account of fisheries and the areas that are dependent on them, including vocational training and regional development schemes. The sector also benefits from EIB loans that finance harbor facilities and coastal installations in particular, and from production or infrastructure projects that contribute to regional development and to the improvement or the structural adaptation of fishing and processing activities.

OBJECTIVES

Objectives 1, 2 and 5b are specifically regional in character; they involve measures restricted to certain eligible regions or parts of regions. The other objectives have no geographic limitations. With the entry of Finland and Sweden as members in 1995, a new objective 6 was established with geographic limitations.

Objective 1 (ERDF, ESF, EAGGF (Guidance), FIFG)

Objective 1 is concerned with economic adjustment of regions whose development is lagging behind and regions whose per capita GDP is less than 75% of the Union average or where there are special reasons for inclusion. It includes some 45.5% of the Union area and 26.6% of the population, compared with 38% and 21.7%, respectively, before 1993.[9] The designation of regions is based on criteria set forth by the MSs. In Objective 1 regions the guidelines are less restrictive and extend to investments that increase the economic potential, structural adjustment and development of the region and where there is a demonstrated need, including expenditures on noneconomic facilities.

Table 10.2
Structural Funds: Functional Structure of Resources for Objective 1 Regions, Percentage Shares, 1994–1999

	Percentage
Infrastructure	31.2
Transport	16.2
Telecommunications	1.5
Energy	2.7
Environment and Water	8.9
Health	1.9
Human Resources	28.5
Education	5.4
Training	19.1
Research and Development	4.0
Productive Environment	38.1
Industries and Services	17.1
Agriculture and Rural Development	15.4
Fisheries	2.0
Tourism	3.5
Other	2.2
Total	100.0

Source: European Union, Commission, Sixth Annual Report of the Structural Funds 1994, COM (95) 583 final, December 14, 1995, p. 17.

Payments relating to Objective 1 rose from 65% of the total funds in 1989–1993 to 68% for the period 1994–1999, not counting Cohesion Fund credits.[10] The share of GDP including the Cohesion Fund, in percentages for 1994–1999, rose to 4.0% in Greece, 3.8% in Portugal, 2.3% for Spain and 2.8% in Ireland.[11]

Objective 2 (ERDF, ESF)

Eligibility for Objective 2 regions (those seriously affected by industrial decline) consists of three criteria: an unemployment rate above the Union average; a percentage share of industrial employment higher than the Union average; and an overall decline in the particular employment category. Objective 2 can be extended to include areas adjacent to Objective 1 regions or areas meeting the main criteria, as well as other areas, in particular in urban districts, that are facing the threat of severe unemployment, problems related to the regeneration of derelict industrial sites, and the impact of the restructuring of the fisheries sector.

Objective 2 regions are generally developed regions whose previously vigorous economies have been weakened by structural change, destroying their economic base and making it necessary to develop alternative activities. They are difficult to revitalize economically because of excessive dependence on declining industries and the poor quality of the environment, such as derelict industrial areas. Infrastructure is in deteriorating condition and the entrepreneurial climate is not favorable to new activities.

Yet Objective 2 areas may be well equipped with basic infrastructure facilities requiring maintenance and upgrading. The research and development (R&D) potential in Objective 2 areas is relatively high in terms of basic equipment, including research centers and universities. But there is a mismatch in terms of these resources and the technological capacity of local businesses.

Out of some 900 areas proposed by the MSs, the Commission selected sixty eligible areas and identified those most seriously affected by industrial decline. The allocation of resources is basically made on unemployment figures.[12] Regions in the United Kingdom, Spain, France and Germany generally receive the largest funding. The areas concerned are primarily subdivisions of basic administrative regions or smaller areas that meet the three basic criteria.

The list of declining industrial areas adopted by the Commission for Objective 2, on January 21, 1994, covers 58.1 million inhabitants, representing 16.8% of the Union's population. For 1994–1996, Objective 2 areas will have ECU 7.2 billion, including Community Initiatives. For 1997–1999, these areas will receive ECU 8.15 billion, an increase of 13.8% over the 1994–1996 period. This amount is 11% of the total Structural Funds for 1994–1999.[13]

Table 10.3
Objective 2 Breakdown, 1994–1996 (millions of ECUS)

	ECUs	Percentage
Productive Environment	3052	45.2
Industry and service	1766	25.9
Tourism	458	6.8
Support infrastructure	827	12.5
Human Resources	2298	34.1
Training, employment	1532	22.5
Training centers, facilities	111	1.7
Research and development	655	9.9
Land planning and site reclamation	937	13.7
Industrial sites	582	8.6
Urban areas	355	5.1
Environmental Protection	388	5.7
Technical Assistance	86	1.3
Total	6761	100.0

Some 77% of the above funding (ECU 5.4 billion) comes from the ERDF and 23% (ECU 1.6 billion) from the ESF.[14]

Source: European Union, Commission, *Sixth Annual Report on the Structural Funds 1994,* COM (95) 583 final, December 14, 1995, p. 41.

Objectives 3 and 4 (ESF)

These are concerned with combating long-term unemployment and with the occupational integration of youth. They reflect the need to help particularly vulnerable segments of the population. Though not restricted regionally, they are combined with the regionally restricted Objectives.

Major changes in Objectives 3 and 4 were made in 1994. The scope of Objective 3 was broadened to take over the tasks previously done by Objectives 3 and 4, and the aims of prevention of long-term unemployment and the vocational integration of young people were extended, without targeting specific categories, to cover all those threatened by exclusion from the labor market. A new Objective 4 was created to take account of new tasks entrusted to the ESF by Article 123 of the Treaty, to facilitate the adaptation of workers to industrial changes and changes in production systems. Objective 4 develops human resources without reference to any particular industrial sector or short-term industrial difficulties. It includes vocational training and advisory measures within the context of retraining measures in the face of industrial changes. SMEs are a particular priority to improve employee's access to continuing training, thereby increasing job rotation. Total funding resources for 1994–1999 are ECU 13.9 billion for Objectives 3 and 4; Objective 3, ECU 12.0 billion and Objective 4, ECU 1.9 billion.[15]

Objectives 5a and 5b (ERDF, ESF, EAGGF [Guidance])

The increased attention given to rural development policy represents a de-emphasis on agricultural subsidies. Instead attention is placed on the introduction of more widespread measures to encourage the development of economically productive activities in rural areas. Such activities include the development of rural industries, tourism and leisure in addition to more traditional incentives to encourage the efficient production of agricultural products.

Adjustment of agricultural structures and development of rural areas are two aspects of single objective closely linked to reform of the CAP. Tighter control of prices and markets must be tempered and offset in such a way that affected persons—farmers (particularly small producers) and the rural community in general—can accept them. At the same time Union action will embrace rural areas not only for production purposes but also more fundamentally in order to preserve an adequate presence there. The Union must help those living in rural areas to convert to alternative activities and more generally must contribute to stimulation of economic activity there.

Whereas the CAP disproportionately rewarded the more productive farmers, the new rural policy seeks to achieve true economic convergence by concentrating assistance on the poorest agricultural regions. Moreover, the assistance is formulated to encourage rural development in its broadest sense rather than to concentrate on production of primary products.

Objective 5a

Objective 5a is horizontal rather than regional in nature. It is closely tied to the reform of the CAP, which in the process of agricultural structural readjustment requires increased financial assistance in the form of structural measures linked to the reduction of agricultural production. The Union must also play a key role in promoting the development of rural areas pursuant to Objectives 1 and 5b particularly through activities designed to promote economic conversion, revitalization and stimulation of such areas. The aim is to develop initiatives that relate not to agricultural production but to supplementary or alternative activities.

The total 1994–1999 financing for Objective (5a) is ECU 6.0 billion, representing 4.4% of the total for all Objectives. The total is divided between the two sectors covered by Objective 5(a): ECU 5.2 billion for agriculture and ECU 800 million for fisheries. The 1994 revisions were designed to expedite the adjustment of production, processing and marketing structures as part of the CAP reform. MSs have greater freedom of choice to implement Objective 5a and enhance flexibility in granting assistance for young farmers, environmental protection and animal welfare. They are intended to be an effective response to new developments in the food industry and to the problem of compatibility between traditional investment and agricultural surpluses.[16]

The Member States have been left considerable freedom in their choice of sectoral priorities, as long as they comply with selection criteria and total funding for each measure. The plans submitted by the Member States reflect some continuity in relation to the previous programming period but the measures envisaged in each sector also show the development of technological innovation in the food industry. This innovation which responds to the priorities defined in the selection criteria, adds more value to products and emphasizes measures aimed at environmental protection, animal welfare and bringing installations into line with Community health and hygiene.[17]

FIFG was created in response to changes affecting the fisheries industry (overexploitation of fisheries resources, businesses heavily in debt, weaknesses in distribution, etc.). It has a total allocation of ECU 2.6 billion for 1994–1999 including Objective 1; 836 million solely for Objective

5a fisheries outside Objectives 1 and 6 areas. The fisheries side of Objective 5a is not confined to specific areas. It has two sides, sectoral and territorial. The aims under Objective 5a are first, to reduce fishing effort and reduce overcapacity, and second, to enhance the international competitiveness of the European fishing industry.[18]

Objective 5b

This objective is concerned with the development of rural areas. Assistance from the three funds though the budget commitment is substantially lower than the allocation for the other objectives. The 5b support represents a departure from past Union regional policy, which has traditionally been associated with factors related to industrialization.

These regions have experienced losses of more than half their population over the past twenty-five years, due in part to the weak diversification of industry and services and the lack of job creation. Rural areas tend not to have very high pockets of unemployment compared with the rest of the Union, often as the result of the outmigration of young people as well as widespread underemployment in the agricultural sector, which has declined in importance. In employment terms the agricultural sector is now about half the size of the production sector in rural areas, where an estimated 25-30% of the total employment is to be found mostly in SMEs.[19]

The general criterion is a low level of socioeconomic development measured on the basis of per capita GDP. Of the three additional main criteria, two must be met for an area to be eligible[20]:

- high share of agricultural employment
- low level of agriculture income
- low population density and/or a significant depopulation trend.

The list of eligible areas can be extended to other areas not covered by Objective 1 that have low development, that is, if they meet one or more secondary criteria.

New rules adopted in 1993 extended the scope of Objective 5b (to facilitate development and structural adjustment of rural areas) and revised selection criteria for defining areas eligible under Objective 5b, giving more importance to depopulation problems and introducing more flexible application of the criteria. The total financing for 1994–1999 is ECU 6.1 billion. Population in the Objective 5b areas increased from 5% of the total population of the Union in 1989 to 8%, or 28.6 million, in 1994. Thus, it will be possible to implement programs that cover a major proportion of the Union's rural areas and provide access to substantial financial resource, making for a real economic impact. A breakdown of the appropriations is:

- Aid to development and diversification of agricultural and forestry activities, 25%
- Aid to economic development, development of industrial estates, small businesses, 25%
- Protection of nature and the environment, 12%
- Rural tourism, 12%
- Renovation of villages and local development, 8%
- Enhancement of human resources (training, outreach work, recruitment aid, etc.), 15%
- Technical assistance, 3%.[21]

Objective 6 (ERDF, ESF, EAGGF [Guidance])

In response to the entry of Finland and Sweden, a new Objective 6 in the Structural Funds was designed to cover the new regions with very low population density. Objective 6 is similar to Objective 1. Austria became eligible to benefit under Objectives 1 to 5b.

Objective 6 was created for regions with a population density of no more than eight inhabitants per square kilometer. The only eligible regions are in Sweden and Finland and cover a population of 1,287,000 with a budget of ECU 741 million for 1995–1999.[22]

Living and working conditions in large areas of the Nordic countries are especially hard and the low population density and long distances shaped a regional policy that aims to maintain population levels, prevent unemployment and protect incomes in the peripheral regions.[23]

PRIORITIES

For 1994–1999, ERDF will provide greater assistance for investments in education and training facilities. There will be closer links between training measures, development of human resources and other priorities of the CSFS and SPDs. ESF measures integrated into development priorities favor the modernization of industrial and service firms, conversion to advanced technology, the development of tourism, and local and rural development.

Priorities for 1994–1999 concern mainly the quest for competitiveness and the fight against unemployment. A vast range of measures and programs has been adopted to support employment and all assistance reflects a dual approach of maintaining and extending the economic base of regions through assistance for investment (47% of appropriations under Objective 1 and 45% under Objective 2) and preventing unemployment through training and retraining those in employment (over ECU 42 billion for the Objectives: Objective 1, ECU 27.2 billion; Objective

2, ECU 1.7 billion; Objectives 3 and 4, ECU 11.8 billion; Objective 5b, ECU 910 million). Increasing competitiveness in regions and firms also involves the stimulation of small firms and R&D, sectors that receive more help from all forms of assistance, both in rural and industrial areas, and in those whose development is lagging behind (small businesses receive 10% of the appropriations under Objective 1 and 17% under Objective 2; Research and Technological Development (R&TD) receives 4% of appropriations under Objective 1 and 10% of those under Objective 2; and 1% of those under Objective 5b. Assistance from the Structural Funds also plays a part in stimulating growth, which is the goal of the Trans European Networks (TENs).

Particular attention has been devoted to the environment. Protection and improvement of the environment will have more resources than in the previous period (Objective 1, over ECU 8 billion; Objective 2, almost ECU 400 million; Objective 5b, about ECU 735 million).[24]

EVALUATION

Benefits

The Commission has estimated that for every ECU 100 billion of aid to backward regions, between ECU 20 billion and 45 billion end up in the other MSs. Investments in the regions receiving aid require purchase of goods, technology and services in the more prosperous regions, giving the Union a basis for requesting assistance from the richer MSs to eliminate regional disparities.[25]

Evidence available from the applications for assistance since 1988 demonstrates that Structural Fund assistance led to a significant improvement in the economic performance of most recipients of Objective 1 assistance. The evidence indicates that gains are likely to accrue from concentrating assistance. In developing further instruments for cohesion, there is a case for targeting some part of Structural Fund assistance on large conurbations within the Objective 1 and 2 regions. To some extent, greater prosperity in these regional centers will promote an increased level of activity throughout the region as a whole as the economic dynamic in the center spreads to the immediate area. At the same time, however, care must be taken to ensure that such support does not create a new type of economic and social problem with potentially unemployed labor being attracted to conurbations, thereby introducing problems associated with overcrowding and social deprivation.[26]

Slow Results

The structural adaptation process cannot be rushed, and the level of funding of the Structural Funds cannot perform miracles in reducing disparities quickly. Adjustment even in a favorable economic environment takes place very slowly; for example, if a region with a per capita GNP of 50% of the Union average were desirous of increasing its level to 70%, a growth rate would be called for above the Union average either of 1.25% for twenty years or 1.75% for fifteen years. The same applies to employment disparities. To reduce the rate of unemployment by five percentage points from 20% to 15%, the region would need an annual employment growth rate of 2.25% for five years, 1.50% for ten years or 1.25% for fifteen years. The impact of structural policy will be detectable only over the longer term. The explicit aim of the policy is to improve the economic opportunities facing the less-favored regions of the EU by enhancing economic infrastructure, human resources and investment opportunities.[27]

While the level of unemployment is used as an indicator to decide regions eligible for Structural Fund support, it is unrealistic to use changes in the level of unemployment in the short run as a measure of the success of the structural actions. If a shift toward targeting unemployment is desired, almost certainly this would require a reconfiguration of the application of the Structural Funds.[28]

National Policies

Structural policies must operate in the context of national economic policies, those being conducted by other member states. Changes in national economic policies or spending programs are likely to outweigh the impact of structural policy. Although Article 130b calls for national and EU policies to be assessed in the light of their impact on cohesion, it remains to be seen who can question, and in what circumstances, the validity of a policy for not contributing to cohesion.[29]

Emphasis on Infrastructure

The ESC is concerned that the effectiveness of the Structural Funds can be impaired by the emphasis in national regional activity on infrastructure investment. As the ultimate objective of the Funds is to help generate economic and social cohesion leading to lasting employment, the ESC stresses the importance of productive investment and training and education of the labor force as key priorities for expenditures.[30] Yet infrastructure improvements in transport and telecommunications reduce locational disadvantages.

Macroeconomic Recessions

There is no provision for the Structural Funds to respond in any meaningful way to unexpected economic disturbances that adversely affect particular regions or sectors or to a general decline in economic activity during a recession. In the face of a sectoral shock that significantly lowers the regional level of economic activity and employment, there is no provision for compensatory financial flows to be made that otherwise could stabilize the level of demand and protect employment. Experience has shown that regions once hit in such a way find it increasingly difficult to restore their previous level of economic activity. The impact of such shocks is likely to overwhelm any long-term support being given through structural programs.[31]

Expansion of the Union

Other countries are seeking membership in the Union. After membership they will be eligible to receive assistance from the Structural Funds. Without a significant increase in the allocations for the Structural Funds, there will be a diminution in the resources available for the regions and loss of funds for the disadvantaged regions already part of the Union. There is the risk that economic and social cohesion among the present member states will decline as the territorial focus of the Structural Funds broadens and that real progress toward cohesion among the new and the current member states will be frustrated.

2000–2006 FUNDING[32]

The Commission has put forward a plan to reform the Union's structural policy for the 2000–2006 period. Structural Fund support for economic and social cohesion will have to be maintained, as in recent years, at 0.46% of the Union GNP to ensure harmonious development, indicating a funding of ECU 275 billion for 2000–2006 (at 1997 prices) for the Structural Funds and the Cohesion Fund. To support enlargement, ECU 45 billion would be set aside. The seven priority objectives (1, 2, 3, 4, 5a, 5b and 6) would be reduced to three: two regional and one horizontal for human resources. Some two-thirds of the Structural Funds would go to Objective 1 areas, which would be strictly limited to lagging regions whose per capita GDP is below 75% of the EU average. A new Objective 2 would encompass regions facing major economic and social restructuring needs, both rural and urban. A new Objective 3 would apply to regions not covered by Objectives 1 and 2, with the goals of assisting MSs to adapt and modernize their systems of education, training and employment. The percentage of the Union population covered by Objective 1 and 2 would be reduced from the present 51% to 35%. The Cohesion Fund would be unchanged. Total transfers from the Structural Funds and Cohesion Fund should not surpass 4% of the GDP of any current or future MS. To make the Structural Funds more effective, simplification of management, flexibility, decentralization and accountability would be required. Cofinancing of a single multi-year program is proposed. Less use of grants is proposed, replaced by low-interest loans, loan guarantees, and equity participation.

Another proposal calls for reducing the current seven objectives to two principal activities. The first would have a geographical dimension focusing both on regions with a lower GDP and regions with unique problems of industrial adaptation and rural development. The second would involve a horizontal human resource development function operating across the Union as a single entity as well as within regions covered by the first activity.[33]

NOTES

1. "The Reform of the Structural Fund," *Trade Union Information Bulletin*, 3 (88), 1988, p. 11.

2. Monika Wulf-Mathies, Commissioner for Regional Policy, "The Structural Funds after 1999," *Inforegio News* 31, August 1996, p. 1.

3. European Union, Commission, *Seventh Annual Report on the Structural Funds 1995*, COM(96)502 final, October 10, 1996, p. 21.

4. Gary Marks, "Structural Policy in the European Community," in Alberta M. Sbragia, ed., *Euro-Politics* (Washington: Brookings Institution, 1992), p. 212.

5. John Bachtler and Sandra Taylor, "Regional Development Strategies in Objective 2 Regions," *Regional Studies* 30 (December 1996), p. 730.

6. Bruce Millan, Commissioner for Regional Policy, speech, Trades House Lecture, University of Strathclyde, Glasgow, September 13, 1991, p. 7.

7. European Union, Commission, *Sixth Annual Report on the Structural Funds 1994*, COM(95)583 final, December 14, 1995, pp. 5–6.

8. Commission, *Seventh Annual Report*, p. 23.

9. Commission, *Sixth Annual Report*, p. 10.

10. European Union, Commission, *The New Regional Programmes under Objectives 1 and 2 of Community Structural Policies*, COM(95)111, 1995, final, p. 8.

11. Ibid.

12. Paul McAleavey and James Mitchell, "Industrial Regions and Lobbying

in the Structural Funds Reform Process," *Journal of Common Market Studies* 32 (June 1994), p. 237.

13. Commission, *The New Regional Programmes*, p. 23.

14. Commission, *Sixth Annual Report*, p. 43.

15. Ibid., p. 57.

16. Ibid., p. 71.

17. Ibid., p. 74.

18. Ibid., p. 76.

19. European Union, Commission, *The Regions in the 1990s Fourth Periodic Report on the Social and Economic Situation and Development of the Regions of the Community*, COM(90)509 final, January 9, 1991, p. 55.

20. European Union, Commission, *Structural Funds and Cohesion Fund 1994-1999 Regulations and Commentary*, 1996, p. 14.

21. Commission, *Sixth Annual Report*, pp. 78–79.

22. Ibid., p. 126.

23. Ibid., p. 125.

24. Commission, *Sixth Annual Report*. p. 6.

25. Marks, "Structural Policy,"p. 191.

26. European Union, Economic and Social Committee, *Opinion on the Future of Cohesion and the Long-Term Implications of the Structural Funds*, CES 246/96, February 20, 1996, p. 16.

27. Ego Schoneweg, "EC Regional Policy and the Outlook for 1992," *Target 1992* 1, Supplement, January 1992.

28. Ibid.; Economic and Social Committee, *Opinion on the Future*, p. 8.

29. Economic and Social Committee, *Opinion on the Future*, p. 8.

30. Ibid., p. 18.

31. Ibid., p. 6.

32. European Union, Commission (London), *The Week in Europe*, WE/28/97, July 17, 1997; and "Structural Funds and the Cohesion Fund from 2000 to 2006,"*Inforegio News* 42, July 1997.

33. Padraig Flynn, commissioner for Employment and Social Affairs, "The European Social Fund: Starting a New Millennium," speech, Centre for European Policy Studies, Brussels, March 4, 1997, p. 4.

Chapter 11

Community Initiatives and Cohesion Fund

BACKGROUND OF COMMUNITY INITIATIVES

A review of the components of the various Community initiatives and predecessor Community programs reveals how much further the European Union has gone than the United States in devising specific programs to revitalize the regions. The unifying element in both the initiatives and the programs is the priority of the Union as opposed to national objectives. In 1984 (Article 7, EEC Regulation 1787/84, June 19, 1984), the purpose of Community programs was defined as to "help in solving serious problems affecting the socio-economic situation in one or more regions. They must provide a better link between the Community's objectives for the structural development or conversion of regions and the objectives of other Community policies." The Community programs, which evolved into the Community initiatives, were initiated by a proposal from the Commission rather than from an MS. Initiatives are transnational programs whose objectives are the same for all eligible regions. However, national, regional or local authorities are involved in drawing up and implementing Initiatives that are of concern to the Union as a whole.

"A principal aim of Community regional policy is to ensure that enterprises in lagging regions, as well as those in industrial regions in decline, can seize the opportunities arising from the completion of the single internal market in 1992. For the most part, Community initiatives are directed towards creating a favorable environment for enterprise development adapted to the needs of the single market and the greater intensity of competition."[1] The Edinburgh European Council in December 1992 stipulated that initiatives must promote cross-border, transnational and interregional cooperation along with aid to remote regions in accordance with the principle of subsidiarity.[2]

WHAT ARE THE INITIATIVES?

Initiatives provide the Commission with the opportunity to take independent action to resolve regional problems on a Union-wide basis. As a result of the reform of the Structural Funds, the Commission was able on its own initiative to propose to MSs that they submit applications for assistance on measures of significant interest and impact to the Union and not covered by the MS development plans. Initiatives have three major features that give them added value as compared with other Structural Fund measures:

• support for the development of transnational, cross-border and interregional cooperation
• a bottom-up method of implementation
• the high profile that they give to Union measures.

Initiatives are an essential feature in structural policies with a real Union dimension, in contrast to Union financial instruments merely supporting national policies. They offer a means by which Union interests and priorities can be reflected in the allocation of Union resources, supplementing the essential MS-initiated priorities. The initiatives contribute to innovation through experimentation with new approaches, and if successful, they can be included in the subsequent mainstream funding.

The Commission is empowered to start Community initiatives designed to:

• help resolve serious problems directly associated with the implementation of other Union policies
• promote the application of Union policies at the regional level
• help resolve problems common to certain categories of region (outlying, remote and cross-border).

Community initiatives start with Commission guidelines inviting MSs to apply for aid for measures of special interest for both regional development and the Union as a whole. On the basis of guidelines, MSs then draw up the operational programs tailored to the situation in the concerned regions. The Union can act on its own when it deems action is necessary to complete the internal market or to help a region prepare for the EMU. The initiatives deal with aspects of regional development relevant throughout the Union and provide the basis for action at the Union level.

Circumstances since 1988 have changed and have been taken into account for the 1994–1999 period. The internal market is in place and an effort is required to ensure that industry benefits from this. In the early 1990s, there was a serious economic crisis, with 17 million unemployed and public finance difficulties that limited public investment. Not only were the weaker regions and the traditional sectors feeling the pressure of competition and economic and social change but the stronger regions and the centers of Union industry felt vulnerable. In the first period there were too many separate Initiatives in view of the available resources and the result was a disproportionate number of high-cost, small programs. The Commission's new policy calls for a smaller number of initiatives. Between 1994 and 1999, they concentrated on seven topics:

- cross-border cooperation and energy networks
- local rural development
- outermost regions
- occupational integration of women, young people and underprivileged groups
- adjustment to industrial change
- urban policy
- restructuring of the fisheries industry.

One view is that the present system of initiatives is "administratively very complex." A new generation of initiatives should be designed with only a few priority themes, and that are: (1) focused on interregional cooperation; (2) of a territorial character; and (3) focused on equal opportunities and human resource development. Greater use should be made of global grants to improve the financial management of the initiatives.[3]

FUNDING

The appropriation for the initiatives during the 1994–1999 period is ECU 13.5 billion at 1994 prices, or 9% of total Structural Fund expenditure. ECU 8.2 billion is allocated to Objective 1 (lagging) regions[4]:

Table 11.1
Community Initiatives Programming, 1994–1999 (billions of ECUs at 1994 prices)

Initiative	Appropriation
Interreg/Regen	2.9
Rural Development	
Leader II	1.4
Regis II	0.6
Employment	
NOW	0.4
Horizon	0.7
Youthstart	0.3
Industrial Change	
Adapt	1.4
Rechar	0.4
Konver	0.5
Resider	0.5
Retex	0.5
Portuguese Textiles	0.4
SMEs	1.0
Urban Policy	0.6
Fisheries (PESCA)	0.25
Reserve	1.6
Total	13.45

Source: European Union, Commission, *The Future of Community Initiatives Under the Structural Funds*, COM(94) 46 final, 2, March 25, 1994, p. 10.

CROSS-BORDER COOPERATION AND ENERGY NETWORKS

Interreg

Interreg covers two different areas. The first is cross-border cooperation to assist border areas within and outside the Union; the second is the completion of energy networks to link them with wider European networks. Interreg strengthens the provisions for technical assistance and support of monitoring and evaluation activities.

Interreg is concerned with completing the regional network policy for energy transmission and distribution in the peripheral areas where such facilities are needed. The objective is the development of networks to carry natural gas and electricity to lagging regions.

LACE

Complementing the Interreg initiative and in partnership with the Association of European Border Regions, the Commission in 1990 set up LACE, (linkage, assistance and cooperation of the European border regions), an observatory on matters relating to cross-border cooperation. LACE provides support services for transfrontier activities, including access to expert advice and assistance, a networking database and training workshops.

LACE is open to all of Europe's border regions. It concerns first and foremost exchanges of experience and information on the regions and covers a number of fields: technical assistance (provision of premises and equipment), promotion of a network of border areas (which may result in joint market research or group purchases) and dissemination and publicity activities, joint market and promotion strategies between enterprises in border regions. A data bank supplements this arrangement.[5]

RURAL DEVELOPMENT

Leader

Leader calls for an integrated approach to rural development at the grass-roots level, projects designed and administered by local partners and exchanges of experience and transnational cooperation. The objective is to find innovative solutions to serve as models for all rural areas. Private funding is added to the Union, national, regional and local funding.

The salient features of Leader are:

- dominance of southern areas
- generally low population densities
- difficult geographical situations.

Between 1994 and 1999, Leader will make it possible for local action groups to undertake economic development activities from which the Union as a whole could benefit. From the ECU 1.4 billion budget, some ECU 900 million goes to the most disadvantaged regions (Objective 1) and ECU 500 million (Objective 5b) to fragile rural areas from which people are likely to move or have already done so.[6] The policy is to stimulate rural development and is designed to help rural associations and local rural governments to better exploit their potential.[7] Eligible measures are acquisition of skills, rural innovation programs networking and transnational cooperation.

OUTERMOST REGIONS

Regis

Regis is designed to diversify the economies of the most isolated or most remote regions of the Union. These include the French Overseas Departments, the Canary Islands, Madeira and the Azores. The initiative operates mainly through the cofinancing of proposals developed by national authorities and approved by the Commission. Loans may be available from the EIB. The specific objectives are:

- to promote economic diversification
- to consolidate the links between these regions and the rest of the Union
- to stimulate cooperation among neighboring remote regions and between them and nearby nonmember countries, especially those having preferential arrangements with the Union
- where appropriate, to increase their capacity to cope with natural disasters
- vocational training.

Priority is given to economic diversification by developing products and services for the local markets, or the markets of neighboring non-member countries and for the Union market.

EMPLOYMENT INITIATIVES

NOW, Horizon, Youthstart

The employment and human resources initiatives are based on an integrated approach bringing together various measures for the revival of employment and are targeted directly at groups facing difficulties in the labor market. There are four interdependent tasks: improving the adaptability of the labor market, improving access to the labor market among disadvantaged groups, raising the supply of human capital, and anticipating and accelerating the development of new job-intensive activities. The initiative draws mainly upon the ESF and to a lesser extent from the ERDF for resources. Though applying to the whole Union, priority is given to Objective 1 areas.[8] NOW is intended to improve equal opportunities for women regarding employment largely through measures for training, access to high-tech and management jobs, and by encouraging them to set up small businesses and cooperatives.

Horizon is directed to facilitating the integration of the disabled and other disadvantaged groups into the labor market. Disadvantaged and at-risk groups consist of drug addicts, isolated and homeless immigrants, refugees, former convicts and the long-term unemployed.

Youthstart is aimed at preventing youth unemployment by promoting access to work, education or training for people under the age of twenty without job qualifications. The basis for Youthstart is twelve national programs adapted to the needs of each MS, with additional resources from Youthstart to develop the innovative/transnational dimension.

ADAPTATION TO INDUSTRIAL CHANGE: ADAPT, SME, RECHAR, KONVER, RESIDER, RETEX

Adapt

Adapt is a program designed to prevent unemployment by creating new jobs and helping workers and enterprises adjust to industrial change. There are no geographical limitations; it is financed from the Social Fund and tied to Objective 4 of the Structural Funds. Its distinguishing characteristics are transnationality, the transfer of know-how, especially to the least advanced regions, and the creation of cooperation networks.

The four interrelated objectives are to assist workers, especially those threatened with unemployment as a result of industrial change, to adapt to increasingly rapid changes in the organization and structure of employment; to help enterprises increase their competitiveness, mainly by encouraging organizational adaptation and nonphysical investment; to prevent unemployment by improving the qualifications of the work force; and to facilitate the development of new jobs and new activities, particularly by SMEs. A new priority has been added to the initial objectives, encouraging action to facilitate the transition to the information society while simultaneously minimizing social exclusion.

SME

This initiative is aimed exclusively at SMEs with a view to encouraging them to adjust to the single market and become competitive internationally. The aim is to assist them to overcome administrative and regulatory constraints, to integrate innovation, to gain access to sources of finance and the most modern management methods, and to prepare an effective strategy. The initiative is directed at businesses in the most disadvantaged regions, those receiving regional, social and agricultural aid under Objective 1. The initiative sets aside 80% of its funding for regions covered by Objective 1 and 20% for Objective 2 and 5b regions. It also takes an interest in other regions insofar as the progress of the most-disadvantaged regions implies cooperation and sharing of experiences with the most-developed regions of the Union.

Because of the SME initiative, the Regional, Social and Agricultural Structural Funds will cofinance various activities undertaken by the MSs in support of SMEs:

- the use of advanced telecommunications services
- the training and retraining of workers
- the spread of better practices and exchanges of experience
- the transfer of technologies, research and innovation
- better access to financial sources.

MSs will have to present the Commission with guidelines, operational programs or requests for global subsidies covering set of projects. Rechar, Resider, Konver and Retex are concerned with the economic diversification of areas overly dependent on particular industries or sectors.

Rechar

Rechar, adopted in 1989, is concerned with the economic redevelopment of the coal-mining areas most severely affected by the decline of the coal industry. Rechar in 1994–1999 gives priority to the environment, new economic activities and human resources to accelerate the adaptation of the concerned areas. Most of the earlier Rechar projects involved investment in infrastructure (56%); promotion of new activities (27%); and training and retraining (17%). The bulk of the investment in infrastructure has been connected to the environment in run down areas and recovery is essential if these areas are to become attractive for living and working. ERDF and ESF assistance was supplemented by contributions from the ECSC and EIB.

Eligible activities have been:

- restoration of the environment
- renovation and modernization of social infrastructures; establishment of new economic activities, particularly SMEs
- promotion of tourism
- vocational training.

ECSC supplementary measures are:

- traditional vocational training;
- prequalification programs to help the least qualified find new jobs
- transitional aid for new employees
- early retirement.

It would be preferable to place more emphasis on supporting non-physical investment projects designed to facilitate the integration of

SMEs into their local commercial environment, particularly with regard to innovation and technology transfer.[9]

Konver

The aim of Konver is to provide economic diversification in areas heavily dependent on the defense sector, both industry and military bases. A Commission study identified twenty-four of the Community's 183 regions in which defense employment was at least double the Community average. Support is available for viable business sectors other than those related to the military. At least 50% of the appropriations goes to Objective 1, 2 or 5(b) regions.

The goal of the Initiative is to diversify by creating complementary economic activities, such as the development of SMEs; financing vocational training or retraining; preserving or implementing the technological potential of these regions; and contributing to the environmental regeneration of military sites and bases.

The program must benefit areas that, even if they do not meet the normal eligibility requirements of the Structural Funds, have employment problems related to changed conditions in the armaments industry and shutting down of military bases. The selection of regions is based on MSs presenting projects to the Commission. Regions not classified as disadvantaged and not otherwise eligible for EU assistance are qualified for funding from this program.

Resider

The 1988 objective of Resider was to contribute to the socioeconomic conversion of the regions affected by the restructuring of the steel industry. It was designed as the principal regional policy measure to compensate for the decline in jobs in the steel industry from 510,000 in 1984 to 407,000 in 1988. The aim was to promote the creation of alternative activities, largely by encouraging the development of SMEs, cleaning up run-down industrial areas, improving the infrastructure, and in general giving support to measures that could contribute to the economic conversion. For 1994–1999, priority is given to the environment, new economic activities and human resources.

Retex

Retex was launched to provide help for regions heavily dependent on and affected by the decline of the textile and clothing industries. In 1992 some 3 million people were employed in the textile industry, which was facing strong international competition. Where these industries are still deemed to have economic potential, one phase of the Initiative is designed to upgrade management, marketing, production and workers' skills. The other phase is to promote diversification toward new types of activities. Measures are designed to improve the production systems and organization of companies, to take better account of the environment (especially more rational use of energy), to develop cooperation and networks among SMEs, to foster cooperation among research centers, technology transfer centers, universities and SMEs for research and development purposes, and to facilitate the access of SMEs for financial engineering.[10]

Urban

The purpose of Urban is to find solutions to problems in depressed urban areas by support for economic and social revitalization, renovation of infrastructures and facilities, and environmental improvement. The solutions should have a demonstrative character on other urban areas. This initiative extends the innovative and pilot actions already started in large and medium-size cities. Some fifty programs will be selected for support, targeting the promotion of access to labor markets for the disadvantaged, creation of new employment opportunities, and improvement in living standards and perception of the areas concerned. Their innovative features must be within the context of long-term urban integration strategies. Two-thirds of the funding has been set aside for Objective 1 regions and the remaining third should go to Objective 2 areas.[11] The initiative has been extended to the most deprived areas in conurbations of more than 100,000 inhabitants, especially to medium-sizd towns. It finances, among other things, integrated development programs featuring a coherent and balanced set of economic development, social integration and environmental protection measures based on local partnership proposals.[12]

PESCA

PESCA is designed for regions dependent on the fishing industry. It assists in the conversion of the fisheries sector and coping with the economic and social results of diversification in these regions through job creation. The fishing industry is facing a severe structural crisis, with overcapacity, high indebtedness of firms and weak economic fabric of many coastal regions. Eligible measures include diversification of the fishing sector (tourism, artisanal fishing) improvement of fishermen's skills or development potential of fisheries products, and the improvement of marketing networks. PESCA principally covers areas dependent on fisheries in Objective 1, 2, and 5b regions. Fifteen percent of the appropriations are available for areas not eligible under any of these Objectives. Half of the appropriations go to Objective 1 regions.

2000–2006 Funding[13]

The Commission has proposed that for 2000–2006 funding, the number of Community initiatives be limited to three and their share of Structural Fund resources would be 5%:

- cross-border, transnational and interregional cooperation
- rural development
- human resources.

COHESION FUND

Background

Living standards vary greatly from one MS to another. In 1990, GDP per capita was two and a half times higher in Luxembourg, the most prosperous MS, than in Greece, the least well-off. In the same year Greece's per capita GDP, expressed in terms of purchasing power, was only 47% of the Union average. In the case of Portugal it was 56%; of Ireland, 68%; and of Spain, 75%. In addition these countries had other problems. They were located on the edges of the Union and therefore needed good means of communication in order to link themselves to the main centers of activity in the single market. But their transport and telecommunications networks were inadequate, as were their energy infrastructure and their means of conducting scientific research and protecting the environment. Further, they had been harder hit by unemployment; Ireland and Spain had the highest unemployment rates.

Measures to reduce economic and social differences often cost more than the MSs in question could afford. To approach the Union averages, the less well-off countries had to continue to invest. Paradoxically, at the same time, they would have to limit public spending in order to prepare themselves for economic and monetary union as envisaged by the Maastricht Treaty. Thus, in the framework of the convergence criteria, they had to limit budgetary deficits.[14]

The four poorest nations, Spain, Portugal, Greece and Ireland, demanded increased economic assistance to permit them to catch up with their richer partners and join the EMU. These four countries, taken together, had a population of nearly 63 million, or nearly one-fifth of the Union's total population. Led by Prime Minister Felipe Gonzalez of Spain, the four won agreement on a legally binding protocol to be attached to the final Maastricht Treaty committing the Union to increase the resources of the Structural Funds and to create a Cohesion Fund for finance, the environment and transportation.

The Cohesion Fund would help the four MSs prepare for EMU by contributing to the financing of trans-European networks (TENs), transportation, telecommunications, and energy infrastructures. By providing this aid, which is in addition to aid from the Structural Funds, the Cohesion Fund would help strengthen economic and social cohesion in the Union. The fund was to provide financial contributions to projects in MSs with per capita GDP of less than 90% of the Union average and that have a program leading to fulfillment of conditions of economic convergence as set forth in the Maastricht Treaty. The Cohesion Fund applies to countries, not regions.

Article 130d "set up a Cohesion Fund to provide a financial contribution to projects in the fields of environment and trans-European networks in the areas of transport infrastructure." The fund did not come into effect until May 1994. It was also decided that the Cohesion Fund will have at its disposal some ECU 15 billion for the 1993–1999 period. The fund would cover between 80–85% of the cost of projects supported, a higher level than provided by the Structural Funds. Countries failing to implement convergence programs run the risk of being refused financial support for new projects from the Cohesion Fund.

Cohesion and Structural Funds

Following the Maastricht Treaty, there are two major instruments to promote cohesion, the Structural Funds and the new Cohesion Fund. These two instruments come under the same heading from a financial perspective, but they have separate allocations, since their operational criteria are different. Both the Structural Funds and Cohesion Fund support the reduction of economic and social disparities.

Structural Funds operate largely through operational programs while the Cohesion Fund finances individual projects, stages of projects or groups of projects. The Cohesion Fund is coordinated with regional aid from the Structural Funds. Geographical coverage of Cohesion Funds is limited to four MSs, but there are no country limits on the Structural Funds. The Structural Funds receive a much larger appropriation: for 1994–1999, ECU 126.3 billion. The Cohesion Fund received ECU 14.5 billion.[15]

Financing from both sources for the same stage or the same item is not permitted, but different stages of a project may be financed separately. A project may not benefit simultaneously from the Cohesion Fund,

EAGGF, ESF or ERDF. Union aid may not exceed 90% of the total expenditure on the same project. The total cost of a project or group of projects may not normally be less than ECU 10 million.[16]

Projects to be considered for Cohesion Fund financing must concern transport infrastructure in the area of trans-European networks or environmental infrastructure. They have to stem from Union policy decisions and should be based on objectives of the Union environmental and trans-European network programs. Since the Cohesion Fund will operate in fields eligible for Structural Fund assistance there is an urgent need to guarantee a maximum of coherence between them.

The other condition of eligibility is prior adoption by the Council of an economic convergence program in the context of the EMU, especially on budget deficits. Implementation of this program will continue to be monitored in the context of multilateral surveillance. The aim is to enable these MSs to shoulder the financial burden arising from Union decisions concerning the environment (e.g., plans to impose Union standards) and transport infrastructure (projects of Union interest covered by blueprints for trans-European networks).

Funding

In December 1992, the budget was set at ECU 15.2 billion for cohesion aid from 1993-1999 with the following indicative allocation: Spain, 52% to 58%; Greece, 16% to 20%; Portugal, 16% to 20%; Ireland, 7% to 10%.[17]

RESULTS

A suitable balance must be struck between transport infrastructure and environmental projects. For the first two years of operation, 1993 and 1994, 45% of appropriations went to environmental projects. The goal for the 1993–1999 period is a 50–50 balance.[18]

Table 11.2
Cohesion Fund Breakdown Between Transport and Environment, 1993

Spain	71:29
Ireland	61:39
Portugal	57:43
Greece	38:62
Total	61:39

Source: European Union, Court of Auditors, *Special Report on the Cohesion Financial Instrument together with the Commission's Replies* 1/95, (January 1995), p. 21.

The Court of Auditors has noted that the Council's decision to allocate finance separately for each project rather than as in the case of the Structural Funds through the CSFs has important consequences. The absence of any necessary links between individual projects financed in the context of cohesion and broader plans represented by the CSFs and programs carries risks that projects will be carried out in isolation and insufficient regard to the impact of infrastructure investment financed by other methods. The Court has questioned whether the small scale of some projects was consistent with intentions to concentrate on major initiatives, particularly in regard to trans-European networks. In view of the long period before projects may be completed, the full effects may not become evident before a considerable time has elapsed.

Projects in theory must be of a sufficient scale to have a significant impact on environmental protection or trans-European infrastructure networks. But the Court of Auditors found few projects of sufficient scale to achieve the objectives of the fund; some are too small scale. The inclusion of such projects seems to be dictated by the urgent need to select projects allowing rapid use of appropriations and by the existence of the more advantageous Cohesion Fund rate of assistance than in the other structural measures.[19]

2000–2006 FUNDING[20]

For the 2000–2006 period the Commission has proposed that the Cohesion Fund be retained in its present form, cofinancing of trans-European transport networks and projects in the environmental field with a per capita GNP of less than 90% of the Union average. The annual funding for the Cohesion Fund for the current MSs would be in the order of ECU 3 billion per year at the beginning of the 2000–2006 period.

NOTES

1. European Union, Commission, *The Regions in the 1990s: Fourth Periodic Report on the Social and Economic Situation and Development of the Regions of the Community,* COM (91)609 final, January 19, 1991, p. 7–1.

2. Ibid., Chapter 7.

3. Padraig Flynn, "The European Social Fund: Starting a New Millenium," speech, Centre for European Policy Studies, Brussels, March 24, 1997, p. 5.

4. European Union, Commission, *Sixth Annual Report on the Structural Funds 1994,* COM(95)583 final, December 1, 1995, p. 90.

5. European Union, Commission, *The Single Market,* 1995, p. 14.

6. "Leader II 1994–1999," *Eurofocus* 18/94 (February 28–March 7, 1994), p. 20.

7. European Union, Commission, *Guide to the Community Initiatives*

1994–1999, first edition, 1994, p. 20.

8. Ibid., p. 22.

9. *Frontier-Free Europe* 10 (November–December 1995), p. 2.

10. European Union, Commission, *Bulletin* 12 (1991), p. 61.

11. European Union, Commission, *Bulletin* 5 (1996), p. 33.

12. Ibid.

13. "The Structural Funds and the Cohesion Fund from 2000 to 2006," *Inforegio News* 42 (July 1997).

14. Peter M. Schmidhuber, "The Cohesion Fund: A Sign of Solidarity in the Future European Union," *Frontier Free Europe* 4 (April 1993), p. 1.

15. European Union, Commission, *Sixth Annual Report on the Structural Funds 1994* COM(95)583 final, December 14, 1995, p. 10 and European Union, Commission, *First Report on Social and Economic Cohesion 1996,* p. 147.

16. European Union, Commission, *The European Union's Cohesion Fund,* 1994, p. 6.

17. Ibid., p. 7.

18. European Union, Commission, *Seventh Annual Report on the Structural Funds 1995,* COM(96)502 final, October 30, 1996, p. 207.

19. European Union, Court of Auditors, *Special Report on the Cohesion Financial Instrument Together With the Commission's Replies* 1/95, January 1995, p. 21.

20. "The Structural Funds," p. 2.

Chapter 12

European Investment Bank and European Investment Fund

EUROPEAN INVESTMENT BANK

INTRODUCTION

The European Investment Bank (EIB) as a financing institution has no parallel in the United States despite the long-standing proposals for the federal government to establish an organization to provide capital, such as a national industrial development bank or a reconstituted Reconstruction Finance Corporation. Despite the continuing need, the 1990s political climate in the United States has not been receptive to proposals for a development bank or a similar type of institution.[1]

During the drafting of the Treaty of Rome, a committee chaired by the Belgian foreign minister, Paul-Henri Spaak, discussed the potential role of the EEC in regional development and considered establishment of a regional fund. Instead, it opted for the establishment of the EIB; previously regional balanced growth had been viewed as an almost inevitable byproduct of the economic growth process. With the reduction of trade, labor and capital mobility barriers, it was viewed as natural that some out-migration of labor would occur from poorer regions and at the same time lower wages and costs would attract capital to less-developed regions.[2]

Article 3(j) of the Treaty of Rome established the EIB "to facilitate the economic expansion of the Community by opening up fresh resources" and the EIB began operations in 1959 under Articles 129 and 130 (now Article 198) as the source of development finance. Its task was to contribute to the balanced and integrated development of the common market.

When EIB was created, reduction of interregional differences through direct and indirect employment creation was a primary target. Unlike national regional policies, which were dominated by industrial grants, the financial principle espoused was that capital could be raised in world money markets where interest rates were low and disbursed as loans in the MSs with endemically high interest rates that hampered regional development. With the highest credit rating EIB can offer relatively lower (unsubsidized) interest rates.

The Bank was created with funds coming from borrowing on international money markets and lending in the form of interest-bearing loans to selected projects in priority regions. Opinion was not favorable to large-scale grants if the costs were to be borne by MSs that were already committed to their own regional strategies.

The EIB was specifically created to deal with spatial development problems at the Community level. A primary factor was the fear that regional problems would become a destabilizing force undermining the Community's long-term political goals. Predictions were that removing intra-Community tariff barriers would increase competition for traditional industries in weak regions unable to meet competition, and monetary union would increase the problems of lagging regions. Thus, there was a need for an intervention agency to counteract the danger that integration measures would increase spatial economic imbalance, cause political friction and block progress toward the integration goal. EIB, as originally envisaged, oriented its lending activities largely toward the less-developed regions of the six members, and particularly the south of Italy. However, the sums of money involved were relatively small and the attraction of EIB loans consisted entirely of the preferential interest rates charged on loans. EIB according to its statutes could not offer any capital grants or subsidies to inputs.[3] Until 1975, when the ERDF was created, EIB was the Community's sole general source of funding for regional development projects and was responsible for the bulk of Community regional infrastructure action. Even after the creation of the ERDF, a majority of EIB loans contributed to regional development. EIB principally supplied long-term capital for financing of infrastructure projects in the fields of transport, energy and telecommunications.

The global loan system was introduced in 1968 and expanded in 1979. Global loans go directly to regional and national financial institutions, which, subject to EIB directives, in turn make subloans to relatively small companies for small-scale investment on projects deemed beneficial to regional development. In 1988, there was a move from loans to large enterprises to SMEs as well as an emphasis on conservation, antipollution and renewable energy sources.

WHAT IS THE EIB?

A distinguishing characteristic of the EIB is its participation in the market both as borrower and lender. It differs from commercial banks in that its goal is not to make profits but rather to contribute "to the balanced and steady development of the Common Market in the interest of the Community" (Article 198e, Treaty of Rome).

In terms of both volume and variety of operations, the EIB is unparalleled among the international financing institutions (IFIs). The EIB is the only IFI that:

- is a significant lender in both developed and developing countries
- operates in a large number of non-member countries
- has a capital ratio of more than 1:1 between subscribed caapital and the aggregate amount of outstanding loans and guarantees
- lends substantial amounts to both public and private sectors.[4]

The EIB is the Union's financing institution, providing long-term loans for capital investments and promoting the Union's balanced economic development and integration. It is a flexible and cost-effective source of finance whose total of ECU 26.2 billion of annual lending in 1997 (ECU 23.0 billion (87.8%) in the Union) makes it the largest international financing institution.

Originally, activities were confined to MSs; later they expanded to include countries with which the Community had associations or agreements. Financing outside the Union, which is not covered in this chapter, totaled ECU 3.2 billion (12.2%) in 1997.[5] In nonmember countries of the Mediterranean and African, Pacific and Caribbean states, the Bank makes loans and grants from its own and EU or MS resources in pursuit of Union economic and financial cooperation objectives.

The SEA, Maastricht Treaty and December 1992 Edinburgh Council enhanced EIB's role in fostering economic and social cohesion. The Maastricht Treaty highlighted and emphasized the identity of the EIB as an autonomous institution. As such, EIB has a major role in helping to promote the EU, particularly as regards economic and social cohesion; promotion of trans-European networks in transport, telecommunications and energy; industrial competitiveness; and protection and improvement of the environment.

While EIB was not given fresh tasks, the Treaty provided an updating of the policy framework within which the Bank operates, and changes the economic and financial context in which it borrows and lends. With a move toward EMU, EIB's lending becomes increasingly important as a source of finance for capital investment assisting internal adjustment within the Union.

The main concentration of EIB's lending has always been in support of redevelopment, an aspect well recognized in the Maastricht Treaty. Its Protocol on Economic and Social Cohesion notes that the EIB "is lending large and increasing amounts for the benefit of poorer regions" and reaffirms that the Bank "should continue to devote the majority of its resources to the promotion of economic and social cohesion."

A unique remit of the EIB is its support of investment that serves a Union objective, contributes to regional development or is of common interest to several MSs. In effect the Maastricht Treaty broadly reinforced EIB's activities in the context of the establishment of EMU among MSs. Operating on a nonprofit basis, the EIB makes loans to facilitate the financing of projects furthering the Union's economic integration objectives.

The amended Treaty of Rome (Article 198e) directed the EIB

to contribute, by having recourse to the capital market and utilizing its own resources. For this purpose, the Bank shall, operating on a non-profit-making basis, grant loans and give guarantees which facilitate the financing of the following projects in all sectors of the economy:

(a) projects for less developed regions;

(b) projects for modernizing or converting undertakings or for developing fresh activities called for by the progressive establishment of the common market, where these projects are of such a size or nature that they cannot be entirely financed by the various means available in the individual Member States;

(c) projects of common interest to several Member States which are of such a size or nature that they cannot be entirely financed by the various means available in the individual Member States.

Article 198e makes specific reference to preferred interaction between the EIB and Structural Fund operations. The EIB has been primarily project-oriented and the Treaty and its Statutes still refer only to project financing.

Capital

According to Protocol A, Article 4, to Article 198e the capital of the Bank is ECU 28.8 billion, subscribed as follows:

	ECU Thousands	Percentage
Germany	5,508,725	19.1
France	5,508,725	19.1
Italy	5,508,725	19.1
United Kingdom	5,508,725	19.1
Spain	2,024,928	7.0
Belgium	1,526,980	5.3
Netherlands	1,526,980	5.3
Denmark	773,154	2.7
Greece	414,190	1.4
Portugal	266,922	1.0
Ireland	193,288	0.7
Luxembourg	38,658	0.1
	28,800,000	100.0

About 9% of the subscribed capital is actually paid in by the MSs (Article 5).

Use of Resources

The EIB's role in furthering the development of less-favored regions is particularly crucial in terms of economic development. EIB is in a position to mobilize the extensive resources required without burdening the budgets of MSs. Through its strict selection and appraisal criteria, resources are channeled in an economically efficient manner to regions and sectors in need of support. The EIB has operated with a strong and deliberate regional bias. "Underpinning regional development is a top priority for the Bankand more than two-thirds of lending is devoted to less-privileged regions."[6]

GOVERNANCE

The Treaty of Rome gave the EIB a legal personality with its own autonomous decision-making bodies, an administrative structure separate from those of the Community and with a considerable degree of independence. The EIB is subject to two distinguishing parameters. As a Union institution, it has a public service to perform; and as a bank it is linked directly to the market. While the EIB has independence in decision-making and in financial aspects, its role as an institution serving the interests of the Union requires close coordination of its activities with the Union's economic policy.

The Board of Governors consists of ministers designated by each MS, usually the finance minister. The Board represents MSs as shareholders of the bank and lays down general directives on credit policy; approves the balance sheet, profit and loss account and annual report; decides on capital increases; and appoints members of the Board of Directors (nominated by MSs), the Management Committee and the Audit Committee.[7]

The Board of Directors ensures that the Bank is managed in accordance with the provisions of the Treaty and the statute and with the general directives laid down by the governors. The directors have sole power to take decisions in respect to loans, guarantees and borrowings and are appointed for a renewable period of five years. Though appointed by the Board of Governors from nominations by MSs, they are responsible solely to the bank. There are 25 directors and 13 alternates. The eight-member Management Committee, with a six-year term, is the executive body under the authority of the president. The Committee oversees the day-to-day business of the EIB.[8]

Method of Operation

Under the Treaty of Rome, EIB was assigned the task of contributing to the balanced development of an integrated Europe, but rather than confining the Bank to a fixed remit, the terms defining its operational framework are general enough to allow EIB continuously to adapt its choice of projects to new challenges facing the Union and to help meet European economic needs in a constantly changing environment. Its mandate is fulfilled through recourse to banking techniques and channels on a nonprofit basis combined with commercial objectives.

All projects must first be eligible for EIB financing in terms of their direct or indirect contribution to European integration. Each project must also be technically viable and offer a satisfactory economic return (as well as an acceptable financial return in the case of productive sector investment). The principle of complementarity governs financing operations, another feature of EIB assistance. The EIB works in close cooperation with other financial institutions and in coordination with various forms of Union aid, especially Structural Funds.

While the EIB has independence in decision-making and in financial operations, its role as an institution serving the interests of the Union requires close coordination of its activities with the Union's economic policy. No decision by a Union institution can exercise authority over the bank; only its governing body has that power.[9]

The Commission is EIB's chief partner within the Union system. Under Protocol A, Article 11, the Commission nominates one director and one alternate director among those to be appointed by the Board of Governors as members of the bank's Board of Directors. The Commission nominates the director general for economic and financial affairs (DG II) for the post of director, and the director general, for coordination of structural policies, (DG XXII) as alternate director. Under Article 21 of the

Protocol, the Commission delivers an opinion on each financing proposal before the bank approves a loan. This opinion considers how the investment project fits in with the Union's economic objectives. Where the Commission has an unfavorable opinion, the Board of Directors may not grant the loan or guarantee unless the decision is unanimous without the participation of the director nominated by the Commission.

Losses should not be incurred as its borrowing and lending activities must enable it to meet its obligations, cover its expenses and progressively build up reserves. The EIB cannot grant any reduction in interest rates. When an interest subsidy is deemed desirable, another Union institution or MS provides the aid (Article 19).

Funding Sources

The Bank obtains the bulk of its resources on the capital markets, where its high AAA credit rating enables it to borrow at the most favorable terms and pass on the savings for the benefit of the borrowers. EIB pays no dividend to shareholders. Profit for 1996 and 1997 was ECU 1.1 billion annually.[10]

During 1997, bond issues totaled ECU 23 billion. Union currencies represented more than three-quarters of the total. Almost all the resources raised were deployed in loan disbursements. At the end of 1997, total outstanding borrowings amounted to ECU 110 billion.[11]

Table 12.1
European Investment Bank Pattern of Resources Raised, 1993–1997 (billions of ECUs)

	1993–1996	1997	Total
Public issues	56.0	22.4	78.4
Private borrowings	2.3	0.6	2.9
Total	58.3	23.0	81.3

Source: European Investment Bank, *Annual Report 1997*, 1998, p. 118.

Over the years the hallmark of EIB lending has been its low-risk profile and reliance on government guarantees particularly and third parties (highly rated private sources). The Bank has earned a reasonable rate of profit, adding to reserves. The profits, which have been retained, build capital and reserves. The size of the profits reflects the loan pricing policy, which is to charge borrowers a rate based on the Bank's own marginal cost of funds plus a small spread to cover administrative costs.[12]

LENDING

The total volume of capital investment in the Union between 1991 and 1995, to which the Bank contributed, was ECU 262 billion, or nearly 5% of gross fixed capital formation (GFCF).[13] The investment makes up a significant share of national GFCFs, especially in those MSs that are totally or partially eligible for assistance under Objective 1 of the Structural Funds: 20% in Portugal and 11% in Greece, Spain and Ireland.[14] Disbursements in 1997 in the MSs totaled ECU 21.1 billion.[15] Some 250 major capital programs and investment programs in MSs were approved in 1997.[16] At the end of 1997, total outstanding lending from its own resources came to ECU 142.4 billion, or 230% of subscribed capital.[17]

Table 12.2
European Investment Bank Financing by Objective, Individual Loans and Global Loans, 1997 (in billions of ECUs)

	ECUs	Percent
Individual Loans	16.8	76.8
Global Loan Allocations	5.1	23.2
Total	7.8	100.0
Objective		
Regional Development	14.6	38.8
Communications	8.8	23.2
Environment	7.2	19.1
Energy	2.6	6.9
International Competitiveness	2.1	5.5
Small/Medium-sized Enterprises	2.5	6.5
Total	37.8	100.0

Source: European Investment Bank, Annual Report 1997, 1998, p. 104.

From 1993 to 1997 EIB regional financing of ECU 64 billion, in conjunction with other Union assistance, has facilitated a total capital investment estimated at ECU 162 billion.[18] The high proportion of assistance for basic infrastructure is explained by the need to remedy the relatively poor capital equipment position in regions lagging in their development. Industrial projects attracted 30% of the total, almost half for SMEs. Numerous projects in the assisted areas also supported the creation of communications infrastructure or met energy policy or environmental protection objectives. During 1997, some two-thirds of EIB funding was devoted to projects contributing to regional development and strengthening the Union's economic and social cohesion.[19]

In 1997, individual loans and allocations from global loans for regional development totaled ECU 14.7 billion, compared with ECU 13.8 billion in 1996. For 1997, they accounted for 67% of aggregate Bank activity. These operations supported projects in the Union, whose total cost ran to some ECU 43 billion.

Table 12.3
European Investment Bank Sectoral Breakdown of Regional Development, 1997 (in billions of ECUs)

	Amount	Percentage
Energy	1.0	6.8
Communications	6.3	42.8
Water Management	2.7	18.4
Urban Development	0.3	2.0
Industry, agriculture	3.2	21.8
Education, health	0.5	3.4
Services	0.7	4.8
Total	14.7	100.0

Individual loans amounted to ECU 11.4 billion and global loans to 3.3 billion.

Source: European Investment Bank, Annual Report 1997, 1998, p. 13.

In 1997, 80% of funding in the Objective 1 (lagging areas) went to upgrading of infrastructure, In Objective 2 (areas affected by industrial decline), Objective 5b (rural areas facing conversion problems) and Objective 6 (sparsely populated Arctic areas) 60% of the funding supported infrastructure and 40% was lent to industry.[20]

In the four MSs with the lowest per capita incomes (those eligible for Cohesion Fund grants), EIB in 1994 contributed to 15% of new capital investment in Portugal, 18% in Greece, 7% in Spain and 9% in Ireland.[21]

The typical EIB loan is long term with a seven-to-twelve year maturity for industrial borrowers and up to twenty years for infrastructure borrowing. Interest rates have been fixed but the proportion of variable loan rates has been increasing.[22]

EIB loans go to projects that meet one or more of the following objectives:

- strengthening economic progress in the less-favored regions
- improving trans-European networks in transportation, telecommunications and energy transfer
- enhancing industry's international competitiveness and its integration at a European level and supporting SMEs

- protecting the environment and quality of life, promoting urban development and safeguarding the Union's architectural heritage
- achieving secure energy supplies.[23]

To qualify for EIB finance, all projects must support European integration, directly or indirectly, and more specifically, one or more of the
previously cited objectives. However, there must also be a satisfactory
profile as regards economic return, technical viability, and in case of productive sector investment and financial return. In addition EIB ensures
that funded projects comply with current legislation as regards the award-
ing of contracts (competitive bidding) and environmental protection.[24]

Since the bank never finances the entire cost of a project, a key principle is that of complementarity. The practice is meant to ensure that the
promoter makes an appropriate contribution, and to help obtain funds
from other sources for investments the Bank considers sound and viable,
such as Structural Funds and other Union financial instruments and
national aid. EIB loans are not intended to replace or supplant resources
that are available elsewhere. The EIB contributes to only part of the
investment costs, as a rule up to 50%.

Its lending depends on the existence of viable eligible projects, interest rates, conditions and liquidity on financial markets, and the general
economic environment. The Bank carries out a rigorous appraisal of each
investment project, not only assessing its consistency with Union policies
but also getting its economic and environmental justification as well as its
financial and technical viability. Only investment can be taken into
account; urban infrastructure projects not directly linked to economic
development such as schools and hospitals are not eligible.

The EIB endeavors to adapt its financial products by offering project
promoters financing tailored to their requirements. Its loans are available
in a wide range of interest rate formats and currencies. The standard
product continues to be a long-term, fixed-rate loan, generally with a
period of grace in respect to repayment of principal, which varies by type
of project.

Individual loans are provided for projects of a certain size. There are
no preset geographical or sectoral quotas, and loans can be made irrespective of the status or nationality of the borrower, to private, public and
semi-public enterprises, local or regional authorities, public institutions,
cooperatives, and so on, or the state itself.

Global Loans

In 1995, global loans totaled ECU 5.2 billion. Global loans constitute an
indirect decentralized financing facility for fostering SMEs that, for practical

and administrative reasons, would not be possible to finance directly with individual loans from the EIB. Intermediaries are used. The minimum allocation is ECU 20,000 for capital investment of ECU 40,000, the corresponding maximum amounts being ECU 12.5 million and ECU 25 million.

Between 1991 and 1995, EIB global loans of ECU 19.6 billion were advanced to over 130 financial institutions and commercial banks, with amounts actually allocated being ECU 16.2 billion. During 1995, 13,801 SME ventures were financed for total of ECU 4.4 billion.[25]

The scope of global loans has been gradually extended in order to adapt to the changing needs of businesses and more broadly based Union and national policies. They now benefit SMEs in industry, agriculture and the service sector as well as small infrastructural works furthering Union objectives. Since 1979, the SME category has been broadened to include investment undertaken by local authorities to develop public utility infrastructure in assisted areas. This financing was broadened in 1980 to encompass investment to reduce oil consumption by promoting more rational use of energy and again in 1986 to investment contributing to protection of the environment.

EIB's strong position as a borrower on capital markets throughout the world is combined with partner banks' knowledge of local conditions and their commercial links. Cooperation and cofinancing with other banks take place in many other ways and are increasingly being used to put together highly specialized financing packages. The financial intermediaries can be of many types but are mainly banking institutions. Banking institutions are concerned primarily with the application of typical banking principles, especially with the capacity to repay loans. In some respects, from the perspective of promoting regional employment or steering funds to key sectors, they may be the wrong people to act as intermediaries.[26]

EVALUATION

The main contribution of the EIB has been its readiness to fund projects in regions where conventional finance is not available and banks may be placed under competitive pressure. But the Bank has not limited its operations to regional development. Much of the industrial and infrastructure investment occurs outside the weaker regions. For those preferring a more interventionist and subsidized approach to regional development, the EIB is considered too commercially oriented toward repayable loans or safe guarantees rather than grants or subsidies.

An appraisal of EIB's activities, especially from the view of a regional dimension, would point to the following deficiencies. The bank is not only concerned with regional imbalance. It has financed projects of joint interest to MSs such as the Airbus and Channel Tunnel projects. Although the EIB is concerned with financing infrastructure improvements, much takes place in developed regions. If one wished to focus financial assistance purely on problem regions, the multipurpose role of the bank would have to be diminished. Yet there is a spillover effect to the rest of the Union from projects that are not directly in problem regions.[27]

From a countercyclical standpoint, the Bank as a market-based institution may not be as active in a recession. Qualified borrowers are fewer just when there is a need for stimulative investment. Repayment problems are exacerbated by exchange-rate problems, which could be ameliorated by a common currency. The insistence on the highest quality financing frees the Bank from any difficulty in evaluating credit risks. However, the establishment of the European Investment Fund (EIF) has resulted in some change in the extent of financing and degree of risk. The question has been raised as to whether an international investment bank is the most effective group to be responsible for regional development. In response it might be questionable if without the EIB there would be another organization or method of financing projects at the same level as the Bank.

Evaluation of the economic and job-creation efforts by region and sector is difficult because of the nature of the investment, that is, infrastructure investment where there is a greater indirect rather than direct effect.[28] It is difficult to quantify precisely the economic impact of the investment in the fifteen MSs as well as by sector. The contribution made to job creation by projects financed is difficult to assess precisely. Yet, account should be taken of the 45,000 jobs expected to be created in SMEs benefiting from ECU 1 billion in subsidized loans in 1995. Another significant factor is the spinoff in terms of jobs created as a result of financing infrastructure projects, which accounts for three-quarters of the Bank activity, as well as the employment safeguarded (not to mention the jobs directly or indirectly created by virtue of the support for industrial and service sector projects).[29]

Funding provided for projects within the Union helped on average to underpin 35% of their aggregate investment costs, which, on the basis of information from the beneficiaries, can be estimated at ECU 53 billion. This capital investment corresponds to about 4% of GFCF in the Union. A 1995 breakdown of total project costs is as follows:

- ECU 21 billion for communications infrastructure
- ECU 10 billion for environmental infrastructure
- ECU 10 billion for energy
- ECU 12 billion for the productive sector.[30]

The continued need for the EIB has been questioned if there is better access to private capital markets. But with tight control of administrative costs, the Bank should survive in the marketplace. More specifically in terms of its public policy role, the availability of risk capital and loan guarantees could be an important component of its future, which may be increasingly in the direction of a wholesale role.[31] Also, interest subsidies could be a major aspect of its future role as administrator.

Though constrained by remit from giving interest subsidies, the EIB acts as a channel for subsidies provided by others for loans made by the EIB. The Bank is taking on greater risk with the management of the EIF; 40% of the ECU 2 billion capital is provided by the EIB. The present EIB is a factor in the promotion of cohesion because it enhances competition and efficiency in lagging financial markets and it acts to pressure the private financial sector.[32]

In terms of applicability of an organization such as the EIB to the United States, a comparison should be made with the Reconstruction Finance Corporation (RFC) experience, which occurred largely during a period of economic decline and global loans with the Small Business Administration. There is unquestionably a role for these types of organizations in the United States, especially for infrastructure. In terms of loans and guarantees for the private sector, other than projects of national interest, do private financial institutions obviate the need for a quasi-governmental financial organization?

EUROPEAN INVESTMENT FUND

Another activity of the EIB is participation in the European Investment Fund (EIF) established in June 1994 as a legally independent entity with a subscribed capital of ECU 2 billion, 40% subscribed by the EIB, 30% by the Union and 30% by public and private banks.[33]

EIF issues guarantees on loans for infrastructure projects of European interest as well as for investment by SMEs. Particular emphasis is given to supporting trans-European networks (TENs), projects in transport, telecommunications and energy. Priority is given to small firms and programs benefiting regions. The limited availability of long-term guarantees in cases where state funding or other guarantees are not available could present difficulties in finding sufficient long-term finance for TEN projects. For SMEs the Fund issues guarantees in the same framework of global loans through banking institutions.

It is anticipated that up to ECU 20 billion of financing can be guaranteed. Subsequently it is hoped that the EIF can participate in equity operations. The Fund operates on a self-sustaining basis and will therefore seek an acceptable return on its capital by charging for its services in line with market practices. The guarantees make it easier for companies to obtain loans to finance large-scale investment projects. The medium- and long-term guarantees are tailored to the type of investment. They cover credit exposure risks incurred by banks and institutions. The Fund is managed by the EIB. Two of the major infrastructure projects are the Malapensa airport in Milan, Italy, and the natural gas project in Portugal.[34]

The EIF in 1994 guaranteed loans totaling ECU 702.7 million, of which ECU 515.3 million were for operations actually signed. In 1995, the loan volume guaranteed was ECU 686.8 million, of which ECU 116.5 million were for transactions actually signed. In 1994, there were only a small number of operations, broken down as follows:

Italy	53.8%
Portugal	20.8%
France	14.7%
Greece	10.6%

Trans-European network projects in 1994 accounted for 85.3% of the total volume signed and 14.7% for small business; in 1995, the figures were 94% for trans-European networks and 6% for small business. The breakdown within the trans-European networks is:

Sector	1994	1995
Transport	17.2%	18.1%
Energy	47.3%	27.7%
Telecommunications	35.5%	54.2%[35]

In 1995, the budget for the period 1995–1999 was set at ECU 2.4 billion.[36]

NOTES

1. U.S. Congress, House Committee on Banking, Finance and Urban Affairs, Subcommittee on Economic Stabilization, *Hearings on Industrial Policy*, Serial 98-47, Part 4 (September 1983), p. 53; and Ira Hirschman, "Can We Pay for What We Plan? Infrastructure Finance in the New York Region," *Metro Planner*, Metropolitan Chapter of the American Planning Association (November/ December 1996), p. 10.

2. Norbert Vanhove and Leo H. Klaasen, *Regional Policy: A European Approach*, 2d ed. (Teakfield, UK: Saxon House, 1987), p. 426.

3. Loukas Tsoukalis, *The New European Economy: The Politics and Economics of Integration* (Oxford: Oxford University Press, 1991), p. 218.

4. *EIB Information* (3rd quarter, 1996), p. 5.

5. *EIB Information* 98, 1998, p. 2.

6. EIB, *40 Years of Lending in Support of European Integration*, 1998, p. 6.

7. EIB, *Annual Report 1997*, 1998, p. 49.

8. Ibid., p. 52.

9. EIB, *Information 66*, November 1990.

10. EIB, *40 Years*, p. 20.

11. EIB, *Annual Report 1997*, p. 7.

12. Patrick Honohan, "The Public Policy Role of the European Investment Bank within the European Union," *Journal of Common Market Studies* 33 (September 1995), p. 315.

13. EIB, *Annual Report 1995*, 1996, p. 21.

14. Ibid., p. 2.

15. EIB, *Annual Report 1997*, p. 7.

16. Ibid., p. 1.

17. Ibid.

18. Ibid., p. 12.

19. Ibid., p. 13.

20. Ibid.

21. EIB, *Information 83*, February 1995.

22. Honohan, "Public Policy Role," p. 317.

23. EU, Commission, *Serving the European Union: A Citizen's Guide to the Institutions of the European Union*, 1996, p. 21.

24. "Loans from the EIB Individual Loans," *Frontier-Free Europe*, Supplement 4 (1993).

25. EIB, *Annual Report 1995*, p. 20.

26. Jeffrey Harrop, *The Political Economy of Integration in the European Community*, 2d ed. (Aldershot, UK: Edward Elgar, 1992), p. 156.

27. Ibid., p. 154.

28. EIB, *Annual Report 1995*, p. 21.

29. EIB, *Annual Report 1995*, p. 21.

30. Ibid.

31. Honohan, "Public Policy Role,"p. 324.

32. Ibid., pp. 326 and 329.

33. "The EIB and the Edinburgh Summit Initiatives," EIB *Information 76*, May 1993, p. 1.

34. European Union, Commission, *Sixth Annual Report on the Structural Funds 1994*, COM(95)583 final, p. 115.

35. Ibid., and European Union, Commission, *Seventh Annual Report on the Structural Funds 1995*, 1996, COM(96) 502 final, p. 209.

36. Ibid, p. 216.

Chapter 13

Research, Technology and Development

ORIGINS

Comparing the EU and the United States in terms of the public role in technology programs to date reveals a more focused approach in the EU. The EU has shown greater concern with the locational impact of research technology and development (RTD), a concern which is minimal in the United States. Starting with the ECSC and Euratom Treaties a comprehensive research and technology policy has developed over the past forty-plus years. The seeds of a European research policy were first planted in 1951 when the ECSC gave the High Authority, now the Commission, the task of making funding available to promote research on coal and steel. Beginning in the 1960s, a number of Community-financed programs were initiated in these sectors.[1]

With the establishment of the European Atomic Energy Community (EURATOM) in 1957, joint European research was placed on a broader basis. Under the Euratom Treaty one of the Community's prime tasks was to develop research and safeguard technical knowledge in the nuclear field. A Community-financed research and training program was installed. A nuclear research establishment was set up in 1957 whose responsibilities were subsequently broadened to cover areas besides nuclear research and now is the Joint Research Center, the Community's research laboratory.

Initially research followed the provision in the EEC treaty for the coordination of agricultural research and the dissemination of agricultural knowledge. In 1974, a new approach was adopted in which the Community's leaders agreed in principle on a general European research and technology policy. In 1983, the individual programs were brought together under the First Community Framework for research, technology and demonstration. The stated objective was to strengthen the scientific and technical bases of Community industry and promote its international competitiveness. The multi-year framework program is a medium-term investment instrument for the programming of activities in research and technological development. It forms a basis and guide for the specific program decisions to be taken during a five-year period.

Research can be carried out in three ways:

- contract research carried out by universities, research centers and industrial firms on a shared-cost basis
- concerted action, in which the Commission acts primarily as a coordinator, ensuring the necessary compatibility and smooth flow of information
- direct action projects, carried out by the Joint Research Center.[2]

The Single European Act explicitly authorized the Community's scientific and technical cooperation by giving the Community formal powers in research and technology. The Single European Act established a European Research and Technology Community and added Article 130f to the Treaty of Rome, which had not given the Commission explicit authority to promote research and development for industry. There was no general policy framework for technology.[3]

High technology was not deemed a replacement or a threat to basic industry. High technology is not the only component of innovation; it can be utilized in basic or smokestack industries, which are likely to be located in lagging regions.[4]

Title XV introduced by the Treaty on European Union stressed the importance of research and technology in the well-being of the Union. Article 130H of the Treaty calls for "the Community and Member States to coordinate their research and technological development activities so as to ensure that national policies and Community policy are mutually consistent." This could be interpreted as a desire to reflect regional and similar policies and avoid fragmentation of research and technological development policies.

According to Article 130f of the Treaty on European Union:

The Community shall have the objective of strengthening the scientific and technological bases of Community industry and encouraging it to become more competitive at the international level, while promoting all the research activities deemed necessary by virtue of other Chapters of this Treaty.

For this purpose the Community shall, throughout the Community, encourage undertakings, including small and medium sized undertakings, research centers and universities in their research and technological development activities of high quality; it shall support their efforts to cooperate with one another, aiming, notably, at enabling undertakings to exploit the internal market potential to the full, in particular through the opening up of national public contracts, the definition of common standards and the removal of legal and fiscal obstacles to that cooperation.

Table 13.1
Fourth RTD Framework Program and European Atomic Energy Community (EAEC) Program Budget, 1994–1999 (in millions of ECUs)

	RTD	EAEC	Total	Percent
First Area of Activity				
Information and				
communication technologies	3,405	–	3,405	27.7
Industrial technologies	1,995	–	1,995	16.2
Environment	1,080	–	1,080	8.8
Life sciences and technologies	1,572	–	1,572	12.8
Energy	1,002	1,254	2,256	18.3
Transport	240	–	240	2.0
Targeted socio-economic research	138	–	138	1.2
Second Area of Actvity				
Cooperation with third countries				
and international organizations	540	–	540	4.4
Third Area of Activity				
Dissemination and				
optimization of results	330	–	330	2.7
Fourth Area of Activity				
Training and mobility of researchers	744	=	744	6.0
Total	11,046	1,254	12,300	100.0

Source: European Union, Commission, *Research and Technological Development Activities of the European Union Annual Report 1995,* COM(95) 443 final, September 28, 1995, p. 100.

RTD PROGRAMS

Research and technological development is considered a key to the future. Since 1985, four RTD framework programs have been the vehicle for all RTD measures in the Union (1985–1988, 1987–1991, 1990–1994, 1994–1998), involving significant expenditure, though the programs account for only 4% of the total public civilian research effort in the Union.[5]

For 1996, the research policy budget totaled ECU 3.2 billion, 3.7% of total financial commitments.[6] The Fourth Framework Program

(1994–1998) has a budget of ECU 12.3 billion. The Fourth Framework Program covers all the research and technological development carried out by the EU during the 1994–1998 period.[7] Subsequently the budget for the Fourth RTD Framework Program was increased by ECU 800 million to take account of the accession of Austria, Finland and Sweden, bringing the total to ECU 13.1 billion for the 1994–1998 period.[8]

To strengthen the links with the Union's regional and structural policies, examples of RTD activities are[9]:

- the choice of research themes, such as decertification, renewable energy, traditional manufacturing, rural areas, marine sciences
- measures in favor of SMEs, for example, the CRAFT initiative (Cooperative Action for Research Technology) begun under the industrial technologies program
- networking measures
- dissemination of research results and technology transfer
- specific actions such as the Human Capital and Mobility Program.

An examination of the nineteen Fourth Framework programs indicates they have differing impacts on regional economic development as compared with spatial impact for the Union as a whole. Within the information technology program, networks of excellence are to be established in order to initiate long-term research. An innovation is the establishment of focused clusters of activities grouping together different well-defined activities.[10]

A network of excellence brings together industry, users, universities and research centers with a common research objective. It combines the critical mass of centers of excellence with the benefits for training and technology emanating from geographical spread. Thirteen networks of excellence involving more than 500 research firms have been started under ESPRIT III (European Strategic Program for Research and Development in Information Technology).[11]

An innovation is the establishment of focused clusters of activities covering a number of technology areas directed toward a well-defined goal. In addition to collaborative research proposals, a cluster may incorporate other types of activity as needs dictate. They can include networks of excellence, associations of suppliers and users, cooperation with Eureka (European Research Coordinating Agency), coordination with national initiatives, international cooperation, dissemination of results or training initiatives.[12]

Four focused clusters have been proposed: open microprocessor systems; high-performance computing and networking; technologies for business processes; and integration in manufacturing. The question is whether they will be directed toward lagging regions.[13]

The basis of the Industrial and Materials Technologies Program is the revitalization of the manufacturing industry by reinforcing its scientific and technological basis through research and development work. The major goals are an increase in the competitiveness of European industry in view of strong international challenges, especially in crucial sectors of advanced technology, and strengthening European economic and social cohesion consistent with the pursuit of scientific and technical excellence.[14] Three research areas have been identified: production technologies for future industries; technologies for product innovation; and technologies for transport means.[15]

A component of Life Sciences and Technology is concerned with agriculture and fisheries. One objective is to increase the viability of the agricultural and agro-industrial sector, especially in the less-developed regions and those regions where agriculture suffers from chronic structural problems. Funding of projects is in response to the interests of rural development, special needs of lagging regions and the reformed Common Agricultural Policy and the Common Fisheries Policy.[16]

The aim of the centralized action for the dissemination and exploitation of knowledge resulting from Union research activities is specifically to give added value to RTD activities. Specific needs of the more peripheral and least-favored regions, have been taken into account, notably through the VALUE (Dissemination and Utilization of Results from Science and Technology Research) and SPRINT (Strategic Program for Innovation and Technology) programs.[17]

Besides activities aimed at promoting leading-edge technology, there is a need for activities aimed at improving the whole of the industrial system and in this respect it is important to integrate the RTD policy effectively into the cohesion objective. This will allow the promotion of RTD capability in the less favored regions and allow them to benefit from the advantages of research and technological development.[18]

COHESION

The Treaty on European Union requires cohesion aims to be taken into account in the economic policies while the cornerstone of the RTD program is the principle of excellence. The cohesion gap in RTD is as great within some MSs as between MSs in the Union. In the MSs least well endowed with RTD facilities, the facilities are mainly located in and around their capital cities or in one other principal center. There is also a significant gap between the advanced countries and the less prosperous MSs with respect to the level of state aid for RTD and innovation.[19]

Within the Union, Germany and France have the highest levels of public expenditure on civilian RTD. In 1993, the MSs spent ECU 50.3 billion; Germany and France together accounted for ECU 30.2 billion, 60% of the total. In contrast, Ireland, Portugal and Greece spent only ECU 672 million, less than 11/2% of the total.[20] Within MSs, spending is disproportionately distributed at the regional level. Almost half the research occurs within twelve "islands of innovation." These islands contain dense networks of enterprises and laboratories and interact in the development of new products and processes.[21]

The imbalances among regions has since 1989 been somewhat lowered, partly due to the Structural Fund expenditures; 5% of the total expenditures have been allocated to RTD-related measures. However, the gap still remains. Yet, almost half the total amount of the contracts under the framework programs goes to only nine regions that account for only 28% of the population.[22]

There are great disparities among MSs, rich and poor, as regards the use of modern information and communication technologies. For example, Portugal spends 2.5% of its GDP on telephone connections, as compared with a mere 0.4% by France, Finland and Italy. The quality of available links is another criterion of ease of access to information technologies. Per capita expenditures on information technologies in the EU came to ECU 317 on average in 1994; Greece was far below the average, with ECU 47, as was Portugal with ECU 85, whereas Denmark invested ECU 591 in 1994. It is not only a reflection of the state of their information technology equipment but also has an indirect effect on the level of training and consequently their ability to use advanced electronics.[23]

STRUCTURAL FUNDS

A specific task of the Structural Funds is to pursue economic and social cohesion. In this context they have had a supplementary role in assisting the less-favored regions with respect to raising their RTD capabilities to Union standards. Activities under the Community research program have not been funded by the Structural Funds.[24] The Structural Funds do not intervene directly in RTD per se but rather see it as a major component of economic development in terms of increased productivity and competitiveness and thus as valuable in narrowing disparities.[25]

An integrated approach has to be devised that develops synergies between the RTD Framework Program and the Structural Funds while respecting the integrity of each policy. Thus, the Structural Funds have contributed to developing capabilities within the less-favored regions, which facilitated their participation in the RTD Framework Program. The RTD Framework Program, largely through the diffusion of technologies, mobility of researchers through networking, and the balance among research activities, contributes to reducing disparities in RTD capabilities.[26]

In general the MSs with Objective 1 (lagging) regions, where the cohesion gap is greatest, have concentrated their resources on building up RTD capabilities rather than on stimulating demand for research by the productive sector. They have tended to emphasize the financing of infrastructures and equipment for research outside the firm, frequently in academic institutions or public-sector research institutes. In the less-prosperous regions it may be necessary to appraise the balance between basic and applied research and the balance between research and its effective dissemination into productive activity.[27] The Commission has begun to explore new paths to support regions in their transition to the information society, such as an interregional initiative for the information society aimed at promoting regional cooperation in this field.

The following six regions face serious problems of structural change: northwest England; Saxony, Germany; north Pas-de-Calais, France; Valencia, Spain; central Macedonia; and Piedmont, Italy. Activities begun in 1994 included the establishment in all six regions of regional-level links with private industry, higher education and the main representatives in terms of pilot groups. These groups have the task of coordinating the preparation of a strategy and an action program and securing the economic, political and financial backing necessary for their realization.[28]

Since 1993, to strengthen competitiveness and cohesion, greater attention has been given to RTD and support from the Structural Funds. Between 1994 and 1999, increased finance for research and development-related measures has been available from the Structural Funds. In the Objective 1 regions, a total of 5% of appropriations (as compared with 3.7% in the previous period) will be used for RTD; and the figure is 12% under Objective 2. In addition the revised ESF regulation provides for the fund to support under Objectives, 1, 2 and 5(b) measures covering training in research, science and technology. The additional spending could be attributed to the overall increase in the Structural Funds.

Greater stress has been placed on the research and technological development aspect of Community Initiatives in two new Initiatives, SMEs and ADAPT.[29] Despite their primary objective of increasing international competitiveness, the programs are also designed to develop RTD capacity in the relatively weak parts of the Union and to strengthen their structural growth. Particularly in the less-developed regions, there is a major need to raise the adaptability of the work force and growth of technological progress of firms.[30]

The search for a better complementarity between RTD and structural policies faces two facts: On one hand there are disparities among the regions in terms of competitiveness, which the Union aims at reducing.

On the other hand regions must have the capacity to take advantage of technological development to ensure competitiveness.[31]

FIFTH FRAMEWORK PROGRAM

Six main themes of the proposed Fifth RTD Framework Program are set out in a draft adopted by the Commission. Covering 1999–2003, the Framework Program will have three thematic programs: (1) resources of the living world and ecosystem, research into health and food, biotechnology and environmental protection; (2) the information society; and (3) competitive and sustainable growth. The remaining horizontal programs deal with international cooperation, dissemination and utilization of results, and training and mobility of researchers. The Commission believes the program should receive the same proportion of EU GNP as the Fourth Program and match the research efforts of the EU's major competitors.[32]

The proposed Commission budget for the Fifth Framework is ECU 16.3 billion, compared with 13.1 billion (adjusted) for 1994–1998, a 3% increase over the Fourth Program in the share of GDP allocated to research. The Commission's policy is to increase funding faster than the growth of GNP through areas such as research because of the added value derived from Union action.

Table 13.2
Fifth RTD Framework Program, Proposed Budget, 1999–2003

	Millions of ECUs	Percentage
Living world and the ecosystem	3,925	3.9
Information society	3,925	23.9
Competitive and sustainable growth	3,925	23.9
Training and mobility of researchers	1,402	8.6
International cooperation	491	3.1
Dissemination and optimization of results	350	2.5
Joint research center	815	4.9
Euratom	1,467	9.2
Total	16,300	100.0

Source: European Union, Commission (London), *The Week in Europe*, WE/30/97, July 31, 1997.

The Fifth Framework Program is intended to mark a shift in emphasis, particularly by focusing on the economic and social priorities for the EU and its citizens, and on maintaining and strengthening the capacity of the EU for scientific and technological research and development.[33]

An Assessment Panel has raised questions about accepting the aforementioned balance with its emphasis on cohesion: "The Panel believes that together with relevance, European added value should be the touchstone for selecting programs and projects in future Framework Programs. It is this criteria that separates work that should clearly be done at the European level from activity that should be sponsored solely within MSs."[34] It would appear that acceptance of the panel's recommendations would lead to further concentration of RTD away from regions the Structural Funds are assisting. An assessment of the proposed Fifth RTD states that it needs to be more relevant economically and socially yet able to provide much more European added value.[35]

A strategy with scientific excellence at its heart should avoid a program decisively colored by the "national or sectoral perspectives" that have characterized past programs.

Examples of added value are:

- the existence of important large-scale research facilities, which no individual MS would develop and support
- promotion of internationally competitive R&D communities in new interdisciplinary areas such as information technology and biotechnology
- creation of strong industrial platforms able to compete or cooperate on a global-level, based on uniform technical standards, for example, mobile telecommunications
- development of pan-European norms and standards of commercial applications.[36]

Changes in the legal framework are proposed that would use qualified majority voting when adopting a Framework Program. The requirement for unanimity results in a program based on national and sectoral interests rather than a strategic program for the Union as an entity. There should be more flexibility in the management of the program to allow a quicker response to changes and scientific advances.[37]

Recommended new management priorities are:

- a more determined approach to the commercial exploitation of research
- more help for SMEs
- applying a systems approach
- using the new technologies to create "virtual" research institutes
- involving the Union in large projects operated by the MSs.[38]

With the EU lagging in terms of total research investment, which in 1995 came to 1.9% of GDP compared with 2.45% for the United States and 2.95% for Japan, the EU has to improve Europe's performance in bringing new products and practices to fruition and to encourage innovation in the EU. Can this be accomplished without neglecting regional considerations?[39]

In response the Commission has proposed that regional cohesion and competitiveness be reinforced through technological development and innovation. Key components of this strategy are providing innovation at the regional level, developing human resources and promoting networking and regional cooperation. Regions are invited to establish an inegrated strategy for RTD and innovation designed for their particular economic structures.

The strategy is directed at identifying ways in which policies can within the framework of the Structural Funds and the Fifth Framework Program or RTD contribute to the growth of less-favored regions. The key elements in attaining these objectives are promoting innovation, improving networking and industrial cooperation and developing human resources.

More specifically the Commission favors integration of RTD and innovation in negotiations on future structural programs. MSs should develop jointly a set of performance indicators for RTD and innovation whereby structural interventions can be evaluated and monitored. Transnational partnerships between centers of excellence in the regions, especially those who have developed fully their technological potential. Creation of a RTD and innovation Web site interlocking regions, MSs and candidate countries.[40]

NOTES

1. Klaus-Dieter Borchardt, *European Integration: The Origins and Growth of the European Union*, 4th ed. (European Union, Commission), 1995, p. 55.

2. Ibid., p. 57.

3. For the evolution of technology policy, see Margaret Sharp, "The Community and New Technologies," in Juliet Lodge, ed., *The European Community and the Challenge of the Future*, 2d ed., (New York: St. Martin's Press, 1993), Chapter 1.

4. European Union, Commission, *Research and Technological Development Policy*, 3rd ed., 1988, pp. 18–19.

5. European Union, Commission, *First Cohesion Report*, COM(96) 542 final, November 11, 1996, p. 69.

6. European Union, Commission, *The Budget of the European Union: How Is Your Money Spent?*, 1996, p. 5.

7. European Union, Commission, *Research and Technological Development Activities of the European Union, Annual Report 1995*, COM(95) 443 final, September 28, 1995.

8. European Union, Commission, *Bulletin* 3, 1996, p. 36.

9. Commission, *Annual Report 1995* 443, p. 10.

10. European Union, Commission, *Directorate General XII, Science, Research, and Development: The Fourth Framework Program*, 1994, p. 4.

11. Commission, *Annual Report 1995*, p. 64.

12. Ibid., p. 64.

13. Ibid., p. 65.

14. Ibid., p. 30.

15. Commission, *Science, Research and Development,* p. 10.

16. Commission, *Annual Report 1995,* pp. 40–41.

17. Ibid., pp. 14–15.

18. European Union, Commission, *Cohesion and RTD Policy—Synergies between Research and Technological Development Policy and Economic and Social Cohesion Policy,* COM(93) 203 final, May 12, 1993, p. 5.

19. Ibid., p. 2.

20. Commission, *First Cohesion Report,* p. 70.

21. Ibid., p. 70.

22. Ibid.

23. Monika Wulf-Mathies, "The Regions and the Global Information Society," *Frontier-Free Europe* 7/8 (July–August 1996), p. 1.

24. Commission, *Cohesion and RTD Policy,* p. 6.

25. Ibid., p. 10.

26. Ibid.

27. Ibid.

28. Wulf-Mathies, "The Regions." p. 1.

29. European Union, Commission, *Seventh Annual Report on the Structural Funds 1995,* COM(96)502 final, October 30, 1996, pp. 214–215.

30. Commission, *First Cohesion Report,* p. 69.

31. Ibid., p. 70.

32. European Union, Commission (London), *The Week in Europe,* WE14/97, April 10, 1997, p. 1.

33. European Union, Commission (London), *The Week in Europe,* WE/06/97, February 13, 1997, p. 2.

34. European Union, *EU Research and Technological Development Activities: 5-Year Assessment of the European Community RTD Framework Programs,* Report of the Independent Expert Panel and Commission's Comments, March 1997, p. 10.

35. European Union, Commission, Directorate General XII, "The Fifth RTD Framework Program: The Five-Year Assessment Panel Calls for a 'New Leap Forward'," Press Release IP/97/163, February 26, 1997.

36. European Union, *EU Research,* p. 11.

37. Ibid., p. 12.

38. Ibid., pp. 13–14.

39. Ibid., p. 17, and "Political Science: The European Union Spends a Lot of Money on Scientific Research. Is This Worthwhile?" *The Economist* 346 (February 12, 1998), p. 79.

40. European Union, Commission, Directorate General XII, "European Commission Encourages Cohesion and Development of Less-Favored Regions Through Research and Innovation," Press Release IP/98/473, May 27, 1998.

Chapter 14

EU Competition Policy

HISTORY

In the EU, in contrast to the United States, there is a defined policy for state aid for regional purposes (Sections 92-94 of the Treaty of Rome as amended).[1] State aid controls are of a constitutional nature and are not based on secondary legislation of the Council. MSs have had to comply with the provisions, modify national laws and circumscribe the availability of subsidies. Although there was no separate title in the Treaty of Rome relating to regional policy, those drafting the Treaty were aware regional problems could be dealt with only if aid policies were monitored. State aid given to shelter national industries represented a serious restriction on competition. Each time aid is granted in one MS, industries in other countries, perhaps even more efficient, are placed at a disadvantage. The response would have been to grant equivalent aid, raise tariff barriers or impose countervailing duties, actions fundamentally incompatible with the Community. It was unrealistic to expect MSs to police themselves, and so some form of control was needed.

Properly controlled, state aid could aid the development of backward regions and meet goals for which the Community lacked adequate funds. Controls limit the freedom to grant unilaterally financial advantages to certain sectors or firms and include provisions whereby national state aids would be monitored by the Commission. Competition policy is implemented with regard for the economic and social climate. "Community competition policy is not an end in itself to be pursued dogmatically; it is an instrument, albeit an important one for achieving agreed Community objectives—economic integration, cohesion, improved standards of living, sustainable growth, social welfare and protection of the environment."[2]

The maintenance of a system of free and undistorted competition was one of the cornerstones of the EEC. Regional aid schemes posed considerable control problems. The basic difficulty was that various regions competed with each other to attract investment. Regional aid became more costly from competitive bidding without appreciably increasing the total flow of investment and gave rise to reciprocal neutralization with unjustified profits for the beneficiary enterprises. Aid tended not to correspond to the relative seriousness of the situation.

The Community was aware that governments can be the greatest violators in terms of restricting competition. Thus, limitations were imposed on national governments, including state aid. Subsidies at the national and subnational level would be monitored and controlled. An issue in the control of regional aid was the need to establish rates of assistance that reflected the severity of regional problems, the need for transparency and the need to restrict regional aid to those areas where it was really justified. The Commission eventually succeeded in attaining a degree of control when in 1971 its communication to the Council laid down principles to govern the way regional aid is approved. The communication had two aims: to lay down general requirements and to prescribe specific aid ceilings. Aid should be transparent; opacity should be progressively rendered transparent or, if not possible, should be dropped. Aid should be regionally specific. It should not normally cover whole territories but should apply to problem regions therein and its intensity should be adjusted to the seriousness of the specific problem.[3] Greater transparency facilitated cooperation of MSs as well as making comparative analysis of the aims, results and justification for state aid easier.

In 1979, the Commission undertook an analysis of regions and categorized them according to their social and economic situation. This system formed the basis of subsequent aid control for regions, not MSs. Aid ceilings were established for each category, according to the gravity and urgency of regional imbalance in a Community-wide context. Ceilings were fixed in net grant equivalent terms and expressed either as a percentage of initial investment or in ECUs. Sections of Article 92 defined the type of state aid considered to be compatible and for which derogations were permitted. Creation of the single market and the need for convergence and cohesion required aid measures to be aimed at overcoming regional disequilibrium. Government assistance to enterprises could be used as a protectionist tool, thus undermining the wider strategy, which rested on the philosophy that the single market must be free and competitive.

Competition was bound to intensify as trade barriers between MSs were reduced. In addition to state aid, the granting of aid by subnational authorities had to be monitored as it aggravates counter-cohesive distortions because authorities in more prosperous parts of the Union are able to offer more generous incentives. "This policy of tightening discipline in richer regions where aid can have a greater distorting effect will be focused not just on regional aid in these regions but also on other general or industry schemes whose impact is felt primarily in such richer regions. Such a reinforced State aid policy will act as a complement to the Community's structural funds."[4]

CONTEXT

Competition policy cannot be understood or applied without reference to its legal, economic, political and social context.

Competition policy so long been a central Community policy that is often forgotten that it is not an end in itself but rather one of the instruments towards fundamental goals laid out in the Treaty—namely the establishment of a common market, the approximation of economic policy, promotion of harmonious development and economic expansion, the increase of living standards and bringing about closer relationship between MSs.[5]

Competition policy is not solely concerned with state aid. Articles 85 and 86 of the Treaty cover anticompetitive behavior by enterprises, as distinct from Articles 92 to 94, which deal with state aid. Article 85 prohibits agreements between undertakings, decisions by associations of undertakings and concerted practices that may affect trade between MSs with the object of preventing, restricting or distorting competition among the MSs. Article 86 prohibits anticompetitive use of monopoly positions by firms. Article 67 of the ECSC Treaty covered interference with conditions of competition. State aid is also concerned with sectoral aids.

State aid has to be distinguished in terms of aid that facilitates growth and adaptation: research and development, training, regional development and positive restructuring. Aid that prevents change or merely exports the problems to other MSs (e.g., rescue aids to preserve bankrupt companies not linked to viable restructuring plans) is not acceptable.

Large and well-developed MSs will always be able to outbid less-developed MSs. The four largest MSs in 1990 accounted for 88% of all aid granted.[6] The four peripheral countries—Greece, Ireland, Portugal and Spain—have granted an annual average of ECU 428 in aid per employed person while the richer central MSs—Germany, France, Italy and the UK—have granted an average of ECU 742 annually.[7]

Between 1992 and 1994, the twelve MSs prior to enlargement devoted at least ECU 95 billion annually on average in state aid to their enterprises. The problem is that the aid is concentrated in the relatively prosperous countries (Germany, Belgium, France and Italy) while the proportion of the less well-off countries (Greece, Ireland, Portugal and Spain) is declining.[8] For 2000–2006, the Commission has proposed reducing the population covered by state aid from 46.7% to 42.7% of the total population. Geographical concentration is necessary to avoid spreading assistance too thinly and to encourage positive action favoring the most-disadvantaged regions. To further enhance the impact of regional state aid on unemployment, it should be granted in the form of investment in production and in direct subsidies as a percentage of wages.[9]

ARTICLES 92–94

The legal basis for competition rules is in Articles 92, 93 and 94 of the Treaty of Rome as amended. Article 92 outlines the policy; Article 93 provides for the supervisory role of the Commission, redress or appeal by the Commission or MSs in the event of disagreement or disputes; and Article 94 covers the role of the Council in making appropriate regulations and the conditions under which Article 93(3) may apply. The articles do not prohibit state aid but give the Commission wide latitude to control state aid and take action against MSs deemed guilty of unfair competitive practices.

Article 92

Article 92 provides the means for regional aid to be deemed compatible with the common market. It sets out the basic principle that state aid is incompatible with the common market, a principle that logically flows from both the letter and spirit of earlier articles in the Treaty, notably, Articles 85, 86 and 90. A blanket exception could not be given since regional aid could become excessive and in turn an unfair competitive advantage.

All industrial projects involving government subsidies must be submitted to the Commission for approval. In practice, governments often go ahead with aid schemes, submitting them for approval only after the money has been paid out or even neglecting to notify the Commission. Aid projects stand a better chance of Commission approval if they help the economic development of a backward region, promote R&D in a key industry or reduce overcapacity in an ailing sector.[10]

Article 92(1) enunciates the basic principles for state aid. State aid granted by a MS "which distorts or threatens to distort competition by favoring certain undertakings or the production of certain goods shall, in so far as it affects trade between Member States, be incompatible with the Common Market." Within this framework, two categories of exception are recognized. One consists of series of aids that are definitely exempted from the general ban (Article 92(2)). The other consists of examples of aid that may also be exempted (Article 92(3)). Aid may be allowed in accordance with specified conditions and as a contribution to Union objectives (economic integration, cohesion, improved standards of living, sustainable growth, social welfare and protection of the environment).

Article 92(2) lists three types of aid compatible with the common market. The Commission has no discretion to refuse authorization.

(a) aid having a social character, granted to individual consumers, provided such aid is given without discrimination as to the origin of the products concerned

(b) aid to compensate for the damage caused by natural disasters or exceptional occurrences

(c) aid granted for the economies of certain areas of the Federal Republic of Germany affected by the division of Germany in so far as such aid is needed to compensate for economic disadvantages caused by the division.

The following may be considered compatible with the common market as covered by Article 92(3):

(a) aid to promote the economic development of areas where the standard of living is abnormally low or there is serious unemployment

(b) aid for major projects of common European interests or to correct serious disturbances in the economy of an MS

(c) aid for development of economic activities or economic areas not adversely affecting trading conditions

(d) aid to promote culture and heritage conservation.

As a general principle the Commission considers that operating aid covering losses to assist firms in economic difficulty is not exempt under Article 92(2)(a) and (3). However, if such aid forms part of a restructuring plan to restore the long-term viability and profitability of a firm, involving abandonment of the loss-making activities, it may be approved pursuant to Article 92(3)(c) as aid to facilitate the development of certain economic activities.

The Commission may in certain exceptional cases and under strict conditions authorize operating aid in regions suffering from serious economic problems and high unemployment and which thus are eligible for regional aid under Article 92(3)(a).

In determining the eligibility of a region for regional aid pursuant to Article 92(3)(c), the Commission in the first stage makes an analysis of the socioeconomic situation of the region based on its GDP and structural unemployment compared with the national average and in the second stage takes into account other relevant indicators. Other indicators the Commission may consider are the contribution the proposed national regional aid map makes to ensure the necessary coherency between the Union's regional aid policy under the Structural Funds and its regional aid policy under state aid rules in Articles 92–94.[11]

It follows that the Commission is in principle hostile toward aid not conditional on initial investment or job creation and that has the character of operating aid. As defined by the Commission, initial investment in fixed assets by way of takeover is limited to takeover of an establishment that has closed down or that would have closed down had such takeover not taken place.[12] Therefore, aid granted for the acquisition of a firm that is not in economic difficulties and that would not have closed without the takeover does not constitute aid for initial investment and may amount to an operation aid for the benefit of the firm. This aid cannot in principle be approved unless it is available only in regions eligible for regional aid pursuant to Article 92(3)(a).[13] The Commission's task is difficult in having to assess and coordinate aid in an unclear background. Successive enlargements have added to the regional diversity and the need for new approaches to controlling regional aid.

Article 93

Under Article 93, the Commission, in cooperation with MSs, has to review constantly all aid systems and propose to MSs appropriate measures needed for the development or functioning of the common market. If the Commission finds a state aid is not compatible with the common market or with Article 92, it declares that the aid should be cancelled or changed within a set period of time.

Article 94

If there is no compliance the matter is referred to the Court of Justice. However, the MS concerned may apply to the Court for annulment of the decision. The Council may intervene under Article 94 if in exceptional circumstances political considerations are deemed to have outweighed all other assessment criteria. MSs are required to notify the Commission well in advance of any plans to introduce new aid schemes or to alter existing ones so the Commission can determine whether they fall within one or the other of excepted categories and therefore may be allowed to proceed. MSs may not implement an aid scheme until the Commission has made a final decision.

Frameworks

Although the Commission has considerable discretion in the field of state aid (and its decisions are difficult to challenge on substantive grounds before the Court) it has increasingly sought to clarify its approach to assessing different types of aid schemes. For the most part, this has taken the form of so-called "frameworks" in different aid areas such as research and development, environmental protection and small firms. These aim to introduce some transparency into the rationale for approving or prohibiting aid proposals of MSs.

PHILIP MORRIS CASE[14]

A precedent-setting decision was made by the Court of Justice in the Philip Morris case, September 1980 (*Philip Morris Holland v. Commission* Case 730/79 [1980 ECR 2671; CMLR 321]), separate from the Philip Morris merger case. Philip Morris International wanted to close its cigarette factory at Eindhoven, Netherlands, and transfer production to another Netherlands location, increasing manufacturing capacity in its proposed location by some 40%, giving it 13% of the total Netherlands cigarette output. Total cost of the new factory would have been just over ECU 60 million and aid proposed by the Netherlands represented between $3^1/2$% and 4% of that total, a relatively low percentage by prevailing standards. Assistance would have been granted under Netherlands law, which applied to all investment projects over a relatively modest level. The Commission stated that the proposed grant to the company was not in a sector facing difficulties or in a region with particular economic problems and thus could not be approved. Philip Morris appealed the decision to the Court of Justice. The Court sustained the Commission decision, stating that approval of the grant would give Philip Morris a competitive advantage over other manufacturers in the Community, which would have to arrange their own finances to cover increases in productive capacity without the benefit of state aid.

The Commission decision was also upheld on the ground that state aid should normally be approved only if it can be established that the aid will contribute to the attainment of one of the objectives specified in Article 92 (3), which under normal market conditions the recipient undertakings would be unable to attain by their own actions. In return for the distortion that the aid implied, the market within the Community must itself receive a benefit that would, at least in the long run, compensate for the aid received. It was the quid pro quo that the Commission and the court were unable to find in the Philip Morris case.

The judgment has frequently been utilized in the Commission's later decisions. It considerably strengthened the Commission's hand in denying approval to aid that does not fall completely into any of the first three categories in Article 92(3). A statement that the national interests of a MS are assisted or that the recipient itself has benefited would be insufficient alone to justify approval. The only kind of aid that stood a substantially favorable chance of approval under this category would be for an MS to show that the result of aid would be ultimately an improvement in market conditions by bringing supply and demand into balance, rather than further continuing the status quo by measures that merely put off unavoidable readjustments. On the other hand, any such schemes falling within those categories but which themselves conflicted with Community policies could not be approved.

SECTORAL

Is there a basic conflict between regional development policy and a policy that addresses sectoral concerns? Regional policies designed to ameliorate distressed areas can conflict with a sectoral policy that results in assistance or investment that disregards regional needs.[15] In a 1970 memorandum to the Council on industrial policy, industrial development was said to justify certain sectoral subsidies, in particular[16]:

- assisting industry in overcoming preliminary handicaps of external competition (advanced technology)
- promoting rationalization or reorganization and the effective use of factors of production by firms
- neutralizing competitive distortions due to actions by third countries apt to cause difficulties for Community industries.

The Commission in the same report faced the question of how to deal with sectoral aid granted for different purposes and to different sectors and enunciated three principles that should underlie all sectoral aids:

- Sectoral action should involve many types of action, ranging from industrial forecasting to subsidizing research and should be complemented by regional and social action.

- Sectoral aid should not be restricted to catastrophic situations, but instead to their avoidance by facilitating conversion to viable economic activities.
- Sectoral action should be more concerned with dynamism of firms and employment than with a particular mode of production. Conversion or diversification of a line of production should be initiated whenever necessary.

The policy on sectoral aid was further defined by the Commission.[17] The Commission stated its approval for aid designed to remedy situations in which market conditions:

- obstruct progress toward certain economic and social aims
- permit these objectives to be achieved only within unacceptable time limits or with unacceptable social costs
- intensify competition to such an extent that it could destroy itself.

It was not clear which situations fall into in the last category and how state aid might remedy them.

Aid granted in the above-mentioned situations would be compatible with provisions of the Treaty on state intervention only if it served the common interest. The Commission, except in very exceptional circumstances, cannot give precedence to one Community policy over others; it must seek rather to reconcile any conflicts arising on a case-by-case basis. Therefore, unless an industry is in a really desperate situation, considerations of industrial policy should not override those of regional policy. The value of regional development aid can be undermined by the availability of state aid of a sectoral character, which by affecting competition within an industry can alter optimal location decisions. Classifications may be somewhat arbitrary. Sector-specific aid thus has to be controlled in both duration and value, temporary and reductive over time. Aid to support firms without reference to restructuring or reconversion programs has to phase out. The aid should not have the effect of increasing capacity or hindering structural industrial change. Its main value lies in easing structural adjustments. Sectoral subsidization should not be disguised in the form of regional development.

Although problems may arise with regard to regional aids, particularly when regions in different MSs attempt to overbid one another in attracting direct investments or when the sectoral composition of regional aids tends to undermine the surveillance of sectoral aids, the real problems are to be found in general and sectoral aids programs. The Commission has tended to take a fairly strict view on general aids. State aids are in principle incompatible with the common market.[18]

There has long been a tradition of sectoral policies that generally have been introduced in response to a particular crisis. But in approving regional aid schemes the Commission normally imposes the condition that the aid must not give rise to sectoral overcapacity at the Union level such that the sectoral problems produced may be more serious than the original regional problem.[19] The Fourth Survey on State Aid covers national aid given by the twelve MSs to the following sectors: manufacturing, agriculture, fisheries, coal and transport (railways and inland waterways). The volume of state aid for these sectors for the period 1990–1992 came to ECU 93.8 billion.[20] The national aid does not include Union funding, such as Structural Funds. For the 1900-1992 period, 41% of the aid went to the manufacturing sector, in 1992 reaching 34.1 billion ECUs in 1991 prices and 3.4% of value added.[21]

Table 14.1
State Aid by Main Sectors, 1990–1992

Sector	Percentage
Agriculture and Fisheries	15
Manufacturing	41
Transport	29
Coal	15
Total	100

Source: European Union, Commission, *Fourth Survey on State Aid in the European Union in the Manufacturing and Certain Other Sectors,* COM(95) 365 final, July 26, 1995, p. 43.

Article 42 of the Treaty of Rome takes account of competition in production and trade in agricultural products by granting aid for the protection of enterprises handicapped by structural or national conditions and within the framework of economic development programs.

RESEARCH AND TECHNOLOGY[22]

The objective of Title XV of the Treaty of Rome is strengthening the scientific and technological bases of industry and encouraging it to become more competitive at the international level. The Commission has traditionally adopted a favorable approach to aid for research and development, recognizing the benefits research and technological development can offer in renewing the growth, strengthening and competitiveness of industry and boosting employment.

The Fourth Research and Development Framework (1994–1998) gives the criteria to be applied in assessing the compatibility of state aid for R&D. They are based on the principle that as the assisted activity gets closer to the marketplace, the potential distortion of competition and effect on trade among MSs because of the aid increases. Thus in evaluating national aid proposals, the Commission in principle seeks lower levels of aid for research and development activities closer to the marketplace. To decide on the closeness to the marketplace, a distinction is made between industrial research and precompetitive development activity. If the development activity is deemed to be nearer to the marketplace, the Commission authorizes lower levels of aid for such activities.

This distinction and definition of eligible costs corresponded to the GATT Agreement on Subsidies and Countervailing Measures signed in 1994. The framework provides criteria for assessing the extent to which the public financing of research and development activities performed by universities or nonprofit public research institutes together with or on behalf of private or public firms constitutes state aid that distorts or threatens to distort competition by favoring certain undertakings or the production of certain goods insofar as it affects trade among MSs and is incompatible with the common market.

Aid should create an incentive for the recipient firm to carry out research and development activities in addition to those carried out by the firm in the normal course of business and without public support. As a general rule aid for precompetitive development may not exceed a lesser proportion of the eligible costs as compared with industrial research. These basic aid intensities may be increased on the basis of the common interest; a bonus could be granted for R&D projects involving SMEs, if the project is carried out in regions eligible for regional aid, or the R&D project is a priority under a Community R&D program.

LEVELS

There is general shift in policy toward granting regional and horizontal rather than sectoral aid.[23] The position of the Union is that there should be a geographical concentration and differentiation of incentives according to the intensity and nature of the problems encountered. Accordingly, the Commission has intervened in setting the levels of aid.

The Union has jurisdiction when a state aid has an appreciable effect on trade among MSs. Where the economic effects are limited entirely to a single Ms, it is normally most appropriately dealt with by the national authorities and thus the Commission has no jurisdiction or reason to intervene such cases. The most generous aid ceiling is for the regions that by comparison with the Union average suffer from abnormally low standards of living or where there is serious underemployment. Lower and differentiated aid ceilings are also allowed in other regions which, while not suffering abnormal and serious problems nevertheless can be regarded as candidates for further development. The Commission adopted on July 19, 1995, a measure on employment aid. To help MSs devise measures that are compatible with the common market, guidelines were set to assess the compatibility of such aid with the Treaty. The Commission gives sympathetic consideration to aid that, subject to certain ceilings, aims to create new jobs in SMEs and in regions eligible for regional aid and to aid that is intended to encourage the recruitment of certain categories of workers experiencing particular difficulties in entering or re-entering the labor market. In view of the urgent need to promote employment, it will adopt an accelerated procedure for processing notifications of employment and training aid schemes.[24] The Commission may approve investment aid in regions eligible for regional aid under Article 92(3)(a) covering up to 75% of the eligible investment costs. Investment aid schemes in favor of firms larger than SMEs can be authorized only if these firms are located in a national assisted areas pursuant to Article 92(3)(a).[25]

To facilitate decisions as to whether an aid distorts trade, the Commission adopted a rule on *de minimis,* which provides that assistance of not more than ECU 50,000 to any one firm over a three-year period is not considered to be aid within the meaning of Article 92 and there is no need to notify the Commission. Any other aid that falls under Article 92 (1) must be notified to the Commission in good time so its compatibility with the common market may be assessed. Normally, MSs notify the Commission of aid projects in the form of schemes, general proposals specifying a minimum level of aid and its purpose or objective. The Commission then decides on overall compatibility of the scheme. Once approved, the MS in question will then be free to decide on the detailed implementation of the scheme. Only in exceptional and particularly important cases does the Commission decide on individual grants of aid to a specific company. Such individual aids may be examined by the Commission either in the context of a more general scheme or as one-time grant.[26]

On December 1, 1997, the Council of Economic and Finance Ministers agreed on measures to combat harmful tax competition. Included is a code of conduct on business taxation, that is, a commitment not to bring in any tax rules that constitute harmful competition and to phase out existing ones. An aim is to eliminate sources of conflict among MSs.

ADMINISTRATION-DG IV

Competition rules are enforced and administered by Directorate General IV of the Commission acting as policeman, prosecutor, judge and lawmaker. DG IV has control of trade and competition policies, state aids, state monopolies, public discrimination and restrictive practices. In recent years as DG IV has become increasingly active in other areas, the Commission control of regional aids has perhaps not attracted the level of attention of other aspects of competition policy.[27]

DG IV must authorize any state aid before it can be implemented. This includes changes in existing incentive schemes. More than 10% of aid registered in 1994 did not comply with this rule, which is considered essential in ensuring that state aid is transparent and, in particular, in preventing aid that is incompatible with the common market from adversely affecting competition.[28] The Directorate can also choose to review existing schemes at any time and a final decision by the Commission that a scheme is not compatible with the Treaty can render an aid scheme unlawful. It can require aid paid out illegally to be reimbursed. Competition can also be distorted when national governments favor certain undertakings by granting aid in whatever form, such as outright grants or special tax advantages. This aspect of competition is of indirect importance to enterprises in the sense that if the Commission finds certain state aid to be illegal, it will intervene against the national government concerned and not against the recipient company.

DG IV arguably enjoys more autonomy and discretion in the area of competition policy than exists in any other Union policy. While the Commission has mainly an advisory role in many other policy matters, power in the field of competition policy is specific and supervisory and the Commission is required to give a decision rather than an opinion, thus enabling the MS involved to challenge the Commission before the Court of Justice under Article 173 of the Treaty. EU law takes precedence over national law, and if there is a conflict between the competition rules and the national law, the former prevails. The only appeal against Commission decisions is to the Court of Justice. The Court will rarely overturn substantive decisions of the Commission stemming from the exercise of its discretionary powers. The Court is slow to contradict Commission decisions that are supported by detailed analysis of factual and economic evidence unless extenuating circumstances can be shown. However, few cases reach the Court of Justice; most disagreements are settled earlier.

The relationship between competition policy and regional policy has been characterized by differences within the Commission itself, arising from different roles and approaches to area designation taken by DG IV (Competition) and DG XVI (Regional Policies). DG XVI is viewed as having a dispersing role in terms of allocating funds for regional policy and DG IV is viewed as having a policing role in monitoring grants. DG IV has seen no reason for spatial coverage under the two policies to be identical, contending that objectives of the policies are different. The Competition Directorate tries to limit state aid to industry. DG XVI prefers that designations as Objective 1, 2, 5b regions should be sufficient cause for exemption from competition policy rules. MSs should also be able to offer regional aid in these areas. Rules on permitted levels of subsidy for different regions generally preserve a fragile truce between the two directorates. The result has been two differently designated areas: Objective 1, 2, 5b areas designated for the Structural Funds and the assisted areas approved by DG IV for regional aid. Challenges for competition policy and the coordination of regional aid are considerable and the Commission has made a commitment to achieve coherence between national and Union regional aid maps. Subsequently a compromise was reached between the two Directorates General to resolve the difficulties arising from their different approaches.[29]

COMMISSION[30]

The Commission seeks to justify its actions on the basis of a formalized approach when undertaking a regular review of regional aid or when assessing proposed assisted area maps. In practice, however, the final outcome is often the subject of negotiation between the MS and the Commission, frequently involving "deals" over temporary designations and future reductions in coverage. As a byproduct of Commission intervention, many of the northern, wealthier MSs have experienced declines in their assisted area maps over the past decade. The position of the Commission in approving assisted area maps is often resented by the MSs, which have frequently been critical of the methodology for approving assisted areas.

The criticism basically has three aspects:

1. Widespread concern over the dependence on quantitative indicators of GDP and unemployment. For example, MSs have argued that the Commission fails to take into consideration completely geographical factors or specific circumstances. A key objective may be to sustain settlement in areas with a declining population; yet problems faced by such areas fail to appear in the Commission's indicators.
2. Territorial units to which the indicators relate. Some designated regions may be too large an entity in respect to industrial restructuring. Data for too large an area can result in problems being concealed.
3. The degree of Commission discretion in approving assisted area maps. The contention is that the use of both quantitative and qualitative criteria gives the Commission considerable room to maneuver. Furthermore, the nature of negotiations between MSs and the Commission can involve a bargaining process with national authorities having options and trading with the

Commission for particular concessions, notably the timing of Commission decisions so as to affect elections within MSs. Historically, regional policy relations between the Commission and several MSs, notably Germany, have been characterized by long-running disputes over the coverage of assisted areas and these sometimes had to taken to the highest political level to be resolved.

EVALUATION

The effectiveness of regional aid can be negated by competition from other state subsidies. For competition policy to be workable in the Union, the Commission has strived to control unrestricted usage of subsidies and ensure that competition policy works to the advantage of backward and declining regions. The Second Survey on State Aids concluded

that sheer volume and proliferation of aids mean that [the] Commission must take into account the negative impact these aids could have on the unity of the common market, competition and therefore the successful completion of the internal market. A firm aid discipline is a prerequisite to the increased competition without which very little of the projected gains from the internal market will be realized. In addition firm aid disciplines will have to be concentrated on aids awarded in the richer regions (be they horizontal or sectoral in objective) and such a policy will therefore increase the aid differentials in favor of the peripheral regions as much as the Commission's favorable policy towards these regions themselves. Competition policy and cohesion are therefore complements and not contradictory.[31]

While the Union on one hand has reformed the Structural Funds with a doubling of the budget and heightened involvement; on the other hand it has the concomitant responsibility of overseeing policies and expenditure of the MSs themselves. There are questions about the efficacy in matching a central decision-making process for determining regional economic development priorities with making funding allocations equitably to widely diverse recipients.

More important, as richer MSs will always be able to afford more subsidies than poorer ones, the poorer ones benefit particularly from firm control of state aids. If industries in the richer MSs are able to benefit from a high level of aid, aid given in the weaker MSs will not go far in achieving the goal of cohesion. Without close control the goal of reducing the gap between richer and poorer states is negated. Completion of the internal market implies increased competition with structural changes in MS economies. The danger is that some MSs will turn increasingly to state aid to protect their industries, since not every industry in every country can be a winner.

The Commission's aim is to reduce the proportion of the population covered, allowing greater concentration of aid and thus making more efficient use of limited resources. The Commission monitors aid intensity so that the variations between the ceilings in the different regions are maintained according to their macroeconomic conditions.[32] Central to the efficient functioning of both the regional development and competition policies is the matter of data availability and reliability. How valid are the indicators, such as per capita GDP or unemployment rates?

There is a problem in isolating and assessing so-called "soft" types of aid. The use of "softer" types of incentives, such as grants for research and development, training and payments for consulting and marketing services, creates new problems. Such incentives are often difficult to assess in competition terms.[33] The state aid question may become less important over time, due in part to fears of the competition watchdog, but it will be much more the result of fiscal austerity as MSs tighten fiscal controls to meet the tough budgetary conditions imposed by EMU.

THE EU AND THE UNITED STATES

In terms of adopting the EU model in the United States for control of subsidies offered by subnational governments, more regulation by a national authority is required than Congress and the states would accept. The Commission's oversight and review require MSs to justify their decisions and they control the effects on resource allocation and trade within the Union. The EU relies on prior review rather than complaints by the aggrieved; a share of the burden of proof is shifted to the subsidizing government, which has to justify why there will be no harm from the proposal.[34]

Though it is unlikely that limits on internal competition can be initiated legislatively in the United States, agreements such as NAFTA and WTO represent steps toward limiting competition that have implications inside the United States. Domestic subsidies will be increasingly scrutinized. Placing restrictions on unlimited subsidies affecting international trade is potentially an important step in controlling subsidies in individual countries. A step in this direction may be the proposal to conclude an agreement between the European Union and the United States on the application of "positive comity principles in the enforcement of their competition laws."[35] The principle of positive comity allows for a party adversely affected by anticompetitive behavior taking place in the territory of another party to request that the second party take action.[36] Will this lead to limits on subsidies?

NOTES

1. For a comparison of competition policies and practices in the EU, NAFA and WTO, see Peter Morici, "Resolving the North American Subsidies War," *Canadian-American Public Policy* 27 (September 1996).

2. European Union, Commission, *Community Competition Policy in 1993* (1994), p. 6.

3. European Economic Community, *Bulletin of the European Communities* (11) 1971.

4. European Union, Commission, *Twentieth Report of Competition Policy* (1991), p. 126.

5. Karel Van Miert, "Framework and Objectives of European Community Competition Policy," speech, European Parliament Committee on Economic and Monetary Affairs, Brussels, February 19, 1993.

6. European Union, *Industrial Policy in an Open and Competitive Environment" Guidelines for a Community Approach*, COM(90)556 final (November 16, 1990), p. 8.

7. EU, *Community Competition Policy in 1993*, p. 40.

8. "Competition: Companies Are Receiving Too Much State Aid" *Eurofocus* (European Union, Commission) 15/97 (April 28, 1997), p. 9.

9. European Union, "National and Union Aid for Their Regions," *Inforegio News*, 48 (January 1998), p. 2.

10. Keith M. Rockwell, "EC Commission in Hot Water Over Selective Subsidy Decisions," *Journal of Commerce* (January 6, 1992), p. 13A.

11. European Union, Commission, Directorate General IV, *Competition Policy Newsletter* 1 (Autumn–Winter 1994), p. 63.

12. European Union, Commission, *Communication on Principles of Coordination of Regional Aid* (OJ C/31), February 3, 1979.

13. EU, *Competition Policy Newsletter*, p. 64.

14. D.G. Goyder, *EEC Competition Law* (Oxford: Clarendon Press, 1988), pp. 380–382.

15. Despina Schina, *State Aids Under the EC Treaty Articles 92–94* (Oxford: ESC Publishing Ltd., 1987), p. 77.

16. European Union, Commission, *Industrial Policy in the Community* (1970), pp. 266–267.

17. European Union, Commission, *Eighth Report on Competition Policy* (April, 1979), p. 124.

18. Jacques Pelkman, *Completing the Internal Market for Industrial Products* (European Union, Commission, 1986), p. 19.

19. European Union, *Competition Policy Newsletter* (Summer 1995), p. 217.

20. European Union, Commission, *Fourth Survey on State Aid in the European Union in the Manufacturing and Certain Other Sectors* COM(95) 365 final (July 26, 1995), p. 38.

21. Ibid., p. 7.

22. European Union, Commission, "The Commission Adopts New Community Framework on State Aid for Research and Development," *Competition Policy Newsletter* 6 (Autumn–Winter 1995), pp. 41–42.

23. European Union, Commission (London), *Background Report State Aids,*

ISEC/B3/95 (March 1995), p. 2.

24. European Union, Commission, *Bulletin of the European Union*, 7/8(1995), pp. 27–29.

25. EU, *Competition Policy Newsletter* (Summer 1995), p. 46.

26. Claus Dieter Ehlermann, "III State Aids Policy," *Frontier-Free Europe* (May 1994) Supplement *Community Competition Policy and Small and Medium Sized Companies*, p. 1.

27. Douglas Yuill et al., "European Regional Incentives 1992–1993," *Journal of Regional Policy* 12 (July–December 1992), p. 503.

28. European Union, Commission, *European Community Competition Policy* (1995), p. 4.

29. Fiona Wishlade, "Competition Policy and Regional Aid," *REGIONS: The Newsletter of the Regional Studies Association* 189 (February 1994), p. 10.

30. Ibid., pp. 10–11.

31. European Union, Commission, *Second Survey on State Aids in the European Community in the Manufacturing and Other Sectors* (1990), pp. 50–51.

32. European Union, Commission, *European Community Competition Policy–1996 XXVIth Report on Competition Policy* (1997), p. 69.

33. Elaine Ballantyne and John Bachtler, *Regional Policy Under Scrutiny: The European Commission and Regional Aid*, Research paper 9, European Policies Research Centre, University of Strathclyde (Britain),1990, p. 26.

34. Morici, "Resolving the North American Subsidies War," pp. 4, 20, 21.

35. European Union, Commission, Press Release IP/97/544, "Commission Adopts a Proposal on EU/US Positive Comity Agreement" (June 20, 1997).

36. Commission, *Report on the Application of the Agreement Between the European Communities and the Government of the United States of America Regarding the Application of Their Competition Laws*, COM(97) 346 final (July 4, 1997).

PART III

NORTH AMERICA

Chapter 15

Canada

BACKGROUND

Canada is a large but sparsely populated country covering 3.9 million square miles. Much of the area is not conducive to settlement. The Yukon and Northwest Territories cover about 39% of the country's area but under 0.5% of the country's population. Historically, the population has been concentrated near the U.S. border due to the area's fertile land and natural resources. The provinces of Ontario and Quebec in central Canada account for 62% of the population. Overall, the population since 1951 has risen in every province, and the greatest growth rate has been in British Columbia and Ontario.[1]

There is considerable variance in the industrial structure of the provinces with respect to the primary and manufacturing sectors.[2] More than half of the GDP is produced in the central provinces of Ontario and Quebec. They contain over 80% of Canada's manufacturing activities because of their varied resource base and proximity to large U.S. markets. The four western provinces account for more than 25% of the GDP. The four Atlantic provinces have experienced little change in their share of GDP.[3]

The division of powers between the federal and provincial governments dates back to Canada's original constitutional document, the British
North America Act of 1867, which, combined with the Constitution Act of
1982, is the basic constitutional document. At the core of regional policy in
Canada is a set of transfer payments to the provinces. These payments orig-
inated shortly after Confederation in the 1870s to equalize fiscal capacity of
the provinces and have become entrenched in the constitution.[4]

Constitutionally, the federal government has strong powers to take
control of matters under provincial jurisdiction and to disallow provincial legislation, but these powers have fallen into disuse. The federal government has the legal right to raise taxes in all provinces by any mode or
system of taxation. It can use revenues to fund federal programs that fall
in areas of exclusive provincial jurisdiction according to conditions laid
down by the federal government under arrangements known as cooperative federalism.[5] Regional economic differences are reflected in the federal division of powers; the division of responsibilities is largely determined by sections 91 and 92 of the Constitution Act of 1982.[6]

Two sections of the Constitution attempt to reduce trade barriers.
Section 121 calls for all articles grown, produced or manufactured from
any province to be admitted freely into each other province. This has
proven to be of limited value since it does not cover restrictions other
than tariffs and similar barriers. Section 91 broadens the exclusive legislative authority of Parliament to regulating trade and commerce and the
currency, two crucial federal powers for the Canadian union. The courts
have not defined section 91 as extending federal jurisdiction to regulating
trade in a province, even when a province's internal policies have a dam-
aging impact on firms outside the province or on individuals seeking to
conduct business in the province.[7]

The framework of regional policy is shaped by the constitution. The
1982 Constitution Act is a commitment to advance economic development by reducing regional disparities and to provide comparable levels
of public services to all Canadians[8]:

Section 36 (1) Without altering the legislative authority of Parliament or of the
provincial legislatures, or the rights of any of them with respect to the exercise of
their legislative authority, Parliament and the legislatures, together with the government of Canada and the legislatures, together with the government of Canada
and the provincial governments are committed to (a) promoting equal opportunities for the well being of Canadians; (b) furthering economic development to
reduce disparity in opportunities and providing essential public services of reasonable equality to all Canadians; (c) Parliament and the government of Canada
are committed to the principle of making equalization payments to ensure that
provincial governments have sufficient revenues to provide reasonably comparable levels of public services at reasonably comparable levels of taxation.

The proclamation of the 1982 Constitution Act contained the Canadian Charter of Rights and Freedoms. Section 6 forms a crucial part of the legal structure. The Charter protects the freedom to move, to live and work in any province subject to laws of general application. But Section 6 fails to guarantee provincial treatment in the full range of Canadians' economic endeavors; it contains an exemption for barriers erected around a province if the rate of employment in that province is below the rate of employment in Canada.[9]

Canada has three levels of government: federal, provincial and local. Only the federal and provincial governments have constitutional standing. The territories have constitutional status and are under federal administration. The federal government appoints the upper house, the Senate; the method of apportioning the Senate seats is a tentative resolution between representation by population and by jurisdiction. The lower house, the House of Commons, is elected by district, giving an approximate representation based on population. Thus, the responsibility for coordinating federal and provincial interests has devolved to casual or unstructured mechanisms, recurrent conferences of ministers and the connected staff machinery, which in total constitute the structures of executive federalism.[10]

Canada is a confederation divided into ten provinces and two territories, with federal and provincial governments being responsible to legislatures chosen by electorates of each jurisdiction. The two northern territories, Northwest and Yukon, enjoy some of the powers of the provinces while being under the jurisdiction of the federal government.

The ten provinces consist of the four Atlantic seaboard provinces of Newfoundland, Nova Scotia, Prince Edward Island and New Brunswick, which constitute Atlantic Canada; the two central provinces, Ontario and the French-speaking province of Quebec; Manitoba, Saskatchewan and Alberta, which make up the prairie region; and British Columbia, the southwestern-most region. Yukon and the Northwest Territories are under direct federal governance. A new territory, Nunavut, made up of the eastern portion of the Northwest Territories, will come into existence prior to April 1, 1999. The 1997 national election indicated that the political parties were to a large extent regionally based. The Cabinet selected by the prime minister traditionally reflects regional interests by including at last one member from each of the ten provinces and the Northwest Territories.

Canada's economy consists of four distinct regional economies: British Columbia, the prairies, central Canada (a tenuous amalgam of Ontario and Quebec) and Atlantic Canada. They relate to each other almost in a zero-sum game. When international commodity prices soar, central Canadian manufacturers are negatively affected; conversely, when natural resource prices fall, Canada's West suffers and Ontario feels no problems.[11] Local governments that have no constitutional recognition include municipalities, metropolitan and regional governments and other entities created by provincial and territorial governments to provide local services. Defense and external relations, criminal law, money and banking, trade, transportation, citizenship and native affairs are federal concerns. Provinces are responsible for education, health and welfare, civil law, natural resources, provincial taxation and local government. Joint jurisdiction exists in such areas as agriculture and immigration.

REGIONS

As in most federal systems, Canada's constitution does not allocate specific responsibility to either federal or provincial levels for economic development or for resolving regional economic disparities. Responsibility of the federal government for economic development concerns the advancement of the country as an entity, while a provincial government's responsibility is the advancement of the particular province. As a result there is an overlap in the responsibilities of the two levels as well as in their activities. Thus, the two levels of government can no longer be considered as if they were precisely divided into two sealed compartments or closed jurisdictions.[12]

There have been concerns over regional disparities since the origins of Canada as a nation. Initially these concerns centered around the inability of the governments of the poorer provinces to provide the same level of services to their citizens as did the governments of the wealthier provinces. For example, at the time of the 1867 Confederation, New Brunswick was given a special ten year grant as recognition of its special financial needs and the same provision was applied to Nova Scotia in 1869. This arrangement gave credibility to the concept of fiscal balance and the redistributive role of the federal government through federal transfers to the provinces. As late as 1948 under Terms of Union between Newfoundland and Canada, the level of public services offered in that province would be at a level comparable to other Atlantic provinces was guaranteed. The crude notions of fiscal equity that existed in the earlier years of Confederation eventually gave way to more sophisticated concepts that were reflected in the emerging transfer structure.[13]

With gross disparities of regional income, there is a long-established tradition to transfer federal subsidies. Almost from the start of the Confederation, the federal government has implemented programs that affected some regions more than others but never were part of a federal regional development policy until the 1960s.[14] Regional development efforts began in March 1935 with the passage of the Prairie Farm Rehabilitation Act to alleviate the growing plight of western farmers.[15]

After World War II the federal government showed increased concern for a regional balance in economic activity as regional differences became more obvious. Previously, the prevailing opinion was that government policies aimed at stimulating national economic growth would benefit all regions. The prosperity in the first decade after World War II also did not engender any sense of urgency on the part of the national government. Because economic growth was rapid and regions shared in the prosperity, the regional problem did not surface as a priority until the recession of the late 1950s forced the federal government to take action to alleviate it. A regional development measure was introduced in 1960 in the form of an accelerated depreciation allowance for firms locating in designated regions.

By the mid-1960s, the proliferation of economic development agencies and measures, duplication, overlap and lack of coordination among individual agencies and between federal and provincial levels of government led in 1969 to the formation of the Department of Regional Economic Expansion (DREE) to assume responsibility for developing and coordinating programs and policies to counter regional economic disparities. DREE has evolved and continued under various forms and titles. Subsequently DREE merged with the Department of Regional Industrial Expansion (DRIE). Over the 1969–86 period, Ottawa (the federal capital) had an extremely important role in planning and directing regional development initiatives.

There were complaints that the programs did not respond to the needs of the regions because they were designed and funding applications were evaluated using standards that could not be generally applied without local input. The wrong kinds of projects were funded and locally worthwhile proposals were ignored.

The second difficulty was that they attempted to satisfy two separate objectives: industrial promotion and regional development. To the less-developed regions, it appeared that DRIE sectoral concerns dominated the decision making process and hence, more funding and assistance were provided for industrial development than for regional development. Regional interests felt that federal assistance should be made available for small-scale, resource-based projects and that selection of projects should be carried out by local offices.[16]

In 1987, the federal government disbanded DRIE and its industrial support programs were amalgamated with those of the Ministry of State for Science and Technology to create the Department of Industry, Science and Technology. The federal government's new approach to regional development emphasized programs and initiatives tailored to foster local economic development opportunity. Federal regional development efforts were entrusted to regionally based development agencies.

The new policy stressed decentralization of administration and authority away from Ottawa to give regional agencies primary responsibility for development within their jurisdictions. Programs and measures would be tailored to suit local needs. Federal regional development responsibilities were decentralized to four separate agencies.[17]

The rationale for creation of separate regional agencies under separate ministers was that the various regions of Canada are distinct and have unique requirements that can be addressed only by regionally tailored (as opposed to nationally designated and delivered) approaches. The new structure incorporated a considerable local element in the determination and implementation of regional development programs. The new department would retain responsibility for regional development in southern Ontario. In the rest of the country, DRIE's regional development responsibilities would be taken over by four regionally based agencies in Atlantic Canada, Quebec, northern Ontario and western Canada. Although the four agencies operate a range of independent private-sector funding programs, much of the federal expenditure on regional development is allocated in partnership with the provinces through federal provincial agreements. Also, each agency has advocacy and procurement functions to maximize federal funding and sourcing in each of the regions.

Atlantic Canada Opportunities Agency (ACOA) covering Newfoundland, Labrador, Prince Edward Island, Nova Scotia and New Brunswick, has responsibility for and coordinates all federal activities relating to economic development in Atlantic Canada and provides a regional perspective in the design and application of national policies and programs. The budget was set at Can $1.05 billion over five years. The agency enjoys considerable freedom to adopt whatever measures it feels may best suit the needs of the Atlantic region.

The Atlantic region has been a primary focus of regional development assistance since the inception of regional policy in Canada. The Atlantic regions since the 1920s have experienced continued deindustrialization, becoming Canada's poorest area with the highest unemployment levels. The maritime economy has been dominated by fishing, lumber, agriculture and mining.

For the poorer Atlantic provinces, there was a very real risk associated with agreements such as CUFTA. Regional development policies and government subsidies, which have been very important to these provinces, are placed at risk if they are interpreted as trade subsidies and hence subject to countervailing duties or other retaliatory actions. They would have included, of course, both industry-specific (e.g., fisheries) and firm-specific (e.g., bailouts of specific firms) policies and subsidies. Even if such policies were not prohibited directly by CUFTA, they could have been indirectly discouraged in the free-trade environment, which puts greater emphasis on competitive market forces.[18]

The Federal Office of Regional Development (Quebec) (FORD-Q) was created to define the nature of federal regional economic development initiatives in Quebec, to administer economic development programs with the government of Quebec and to implement business support programs. Its five-year budget was set at Can $1.3 billion.

Federal Economic Development Initiative (Northern Ontario) (FedNor) was established to promote economic development in northern Ontario and to provide the federal government with local input and advice on policies, programs and services affecting the region and to raise the direct involvement of the regional and local community in decision-making. FedNor was given the mission of encouraging economic growth and diversification, job creation and income generation by supporting private-sector initiatives. As compared with ACOA, FORD-Q, or Western Economic Diversification (WD), FedNor is a smaller program. The FedNor allocation was Can $55 million in 1987 for a five-year period and was supplemented by Can $14 million in 1990 and an additional allocation of Can $29 million in April 1992 for another five years.

The mandate of WD, covering British Columbia, Alberta, Saskatchewan and Manitoba, was to help move the western economy away from the volatile resource and agriculture sectors and to lessen its dependence on primary resources by assisting the development of new and diversified industries. The initial budget was set up as a Can $1.2 billion five-year fund.

INSTITUTIONAL FRAMEWORK

Industry, Science and Technology

The Department of Industry, Science and Technology (ISTC) was established on February 23, 1990, with a mandate to promote national competitiveness and industrial excellence, to build Canada's scientific, technological, managerial and production base and to bring out the talents required to safeguard Canada's place in the first rank of industrial nations.[19] The creation of the department was a new way for business to receive government aid. Creation of the department represented the final rejection of the idea of an all-encompassing, government-led industrial strategy.

In its 1989–1990 Annual Report, regional development was not cited specifically as a main responsibility of ISTC. The new approach to industrial revitalization in Canada included a renewed and decentralized emphasis on regional development, as witnessed by the formation of the four regional development agencies.

During the 1980s there was some attempt made by the federal government to consolidate its grant programs to promote R&D and innovation. The tangible benefits of such programs at the federal and provincial government levels proved difficult to identify; a case may have been that until the early 1990s the science and technology initiatives were to an extent involved with regional development.[20]

It can be debated whether the scaling down of regional development programs is a suitable policy to help rationalize the relatively large and fragmented set of government programs designed to promote innovation and structural readjustment. Such programs have long been criticized as mixing regional development goals with science and technology objectives, with the result that their effectiveness in stimulating industrial innovation has been reduced.[21] Yet the European Union has sought to coordinate regional development with research in technology.

Industry Canada

In 1993, there was a further restructuring of the federal government's key economic development agencies into Industry Canada under the direction of the Minister of Industry. Industry Canada has a prominent role in the reduction of internal trade barriers and brings together the previous responsibilities of Industry, Science and Technology Canada in promoting international competitiveness and economic development.

The 1994–1995 industry and science development programs consisted of the following estimates (in thousands of Can $)[22]:

Industrial and aboriginal programs	515,912
Industry and science policy	59,949
Regional operations	391,197
Communications research	90,165
Corporate and advisory services	89,261
	Can $1,146,484

Until the 1989 Expenditure Review Committee (ERC) process was instituted, there was no formal overall allocation of federal regional development funds among regions. Spending patterns were dictated more by the nature and geographic coverage of the various program instruments involved. In the context of the 1989 ERC process and the 1989 federal budget, a five-year funding framework was established for total regional development funding and for its allocation among the individual regions. This was a first. Separate and not synonymous with the aforementioned regional budgets, the framework included funding directly associated with the federal agencies as well as that related to agreements administered by other government departments.

The agencies' mandates provided for similar types of functions within their respective regions:

- formulating regional development policies and approaches
- developing and implementing new programs tailored to the needs of each region with an emphasis on SMEs
- advocating and coordinating the interests of its region in the development of national policies and programs
- coordinating all federal regional development activities in the region
- ad hoc issues management in respect of regional development problems and projects notably where a variety of interests and departments are involved.[23]

From the outset, objectives, instruments and approaches of the agencies varied. ACOA pursued more traditional regional development program spending approaches. WED was more selective (it is considered more businesslike), and focused on diversification opportunities. FORD-Q dealt with more traditional rural development problems in resource-based regions and with industrial adjustment and "new economy" issues facing Quebec's industrial base in a sensitive federal provincial environment.

PROGRAMS

Foreign Investment Review Agency

As foreign investment became more significant, there were suggestions that efforts be made by national governments to direct the facilities and jobs toward the neediest areas. For example, Britain instituted a system of Industrial Development Certificates in 1946, no longer in effect. In 1973, the Foreign Investment Review Agency (FIRA) was instituted in Canada to screen foreign investment so as to maximize the benefits for the country. The Grey Report, which was instrumental in the establishment of FIRA, stated that the review process could facilitate the government's desire to improve economic conditions in the slow-growth regions. The review agency could consider location in a slow-growth region as a positive benefit when assessing the net impact of investment in Canada. FIRA could negotiate legally binding agreements with investors to require them to satisfy export targets or Canadian content-quotas.[24]

In terms of applicability to the United States, the General Accounting Office (GAO) concluded that it was a not a suitable model for U.S. adoption.[25] A congressional committee recommended that Congress favorably consider proposals for a screening agency.[26] A report prepared for the U.S. Department of Housing and Urban Development recommended that seri-

ous consideration be given to the establishment of a board similar to
FIRA.[27]

A 1983 GATT finding determined that FIRA restrictions on foreign
investment violated GATT Article III in that it had discriminatory trade
effects but did not mention the investment measures per se. This experience suggested that it would be preferable to recast what were basically
investment issues into trade-related issues.[28] In 1985, Investment Canada
replaced FIRA, reduced the number of investments reviewed by 90% and
provided an environment more conducive to foreign investment.[29]

Attempts to direct foreign investment to particular locations by
national governments are likely to be contentious. Foreign investors often
have a choice of locations worldwide; also, states or provinces may resent
efforts to steer the investment elsewhere within the country. A more realistic approach may be efforts to limit the competition or bidding for the
investment in facilities.

Community Futures[30]

Often the impact of change in a community is of such magnitude
that the employment needs of individuals can be approached only from
the standpoint of the economic future of the community. This is particularly pertinent for those communities undergoing long-term shrinkage of
employment, single-industry communities facing closures or shrinkage,
communities facing structural changes in their economic base rural or
remote communities.

As a response Community Futures (CF) was initiated in 1986 by the
Ministry for Employment and Immigration; it is a locally based, self-help
program assisting communities to work toward economic development,
particularly for small communities. Community Futures links the core
Canadian approaches of a regional focus, strategic planning and social
support. It uses a partnership model with a high level of voluntary sector
involvement to promote collaboration among three main sectors: public,
private and social, including financial institutions and the education system. The federal government provides funds to a local committee to be
used for planning and for business and infrastructure development. The
program embodies two broad threads of Canadian policy: comprehensive planning for development and a focus on linking groups into a single development unit. More specifically it covers a fund for innovative
measures to generate new areas of activity; creation of business support
centers to help promoters of small businesses start up projects; assistance
for starting up in self-employment; and targeting people on unemployment benefits or welfare.

Initial infusions of the federal assistance in the form of money and technical assistance are viewed as seed capital that allow a community to begin growing. The program utilizes local labor markets to define regions and management of a Community Futures Committee selected from local leaders. Federal funds are provided over a five-year cycle with few strings attached in terms of specific uses. The five-year life of the federal commitment allows more long-range planning than a program funded by annual appropriations. A community must develop a strategic plan that shows how federal assistance can be used as leverage for development. Communities can focus on eliminating major gaps in infrastructure, on facilities enhancing employment skills of the local labor force, or on directly assisting local businesses.

CFs supplement more traditional programs that provide education and training to workers and facilitate job searches. These traditional programs are similar to the U.S. Job Training Partnership Act (JTPA). By contrast CFs focus on the community rather than the individual. Improving the skills of the labor force and the capacity of the community increases the odds of successful economic development. How effective is the program in comparison with the U.S. Empowerment Zone program?

The goal of the program is to stimulate cooperation within each region by providing a carrot in the form of a multimillion-dollar assistance package and direct technical assistance. Federal assistance allows the development process to reach a takeoff point where it can become self-sustaining. For some communities this will take a second five-year cycle of funding. The federal government views this investment as a better alternative than simple income transfers in the form of unemployment insurance and welfare payments.

AGREEMENT ON INTERNAL TRADE

With the growing need for curbing the internal competition for industry, Canada put into effect the Agreement on Internal Trade (AIT), which could serve as a model for comparable legislation in the United States. The agreement also serves to indicate the importance of regional economic development in Canada as compared with the United States.

While Canada has been concerned with external trade barriers and has steadily lowered its trade restraints with other nations, notably the United States, its thorniest trade problems have been among the ten provinces themselves. The constitution, while ensuring basic mobility rights among the provinces, leaves untouched a number of obstacles to economic mobility, to which the AIT partially responds.

A key concern has been that the growing economic importance of the provinces would have the often unintended effect of weakening one of the original purposes of the Confederation, that is, ensuring reasonably unimpeded access to markets across Canada for Canadian goods and services as well as for Canadian labor and capital.

Some 500 trade barriers are estimated to have cost Canada about Can $5.2 billion in lost investment and reduced efficiency. The barriers have proven resistant to change due to the tendency of provinces to go their own way in political and economic matters.[31] Internal barriers to trade in Canada among its provinces have been evaded by exporting to the United States, then reimporting the product.[32]

Compared with international trade arrangements, removing interprovincial barriers is difficult in that Canada is a single country. Under international trade treaties reciprocity arrangements can be enforced with the threat of trade retaliation but this cannot be done with provinces.

Increased interest in internal trade barriers sufficiently stimulated the interest of the Canadian government to initiate negotiations in 1993, followed by the 1994 AIT. The agreement went into effect in July 1995 though all provisions were not approved immediately by the federal Parliament or the provinces. It was endorsed and enacted into federal law in 1996 (Statutes of Canada 1996, Chapter 17, Bill C-19, assented to June 20, 1996, Second Session, Thirty-fifth Parliament, 43 Elizabeth II, 1996). The enactment provided for the appointment of a federal representative to the Committee on Internal Trade and payment of the federal government's share of expenditures. Existing law was amended to bring it in conformity with the federal government's obligations under the agreement.

Signatories are the government of Canada together with the governments of Newfoundland, Nova Scotia, Prince Edward Island, New Brunswick, Quebec, Ontario, Manitoba, Saskatchewan, Alberta, British Columbia, the Northwest Territories and the Yukon Territory. "Party" means a signatory to the agreement and "non-party" covers a foreign sovereign state.

The agreement attempts to resolve undue barriers to trade and mobility due to both federal and provincial practices. Under the agreement, provinces are not to erect any trade barriers among themselves and are to work toward improving their performance in ten sectors. They are committed to setting up a dispute resolution system similar to the panel structure under NAFTA.

What Is the AIT?[33]

AIT is based on the operating principle that Canadian governments should ensure free movement of persons, goods, services and investments across the country. Guiding principles and administrative policies of the agreement are that new barriers in internal trade will not be established and cross-boundary movement of persons, services, goods and investment within Canada will be facilitated. They will be treated equally irrespective of where they originate in Canada. General rules prevent governments from erecting new trade barriers and require reduction of existing ones in areas covered under the Agreement. A formal dispute mechanism is provided that is accessible to individuals, business and governments.

Reciprocal nondiscrimination (i.e., equivalent treatment for all Canadian persons, goods, services and investments), requires governments to provide treatment that is no less favorable than the "best-in-Canada" treatment. The right of entry and exit prohibits governments from adopting or maintaining measures that prevent or restrict the movement of persons, goods, services or investments across provincial or territorial boundaries. Governments have to ensure that their policies and practices do not have the effect of creating obstacles to trade. In pursuing certain nontrade objectives, there may be legitimate goals and thus it may be necessary to deviate from the preceding trade rules.

The AIT includes a basis for reconciliation by providing a means of eliminating trade barriers caused by differences in standards and regulations across Canada. To make the AIT transparent, it includes provisions such as publication and notification to ensure that all information is fully accessible to interested parties. Canadian firms are better able to make business decisions based on market conditions rather than on restrictive government policies.

An important provision relevant to regional economic development covers the code of conduct, preventing governments from giving incentives to specific enterprises as a means of luring them away from other Canadian jurisdictions (poaching). The use of incentives, which could be harmful to the economic interests of other parts of Canada, is discouraged; governments cannot provide relocation incentives to firms in other provinces and agree to avoid providing subsidies that harm firms in other provinces.

Institutionally, at the ministerial level the Committee on Internal Trade is the main body that oversees implementation and operation of the agreement. The Secretariat, based in Winnipeg, provides administrative and operational support to the Committee on Internal Trade and the Working Groups or Subcommittees. Under Article 1600, the Committee on Internal Trade was established to supervise implementation, assist in resolving disputes and approve the annual budget.

Regional Economic Development

Article 1801 recognizes that measures adopted or maintained by the parties that advance regional and economic development objectives within their own jurisdictions, provided they are part of a general framework of regional economic development, can have a significant role in encouraging long-term job creation, economic growth, and industrial competitiveness and in reducing economic disparities. Regional economic development programs, subject to certain conditions, are not limited by the restrictive provisions of the agreement.

Incentives

Article 607(1) does not prevent a party from conditioning the receipt of an incentive on a requirement to carry out economic activities in its territory or to create or maintain employment.[34]

Annex 608:3, Article 9 states that each party shall endeavor to refrain from engaging in bidding wars to attract prospective investors seeking the most beneficial incentive package.

Under Annex 608:3, Articles 4–7, incentives are prohibited that in law or in fact are contingent on and would directly result in an enterprise located in the territory of any other party relocating an existing operation to its territory. Incentives are not prohibited where a party can demonstrate that the incentive was provided to offset the possibility for relocation of the existing operation outside Canada and the relocation was imminent, well known and under active consideration. No party shall provide an incentive the primary purpose of which is to enable the recipient enterprise to undercut competitors of another party in obtaining a specific contract in the territory of a party.

Annex 608:3, Article 8 states that economic development may include the provision of incentives though the parties acknowledge that certain incentives may harm the economic interests of other parties. Thus, they should take into account the economic interests of other parties in developing and applying their incentive measures, and shall endeavor to refrain from providing an incentive that:

- sustains for an extended period of time an economically nonviable operation whose production adversely affects the competitive position of a facility located in the territory of another party
- increases capacity in sectors where the increase is not warranted by market conditions
- is excessive, either in absolute terms or relative to the total value of the specific project for which the incentive is provided, taking into account such factors as the economic viability of the project and the magnitude of the economic disadvantage that the incentive is designed to overcome.

Under Annex 608.3, Article 5, an exception is where the party can demonstrate that the incentive was provided to offset the possibility for relocation of the existing operation outside Canada and the relocation was imminent or under active consideration.

Disputes

Article 1711 states that the formal dispute settlement mechanism applies to governments and the private sector, which has to use governments to represent them in actions.

A Committee on Internal Trade was established to supervise implementation, assist in resolving disputes, and approve the annual budget. It consists of representatives from each party. The Secretariat is chosen by the committee, funded 50% by the federal government and 50% by provincial governments. The share of each province is determined by the size of its population relative to total population.

For disputes between governments, retaliatory action may be taken as a last resort only after consultation with the Committee on Internal Trade.

The dispute settlement provisions were closely modeled on those in the Tokyo Round of GATT and NAFTA. Considerable emphasis is placed on settlement of disputes by consultation and mediation between governments. Where these diplomatic techniques fail, disputing parties are to resort to ad hoc panels of experts, rather than to a permanent tribunal or to the courts. Although the agreement does allow, in some circumstances, retaliation against a government that fails to adhere to the ruling of a dispute panel, there is no provision for binding enforcement through an award of damages, an injunction or some equivalent order.

One significant difference between dispute settlement under the agreement and that under equivalent WTO and NAFTA provisions is that the agreement affords some avenue for private parties to press complaints against governments through a government's taking up their cause.

Legal Status[35]

AIT is a nonbinding political accord among the federal, provincial and territorial governments directed to removing internal trade barriers in Canada. "While federal and provincial implementing legislation is needed to give legal force to the AIT, most such existing or proposed legislation does not make the AIT's provisions directly applicable nor does it give them a legal status superior to that of ordinary statutes."[36]

The AIT closely tracks the types of obligations or commitments that are found in international trade treaties with respect to trade between sovereign countries. Thus, in many areas such as services, investment and government procurement, provincial measures that discriminate against out-of-province economic entities are prohibited or disciplined. AIT sets out nonlegal obligations in legal language. AIT has a formal dispute settlement mechanism, to which private parties have limited access and governments have broader access. "However, the formal rulings of these dispute panels have no legal effect."[37]

Differences of opinion exist on whether the nonlegal status of AIT is a significant handicap in reaching its goals. One contention is that AIT is likely to have an impact on law and government policy since governments will feel obligated to comply regardless of whether there is a legal commitment. The progress toward implementation has not been rapid. Another viewpoint is that the economic impact of provincial barriers is not significant. Yet though these barriers may actually have a modest economic role, their existence is at odds with the concept of a Canadian union.

Evaluation

In terms of regional development, the agreement recognizes that measures of the parties, part of a general framework of regional economic development can play an important role in encouraging long-term job creation, economic growth, and industrial competitiveness and in reducing economic disparities. The agreement does not apply to a measure adopted or maintained by the federal government or any other party that is part of a general framework of regional development subject to certain specified conditions.

The general rules of AIT offer a good balance between acknowledging the full rights of governments to take measures to achieve legislative objectives in their respective spheres of authority and seeing that these measures do not become unnecessary obstacles to trade across internal borders. "It also contains some interesting institutional innovations, such as a dispute settlement mechanism to which—unlike most such mechanisms in international trade agreements—firms and individuals have some access, albeit through a convoluted process involving the complainant's provincial government and/or an independent screener."[38]

Although the AIT has made some progress toward removing barriers in a number of sectors, favorable judgments in almost all cases about the liberalizing effect of the agreement have to be conditional. Too many implementation details have been postponed for subsequent negotiations under the supervision of government officials responsible for particular sectors without any deadlines, as well as being subject to a rule of unanimity among participating governments for all decisions.[39]

A major stumbling block in implementation is jobs. In a nation with a 9.6% unemployment rate as of January 1996, provincial premiers have a hard time eliminating rules that protect local suppliers of goods and services. Wide gaps exist in the agreement; for example, procedures for filing complaints are highly bureaucratic, and there are no binding enforcement measures and no awards for damages. A company that believes it has been discriminated against cannot sue directly; it must be represented by its provincial officials. The sections on discrimination on government procurement are limited to direct purchasing by provinces; they do not cover provincially owned crown corporations, municipalities, hospitals and other public agencies.

A concern over providing sufficient latitude to provinces to engage in regional development policies pervades the entire agreement and unnecessarily complicates and obfuscates many of the rules to which the parties are ostensibly committing themselves. A more straightforward approach would remove regional development considerations. There would be a blanket exemption for all direct government subsidies.[40] "The very notion of regional economic development remains a substantial mystery, given the absence in the agreement of a definition of developed and developing provinces."[41]

Applicability to the United States

The goals of the agreement are worthwhile and are a starting point from which the United States could explore the possibility of initiating a similar program. The focus would be on monitoring and deterring the use of unlimited incentives and subsidies in the competition for industry. A crucial factor in the United States is the difficulty in having fifty states reach an agreement, compared with only ten provinces in Canada. In Canada local governments are creatures of the provinces and to a large extent financially dependent on the host province; they have restricted powers. In the United States there are more than 3,000 counties and tens of thousands of individual municipalities. Local governments in the United States, depending on state constitutions, have more flexibility and authority than their Canadian counterparts and are more prone to independent action.

RESULTS OF PROGRAMS

Historically, though there have been marginal successes over the years, more often Canada's regional development programs have not reduced disparities. Dissatisfaction with the programs has led to periodic reorganizations of federal efforts in this field; many reflected the desire of the various administrations to put their own mark on regional development policy. However, many regional development programs have simply sought to create jobs without achieving the necessary changes in the fundamental structure of the local economies that would ensure long-term opportunities for growth. Creation of jobs usually implies that growth has occurred. Economic growth, however, should not be confused with economic development, since the former does not signify any alteration in a region's future prospects. Economic development, on the other hand, implies a fundamental change in an areas's ability to create wealth. Effective regional development policies should result in much greater opportunity for self-sustaining growth.[42]

Since 1987, there has been a strong commitment to a decentralized approach to regional development without a homogeneous national regional policy. Emphasis on decentralized programs may conflict with overall national needs for convergence. "Only taxes, transfers and, possibly, other government programs are left to close further regional gaps. It thus appears that the Canadian industrial structure and/or barriers to factor mobility will have to change in some fundamental way if they are to have a significant impact on regional disparities."[43]

NOTES

1. OECD, *Regional Problems and Policies in Canada* (Paris: Organization for Economic Cooperation and Development, 1994), pp. 9–11.

2. Ibid., p. 13.

3. Canada, Statistics Canada, *Canada Year Book 1994* (Ottawa, 1993), p. 601.

4. David Freshwater,"Canadian Rural Policy Mostly a Regional Matter," *Rural Development Perspectives* 7 (June–September 1991), p. 13.

5. OECD, *Regional Problems*, p. 17.

6. Alain-G. Gagnon, "The Dynamics of Federal Intergovernmental Relations: Delivery of Regional Development Programs in Canada," *Regional Politics and Policy* 1:1 (1991), p. 2.

7. Daniel Schwanen, *Drawing on Our Inner Strength: Canada's Economic Citizenship in a Era of Evolving Federalism* (Toronto: C. D. Howe Institute, June 1996), Commentary 82, pp. 5, 6.

8. William B. P. Robson, *Dynamic Tensions Markets, Federalism and Canada's Economic Future* (Toronto: C. D. Howe Institute, 1992), p. 84.

9. Ibid., pp. 58–59.

10. Carolyn J. Tuohy, *Policy and Politics in Canada   Institutionalized Ambivalence* (Philadelphia: Temple University Press, 1992), p. 7.

11. Stephen Blank and Stephen Krajewski with Henry S. Wu, *U.S. Firms in North America: Redefining Structure and Strategy* (Washington: National Planning Association, 1995), p. 14.

12. Donald J. Savoie, *Regional Economic Development Canada's Search for Solutions,* 2d ed. (Toronto: University of Toronto Press, 1992), p. 14.

13. Doug May and Dane Rowlands, "Atlantic Canada in Confederation:

Uncharted Waters With Dangerous Shoals," in Norman Cameron et al., *From East and West Regional Views on Reconfederation* (Toronto: C. D. Howe Institute, 1991), Canada Round Series 6, pp. 16–17.

14. Guy Beaumier, *Current Issue Review, 88-13-E*, Canada, Canada Communications Group, Library of Parliament, Research Branch (November 30, 1988, revised February 23, 1995), p. 1.

15. Ralph Matthews, *The Creation of Regional Dependency* (Toronto: University of Toronto Press, 1983), p. 104.

16. Beaumier, *Current Issue Review*, p. 11.

17. OECD, *Regional Problems*, p. 55, and "New Agencies Under Attack," *Financial Times of Canada*, January 11, 1988, p. 16.

18. Morley Gunderson, "Regional Dimensions of the Impact of Free Trade on Labor," *Canadian Journal of Regional Science* 13 (Summer–Autumn 1990), p. 251.

19. Statistics Canada, *Canada Year Book 1994*, p. 550.

20. OECD, *Economic Surveys 1994–1995 Canada* (Paris: Organization for Economic Cooperation and Development, 1995), p. 95.

21. Ibid., p. 109.

22. Canada, Minister of Supply and Services, *The New Face of Government: A Guide to the Federal Government*, 2d ed. (1994), p. 50.

23. Canada, Department of Finance, *Background on Regional Development Funding and the Regional Agencies*, RHR 25/DOC, Internal Background Paper (1995), p. 9.

24. Canada, Information Canada, *Foreign Direct Investment in Canada* (1972), p. 471 and Morris L. Sweet, *Industrial Location Policy for Economic Revitalization National and International Perspectives* (Westport, Conn.: Praeger Publishers, 1981), pp. 77–79.

25. U.S. General Accounting Office, *Should Canada's Screening Practices for Foreign Investment Be Used by the United States?* ID-79-45 (September 6, 1979).

26. U.S. Congress, House Committee on Government Operations, *The Adequacy of the Federal Response to Foreign Investment in the United States: Twentieth Report*, 96th Congress, 2d sess., House Report 96-1216, August 1, 1980, p. 45.

27. Robert B. Cohen, *The Impact of Foreign Direct Investment on United States Cities and Regions*, report prepared for the U.S. Department of Housing and Urban Development (Arlington, Va.: Analytic Sciences Corp., 1979).

28. Michael Hart, "A Multilateral Agreement on Foreign Direct Investment: Why Now?" in Pierre Sauve and Daniel Schwanen, eds., *Investment Rules for the Global Economy Enhancing Access to Markets* (Toronto: C. D. Howe Institute, 1996), Policy Study 28, p. 70.

29. Beth V. Yarbrough and Robert M. Yarbrough, *Cooperation and Governance in International Trade: The Strategic Organizational Approach* (Princeton: Princeton University Press, 1992), p. 101.

30. Andre Joyal, "Canada's Commitment to Community Development," *LEDA Magazine* 9 (European Commission, Directorate General for Employment), (Summer 1994), p. 12; Canada, Advisory Council on Adjustment, Adjusting to Win, Community Futures Program (1989); and Morley Gunderson, "Labor Adjustment Under NAFTA Canadian Issues," in *Adjusting to NAFTA: Strategies for Business and Labor*, North American Outlook (National Planning Association) 5 (February 1995), p. 14.

31. Aviva Freudmann, "Free Trade in Canada Not in My Province," *Journal of Commerce* (February 14, 1996), p. 1.

32. David Howard Davis, "The Problems of Borderless Communities," *Public Administration Times* 16 (November 1993), p. 10.

33. Canada, Industry Canada, *Summary Agreement on Internal Trade,* July 18, 1994, and E. Wayne Clendenning and Robert J. Clendenning, *Analysis of International Trade Dispute Settlement Mechanisms and Implications for Canada's Agreement on Internal Trade,* Industry Canada, Occasional Paper 19, November 1997.

34. Michael J. Trebilcock and Rambod Behboodi, "The Canadian Agreement on Internal Trade: Retrospect and Prospects," in Michael J. Trebilcock and Daniel Schwanen, eds., *Getting There: An Assessment of the Agreement on Internal Trade* (Toronto: C. D. Howe Institute, September 1995), Policy Study 26, p. 52.

35. Robert Howse, *Securing the Canadian Economic Union: Legal and Constitutional Options for the Federal Government* (Toronto: C. D. Howe Institute, June 1996), Commentary 81, pp. 170, 181.

36. Ibid., p. 1.

37. Ibid., p. 2.

38. Schwanen, *Drawing on Our Inner Strength,* p. 6.

39. Ibid.

40. Trebilcock and Behboodi, "The Canadian Agreement,"p. 56.

41. Ibid., p. 83.

42. Beaumier, Current Issue Review, pp. 12–13.

43. Serge Coulombe and Frank C. Lee, *Long Run Perspective on Canadian Regional Convergence,* Industry Canada, Working Paper 11 (May 1996), p. 20.

Chapter 16

Mexico

INSTITUTIONAL

Despite its formal title, the United States of Mexico has a type of federalism much different from those of Canada and the United States; Mexico's is much more centralized. Thus, there is a different national and subnational power arrangement, which affects regional economic development. The result of the federal centralization and associated central financial controls is to proscribe the extent of autonomous subnational economic development activity in Mexico. In contrast, the provinces and states in Canada and the United States are key participants in the economic development of their respective nations; they have wide latitude to act independently if they so desire.

The 1917 constitution, Article 40, established a federal republic "composed of free states, and sovereignty in everything pertaining to their internal regime," but the states have barely maintained their sovereignty.[1]

Crucial to the consolidation is the high degree of power enjoyed by the president; the legislative and judicial branches have until recently been rubber stamps of the executive. To illustrate, in contrast to Canada and the United States, where there was vigorous debate over CUFTA and NAFTA, there was little opposition expressed in Mexico. The reason for the silence was the power exercised by the Mexican president.

Further examples of the crucial powers unavailable to the United States and Canada national governments but available to the Mexican executive are the ability to remove from office any state governor for specific but wide-ranging reasons and dedication of the principal types of tax receipts to the federal government, which then allocates certain revenues to the states.[2]

The constitution gives the president direct control of numerous parastatal enterprises and agencies, through which the government operates indirectly. State and local governments are strongly subordinated to the federal administration in Mexico City. But the most important key to the subordinate status of the states is their economic dependence. The federal government claims the biggest slice of the tax revenues and has taken over or created innumerable organizations to generate goods and services of all types. A considerable part of this budget is used in the provinces but by means of a multiplicity of institutions through which the federal government directly delegates power or through agreements made with the governors, all of which must be annually renegotiated. Governors assume the role of formal mediators and their success in this mediation is the measure of their power. Yet, no matter how successful this negotiation might be, federally provided public expenditure will not on the whole be administered by local actors but by federal agencies that penetrate and organize the territory of each state in their own way.[3]

The concentration of fiscal power has as its counterpart the increasing importance of centralized government agencies that intervene locally. Some of these are large state economic corporations that manage both local agricultural and industrial development in different regions. These corporations bypass municipal and state government; their officials are responsible to the centralized agencies in allocating funds or managing development schemes.[4]

Each successive layer of government is substantially weaker, less autonomous, and more impoverished than the levels above it. In 1991, it was estimated that the federal government accounted for 78% of total government expenditure. Almost all taxes are collected by the federal government. Part of these revenues are redistributed among the states and municipalities according to a formula based on a state's capacity to raise revenue directly and its population.[5]

Constitutionally states and municipalities have a significant degree of autonomy, but not so in practice.[6] Most municipalities get 80% of their revenue from federal and state governments and only 20% from local sources.[7] Most important for state and local leaders, particularly along the more industrialized northern border, is that only a small percentage of the tax revenue is returned.

Total debt of the thirty-one states was estimated to be almost $4 billion at the May 1995 exchange rate. Most of the debt has been incurred by states and local communities through commercial bank loans at variable interest rates. Mexican states and municipalities do not float government bonds to pay their share of public works projects primarily financed by the federal government.[8] Paradoxically, while Mexico in recent years has privatized banks and telecommunications and is now moving to decentralize port management and auction off the state railroad, equivalent decentralization of fiscal authority to state governments has lagged.[9]

CHANGES

President Ernesto Zedillo made promises during the 1995 election to hand over powers to the legislature and state governments. Mexico City has been given the power to elect its mayor. After six decades of central government rule, Mexico is cautiously moving to decentralize government decision-making and give states greater power to collect and use tax revenue.[10] The lack of a strong president leaves a void to be filled by provincial political leaders.[11] The result could be more economic power for the states or, in other words, development of a regional structure in Mexico.

Decentralization and emergence of a new federalism are important for Mexico because the existing structure of state-federal relations has hampered regional development and led to pilfering and inefficiency. That in turn has created structural economic and infrastructure problems that continue to frustrate trade and transport.[12]

In the 1997 elections the dominance of one political party at both the national and state levels changed radically, resulting in a new division of political power and a diminution of federal power to the benefit of the states. An example of the change was the August 1997 announcement of a new poverty program, El Progresa, which in contrast to Solidarity, will be administered by the states and not the federal government.

REGIONS

Mexico is a constitutional federation of thirty-one states and the Federal District of Mexico City, and 2,377 municipalities (*municipios*) characterized by a highly centralized administration, with federal programs accounting for most areas of government activity. The administrative boundaries are the basic regional division and in Mexico, the major administrative units are the states and the Federal District (Mexico City). The primary administrative unit below the scale of the state is the *municipio*. This administrative structure, although it does not necessarily match other natural, cultural or social regional bases, has in itself created and emphasized regional differences. Federal and local government investment varies considerably by state, encouraging certain types of regional

development, and productive activities. Censuses and other government
reports usually organize statistical material by state and guide perceptions and plans in differentiating regions. Thus, the concepts of administrative and economic regions are solidified and unified.[13]

Section VI, Article 115, Title V of the constitution makes provisions for
planned development. "When two or more urban centers situated in municipal territories or two or more states form or tend to form a demographic
continuity, the respective Federal, State and Municipal Governments within
the area of their jurisdiction, shall plan and regulated in a coordinated manner the development of said centers, according to the applicable federal law."

Defining Mexico's regions:

* Northwest—Baja California (Norte and Sur), Nayarit, Sinaloa and Sonora
* North—Coahuila, Chihuahua, Durango and Nuevo Leon
* Gulf—Tamaulipas and Veracruz
* Center (north)—Aguascalientes, San Luis Potosi and Zacatecas
* Center (west)—Colima, Guanajuato, Jalisco and Michoacan
* Center—Hidalgo, Morelos, Puebla, Queretaro and Tlaxcala
* Valley of Mexico—Federal District and Mexico State
* South and Southeast—Campeche, Chiapas, Guerrero, Oaxaca, Quintana
  Roo, Tabasco, and Yucatan[14]

The centralization in Mexico is imposed on a markedly varied group of
regions with differences in economic development, populations and natural
endowments. Yet the centralization is limited by the historic regional diversity. The existence of natural resources and the physical limits imposed by
mountains, and waterways cannot be ignored in the determination of regions.

Over 60% of the population live in urban areas. The population growth
in rural areas is beneath the national average. Medium-size cities are growing at a faster rate than large cities. The country's future will be irrevocably
urban. The president sought to consolidate a system of cities that will allow
full advantage to be taken of the economic potential, soil availability, water
and infrastructure of the country's eighty largest population centers.[15]

There is concern that the historical divide in the country is growing
and the north's success will not translate into progress for the rest of the
country. In the north, median income is nearly twice what it is in the
poorest states of Mexico's south and the northern unemployment rate is
two percentage points lower than the national average.[16]

Mexico City

Located in the geographic center of the Mexican Republic, the metropolitan zone of Mexico City consists of the Federal District and 27

urbanized municipalities of the State of Mexico. The total population of the metropolitan area is over 15 million people and some 8.5 million people in the inner core out of a total population of 81 million.

As the country's nerve center, Mexico City has always had a political weight disproportionate even to its enormous size. In view of its size and economic importance, the district's annual budget is considerably larger than that of the states and the mayor is perhaps the second most powerful official in the country and considered to be a member of the Cabinet. The government has discouraged the establishment of new industrial facilities in the metropolitan areas of Mexico City, Monterey and Guadalajara because of the excessive concentration of industry and overpopulation.[17]

The federal government offers a tax incentive to industries to locate outside the metropolitan areas of Mexico City, Guadalajara and Monterey. Some individual state governments are willing to grant incentives to attract new industries to specific areas within their borders, often in the form of reduced prices for land in industrial uses and reductions in property taxes.[18]

INCENTIVES

Tax and nontax incentives are granted on the basis of location and regional priorities, pursuant to Mexico's general strategy of decentralization and regional development. For purposes of granting federal tax incentives for promotion of industrial decentralization, Mexico is divided into four geographic zones.[19]

Zone I

Zone I consists of 109 specific municipalities, is considered a zone of maximum national priority and includes municipalities where it it is believed to be easier to achieve industrial development because the necessary infrastructure already exists.

Zone II

Zone II is considered a maximum priority for state purposes and includes municipalities specified in agreements to be concluded between federal and state governments.

Zone III

Zone III is a regulated zone divided into two subzones: III-A, labeled for controlled growth (53 municipalities), and III-B, considered as merely for consolidation (163 municipalities).

Remainder of the Country

This zone includes all municipalities not specifically included in the three aforementioned principal zones. These incentives have been available only to Mexican majority-owned companies.

Eligibility

Only those Mexican majority-owned entities considered small and micro-size industries are eligible. For this purpose, a small industry is one with a labor force of up to 100 employees and yearly gross sales of up to Ps400 million. Incentives are available only to companies whose foreign ownership does not exceed 49% of its capital.

In May 1989, the government significantly liberalized foreign investment regulations. Where a project does not comply with the regulations but it does bring significant economic benefits (e.g., it helps in the development of less-industrialized regions), it fits the category of investment being sought.[20]

PROGRAMS

In contrast to the United States and Canada, Mexico has had national economic plans, even preceding the National Development Plan for 1995–2000. In the past the Mexican administrations may have overconcentrated on macroeconomic policies, and thus have overlooked the regional dimensions of development as well as ignoring problems such as the emigration of workers to the United States.[21]

The discussion of regional policies has frequently been limited to nominal or rhetorical remarks on the spatial allocation of the national government's spending and investment. There has not been much evidence of a strategic will to converge resources on developing specific areas of the country.[22] The Mexican government has demonstrated limited capacity to implement planning, and to achieve accomplishments, as witnessed by the failure of its programs of regional development and agricultural modernization.[23] But when President Zedillo took office in

December 1994, he emphasized the importance of regional economic development.

First of all, I see regional development as a key element in my National Poverty Abatement Plan. Regional development hinges on what I have called a new federalism and it will be forged out of change—political, social, legal and economic change. We must experience a profound reallocation of real power, authority, responsibilities and resources from the omnipresent federal government to the state and municipal bodies. By decentralizing the federal government and shifting responsibility for public expenditure and investment funds to state and municipalities, we well be able to better address the individual concerns of each community. The regional development strategy includes: providing credit and savings services through local financial institutions; deregulating at the local level; investing heavily in infrastructure; and communicating regularly with state and local authorities. In short, we are looking at a transfer of responsibilities, resources and decision-making powers, investment in infrastructure; and promotion of priority regional projects.[24]

DEVELOPMENT PLANS

The 1989–1994 National Development Plan (NDP) was an instrument through which the government defined its national objectives and strategies needed, based on various proposals made in public consultation forums and commitments made by President Salinas de Gortari during his political campaign. One of the guidelines referred to the creation of productive jobs and protection of workers' standard of living. The National Development Plan went far beyond regional economic development and was a blueprint for attaining national objectives. Included in the NDP strategy was the elimination of extreme poverty through the National Solidarity Program (Programma Nacional de Solidaridad, PRONASOL). An optimistic evaluation was made on the use of public resources, but what should be observed is the emphasis on "balanced regional development."

Mexico has succeeded in stabilizing its economy by means of fiscal discipline and the general agreement of the economic sectors. In addition, it has renegotiated its debt to eliminate the excessive burden that it imposed on the economy and on the labor of each and every Mexican. The resources made available by that renegotiation, and those derived from the process of selling or liquidating enterprises, are being allocated to the creation of social infrastructure, to the support of economic growth, to the creation of jobs and to the achievement of more balanced regional development.[25]

PRONASOL, the antipoverty program, was the trademark of former President Salinas, who spent $15 billion on the program during his term of office. Critics contended it accomplished little. At the start of the Salinas term, there was widespread unemployment as older, uncompetitive businesses closed. Peasants could not compete when the Mexican market was opened to farm products from the United States and Canada. The stadiums and small public works projects were a temporary ameliorative and kept them loyal to the government. But little was accomplished to reduce poverty; rather than creating permanent jobs, it provided temporary employment on public works. The 1995 annual budget was set at $1.6 billion. President Zedillo replaced PRONASOL with the Alliance for Well Being, thousands of small local committees that with the states decide what is needed even if it is a baseball stadium. The criticism, as with the Salinas program, is that political purposes are primary as opposed to social and economic development. There is little central control in use of the money.[26]

The 1995–2000 NDP has five components: sovereignty, rule of law and nation of laws, democratic development, social development and economic growth.[27] The emphasis is on economic growth and to a lesser extent on social development. The plan gives priority to industrial or sectoral policy over regional policy. The fundamental strategic objective of the plan is to promote vigorous and sustainable economic growth to strengthen national sovereignty and, to a lesser extent, social well-being. High economic growth is an essential condition for promoting all aspects of the country's development.

There are five major strategy guidelines to promote sustainable economic growth:

1. Make domestic savings the cornerstone of national development financing and assign foreign savings a complementary role for the purpose of promoting productive investment.
2. Establish conditions to favor and preserve stability and certainty for economic activity.
3. Promote efficient use of resources for growth.
4. Implement an environmental and natural resources policy conducive to sustainable economic development.
5. Sectoral policies.[28]

Industrial Development. The NDP proposes a set of instruments and strategies that are an indispensable part of industrial policy. The sectoral program is designed to offer a framework for the country's industrial development over the coming years, with emphasis on the promotion of microeconomics and SMEs. In addition, the plan proposes to strengthen the development of the most backward subsectors and branches of industry and to promote the efficient development and integration of the most backward regions by identifying and increasing their competitive advantages.

Mining. Mining policy will be based on a regulatory framework offering investors legal certainty. The plan is aimed at maintaining a pace of expansion in keeping with sustainable development and at making the most of the extensive capacity of the mining industry to create jobs, supply the domestic market and generate inflows of foreign exchange.

Tourism. The development program for the tourism sector recognizes that tourism activities are the fastest-growing and most viable option for developing some of the country's regions due to the relative advantages stemming from proximity to many markets and, above all, from the unique resources.[29]

Agricultural and Livestock Policy. The central objective of the agricultural and livestock policy is to increase the net income of producers. To that end, measures will be established to improve production infrastructure, training for agricultural workers and financial services, and to afford certainty in terms of land tenure. To supplement the producers' income, direct supports will continue to be provided for promoting the capitalization and technological development of the sector. For its part, the policy for pricing agricultural and livestock products will be designed to permit the creation of regional markets, the productive reconversion of regions offering comparative advantages, the expansion of chains of production and the adequate supply of corn and beans.[30]

MAQUILADORAS

Maquiladoras merit attention as a prototype of regional economic development. Though maquiladoras began as an economic development program applicable to a specific region, the coverage was subsequently extended to the country as a whole. In December 1989, regulations were further liberalized, allowing maquiladoras to receive automatic authorizations to locate plants in any area zoned for industrial development.

Maquiladoras are assembly plants operating in Mexican territory under special customs treatments and liberal foreign investment regulations. Maquiladoras import into Mexico (duty-free on a temporary, in-bond basis) machinery, equipment, parts, raw materials and other components used in the assembly or manufacture of semifinished or finished products. These products are then exported back to their country of origin or to a third country.

Originally a coordinated U.S.-Mexico effort, the in-bond program has greatly benefited from U.S. Tariff Items 9802.00.60 and 9802.00.80, which allow for duty-free re-entry into the United States of goods assembled in another country from components of U.S. origin. Duty is paid only on components that are not of U.S. origin and the value added in assembly or in manufacture in Mexico.

The program evolved from the earlier Bracero Program, in which, beginning in 1951, the United States in cooperation with Mexico allowed Mexican citizens to enter the United States legally as seasonal agricultural workers; it was terminated in 1964. To compensate for the discontinuance of the program and to lower Mexico's high unemployment rate, the Mexican government proposed a plan whereby industry would be induced to locate on the Mexican side of the border.

The Border Industrialization Program (BIP), commonly known as the maquiladora program, was established in 1965 to address the need for job creation and an improved standard of living along the Mexican side of the U.S.-Mexican border. It was especially key in that the Bracero Program had permitted up to 200,000 Mexican workers per year to enter the United States to perform farm work. An objective was to compensate by attracting foreign investment, mainly from the United States.

This program was a major step away from economic protectionism and looked toward stimulating economic development in the stagnant areas of northern Mexico. Though there were limitations on foreign-ownership, 100% foreign owned production facilities were permitted on condition that the total output of these facilities were to be exported. A hope for the program was that BIP would work as a full-blown regional policy that would turn the traditionally backward and isolated north frontier, dependent as it was on supplies from north of the border, into a dynamic growth pole for the whole northern region, if not the whole country.

Before the advent of maquila industry, few of the cities on either side of border could be characterized as industrial, although states in which they were located did have some industry. Communities north of the border in the United States were for the most part traditionally poor and backward, except for San Diego.

Backwardness of most of the Mexican borderlands in comparison with northern and central regions had long been recognized. Despite the obvious benefits from export to the United States, there was a strong consensus in Mexico that it was dependence on its rich and powerful northern neighbor that was at the root of the problem. This was the theme that was to exercise the Mexican government with particular force from the 1960s onwards and was to be instrumental in the creation of a series of innovative administrative vehicles to promote border development.[31] In 1995, the trade balance of Mexico's maquiladora (in-bond) sector was $5 billion, or 63.8% of the country's trade surplus and in the same year (1995) the total number of maquiladoras throughout Mexico grew to 2,782. The fastest-growing sectors were auto parts and electronics assembly with respective growth rates of 23.8% and 25.8%.

In 1994, the maquiladora industry contributed nearly $6 billion in foreign exchange to Mexico, making it the second-largest source of international reserves. The share of total manufacturing employment was 26% in 1994, up from 5.1% in 1982.[32]

The maquiladora labor force in December 1996 was 803,000, of which over 80% was concentrated in the five border states of Chihuahua, Sonora, Baja California, Tamaulipas and Coahuila.[33] In December 1993, the maquiladora labor force was 546,588.

The 1994 peso devaluation effectively reduced labor costs. The daily minimum wage was US $5.25 and a year later was US $2.59. Wages paid along the U.S.–Mexican border are 25% higher than those paid farther south. In April 1996, the minimum wage was increased 10%.[34]

Over time the role of maquiladoras has been changing; it is no longer simply a device by which a multinational firm can reduce the labor costs associated with its relatively labor-intensive production. Rather they are evolving into a mechanism by which a multinational firm can not only reduce its labor costs but also increase productivity of its manufacturing activities. This may have been accomplished by an increased investment in the technology used in the manufacturing or assembly processes, by an increased investment in and reliance on information technology or both.[35] Maquiladora industry has moved well beyond the constraints of heavily labor-intensive plants, simple manual assembly operations and low-level technology. Technology transfer has brought increasingly sophisticated and innovative proceeds in the plants.

Effects

Geographic diversification has been a trend in the industry. Since 1972, when the Mexican government began allowing the establishment of maquiladora plants in non-border or interior areas, they have been found throughout the country but are still concentrated in the border region. The movement to the interior was facilitated by lower wages and promises of less worker turnover. Besides cutting labor costs, a move to Mexico's interior would bring maquiladoras in close contact with the populated Mexican cities of the country's middle. The growing interest in moving from the border created a climate of competition, with individual states eager to lure foreign firms. Mirroring the competition in the United States, Mexican state governments promised to pay for worker training programs and to subsidize land costs. At least one Mexican state government went so far as to give verbal guarantees that workers will not cause any trouble. Sonora, like other states, launched a recruitment campaign involving private and public sector monies.[36] Regulations allow companies to sell domestically up to 50% of their production, on a government-approved basis compared with previous limits of 20%.[37]

Future

Eventually the name of the maquiladora program will be changed to the Export Manufacturing Industry and will officially be part of Mexico's domestic manufacturing industry. Yet maquiladoras along the border are expanding when many thought they were beginning to lose their significance. The program will change under NAFTA in two phases, 1994 through 2000 and beginning in 2001. The basic operating framework will not change in the first phase but access to domestic markets will be gradually liberalized. By 2000, maquiladoras will be able to sell to the domestic market 85% of the value of their export production in the preceding year, up from 50% in 1993. In 2001 they will be allowed to sell 100% of their production domestically.[38]

NAFTA's more important change to the program occurs during the second phase, when the provision that essentially defines the program of duty-free importation of inputs into Mexico, regardless of origin, is abandoned. Maquiladoras in 2001 will lose the special tax status that allows them to import duty-free and pay levies only on the value added to products. After 2001, maquiladoras will be treated like any other manufacturers. North American rules of origin will determine duty-free status for a given import, while duty drawback provisions will apply to non-North American inputs. Mexico's intent in general after 2000 will be to ensure that maquiladoras continue to find the investment climate sufficiently attractive to remain in the country.

NAFTA's local content stipulations will require maquiladora operations that buy raw materials or components from third countries like Asia to buy directly from North American companies or have their source establish operations in North America if they wish to export duty-free to the United States or Canada.[39]

The word "maquila" will gradually disappear as companies begin to buy their materials from North America; there is no future for in-bond plants in a free-trade zone. What will eventually remain of the industry attracted to the border region by the maquiladora program? Will it have served as the basis for a regional economy, possibly overlapping the two national borders?

The dominance of the border for coproduction will not disappear. The border's locational advantage is proximity to the United States, which cuts down on transportation problems and costs. There is the factor of inertia for plants already in place. A shift would require upgrading Mexico's transportation and communications, which will not be immediate.[40]

When the Mexican peso lost much of its value against the dollar after the December 20, 1994, devaluation, maquiladoras raised exports to maximize returns, as their fixed costs, like labor, remained in pesos while the earnings were in dollars. A weak peso and benefits from manufacturing in a NAFTA country combine to produce a boom in companies locating or expanding along the U.S.-Mexican border.

Other scenarios are that maquila industries will move inland and produce for local markets once the country begins to trade freely with the United States. High-tech production will remain near the border where the skilled labor pool is located, while labor-intensive manufacturing requiring relatively low skills will concentrate further inland. Manufacturers also may want to stay in the border regions because of its established infrastructure. While the government is building new toll roads inland, telecommunications services in those areas are spotty.

Maquiladora industry can be expected to keep growing until the NAFTA provisions are fully implemented. Maquiladoras will develop more North American strategies, consolidating operations and entering into more joint ventures.

NOTES

1. Guillermo de la Pena, *Local and Regional Power in Mexico* (Austin: University of Texas, Mexico Center for Latin American Affairs, Papers on Mexico, Prepublication Working Papers 88-01, 1988), p. 15.

2. Price Waterhouse, *Doing Business in Mexico Information Guide, 1993 and Supplement,* June 30, 1994.

3. De la Pena, *Local and Regional Power,* p. 16.

4. Bryan Roberts, "The Place of Regions in Mexico," in Eric Van Young, ed., *Mexico's Regions Comparative History and Development* (San Diego: University of California, Center for U.S.-Mexican Studies, 1992), p. 238.

5. *OECD Economic Surveys Mexico* (Paris: Organization for Economic Cooperation and Development, 1995), p. 68.

6. Ibid., p. 150.

7. Tom Barry, ed., *Mexico A Country Guide,* 1st ed. (Albuquerque: Inter-Hemispheric Education Resource Center, 1992), p. 13.

8. Anthony DePalma, "Economic Crisis Hits Mexico's States With Some Nearly Broke," *New York Times,* May 10, 1995, p. A13.

9. Kevin G. Hall, "Mexico to Give States Greater Power," *Journal of Commerce* (August 21, 1995), p. 1A.

10. Ibid.

11. Matt Moffett, "Political Vacuum as Mexico's Leader Cedes Some Authority, Power Scramble Begins," *Wall Street Journal,* March 25, 1996, p. 1.

12. Hall, "Mexico," p. 1A.

13. Diana Liverman and Altha Cravey, "Geographic Perspectives on Mexican Regions," in Eric Van Young, ed., *Mexico's Regions Comparative History and Development* (San Diego: University of California, Center for U.S.-Mexican Studies, 1992), p. 45.

14. Alberto Ariz Nassif, "Regional Dimensions of Democratization," in

Wayne A. Cornelius, Judith Gentleman and Peter H. Smith, eds., *Mexico's Alternative Political Futures* (San Diego: University of California, Center for U.S.-Mexican Studies, 1989), Monograph Series 30, p. 88.

15. President Carlos Salinas de Gortari, *Third State of the Union Report*, November 1, 1991.

16. Abstract from Atlanta Journal and Constitution, August 14, 1994, in NAFTA Digest 3 (September 1994), p. 8.

17. Price Waterhouse, *Doing Business in Mexico*, p. 28.

18. Ibid., p. 22.

19. Ibid., pp. 36–39.

20. Gray Newman and Anna Szterenfeld, *Business International's Guide to Doing Business in Mexico* (New York: McGraw-Hill, 1993), pp. 113–115.

21. Jesus Tamayo and Fernando Lozano, "Mexican Perceptions on Rural Development and Migration of Workers to the United States and Actions Taken, 1970–1988," in Sergio Diaz-Briquets and Sidney Weintraub, eds., *Regional and Sectoral Development in Mexico as Alternatives to Migration* (Boulder: Westview Press, 1991), p. 383.

22. Jesus Tamayo and Fernando Lozan, "The Economic and Social Development of High Emigration Areas in the State of Zacatecas: Antecedents and Policy Alternatives," in Sergio Diaz-Briquets and Sidney Weintraub, eds., *Regional and Sectoral Development in Mexico as Alternatives to Migration* (Boulder: Westview Press, 1991), p. 19.

23. Roberts, "The Place of Regions," p. 239.

24. "Mexico Investor Mexico's New President Looks Ahead," *New York Times*, December 1, 1994, p. D9.

25. Presidencia de la Republica, Direccion General de Comunicacion Social, *The Mexican Agenda 1991*, pp. 70–71.

26. Anthony DePalma, "Anti-Poverty Program Under Fire in Mexico," *New York Times*, July 3, 1995, p. 5.

27. Presidencia de la Republica, Direccion General de Comunicacion Social, Poder Ejecutivo Federal, *National Development Plan 1995–2000*.

28. Ibid., p. 39.

29. Ibid., p. 44.

30. Ibid., p. 45.

31. Leslie Sklair, *Assembling for Development: The Maquila Industry in Mexico and the United States* (Boston: Unwin Hyman, 1989), p. 26.

32. Lucinda Vargas, "Maquiladoras: Mexico's Bright Spot," *The Southwest Economy* 5 (Federal Reserve Bank of Dallas) (September–October 1995), p. 9.

33. *NAFTA Digest* 6 (April 1997), p. 5.

34. "Maquila Update," *NAFTA Digest* 5 (March 1996), p. 6.

35. Stephanie A. M. Smith and Stephen E. Lunce, "Information Technology Usage by Maquiladoras," *NAFTA Digest* 5 (March 1996), p. 1.

36. U.S. International Trade Commission, *The Likely Impact on the United States of a Free Trade Agreement with Mexico*, Publication 2353, Investigation No. 332-2997, February 1991.

37. "Maquiladora Industry Generates $3 Billion a Year," *Wall Street Journal*, April 30, 1991, p. A19.

38. Vargas, "Maquiladoras," p. 10.

39. *NAFTA Digest* 4 (July 1995), pp. 5–6.

40. Sidney Weintraub, *NAFTA: What Comes Next* (Washington: Center for Strategic and International Studies, 1994), p. 49, and "Perspective: Does Moving Pay?" *Investor's Business Daily*, August 10, 1998, p. A6.

Chapter 17

Evolution of U.S. Regional Policy

INTRODUCTION

Regions since the early years of the nation have, in varying degrees, benefited directly and indirectly from federal activism. But the U.S. has never had a consistent long-range regional policy with adequately funded programs specifically directed to the distribution of economic activity and the resolution of spatially based structural problems. But historic factors have played a part in determining the present regional configuration.

In a broad sense they include such early events as New England's threat to secede during the War of 1812, the differences between Senator John C. Calhoun and President Andrew Jackson on tariffs, the disputes leading to secession and differences over how to deal with the postwar leading to secession and differences over how to deal with the post–Civil War Reconstruction.[1]

Compared with other countries, the United States began without a deep-rooted regional structure. At its inception, the United States did not have to accommodate long-standing historical patterns, such as ethnic differences, feudal boundaries or institutions, as the United States was not constructed from the unification of historically distinct regions. The

roughly 160 years between the end of the Revolution and the close of
World War II have been rife with examples of federal actions and policies
that, perhaps unintentionally, have selectively affected subnational economic development.

Two important features of the federal development activities in the
century and a half before World War II separate them from the pattern of
federal involvement after 1945. One is that the earlier activities were
largely episodic and had a certain accidental quality. Few of these efforts
were designed with subnational economic development goals as the
prime objective, whereas various New Deal and post-World War II
renewal and redevelopment programs represented more sustained and
planned commitments of national scope. The second feature was that
those federal activities usually represented responses to projects initiated
at the state or local level. In both respects, involvement of the national
government was consistent with the decentralized nature of the federal-
state relations before the transformation in the Depression era.

THE NINETEENTH CENTURY

The first decades of the 1800s were marked by debates between
Thomas Jefferson and Alexander Hamilton on issues of law concerning
commerce and land, policies of exploration or settlement of disputed borders and acquisition of new territories. The early U.S. programs involving regional development were based on the concept of relating economic development to construction of national roads and canals. The federal
treasury was considered a rich source of subsidies for an endless list of
projects for canals and roads in various states. One of the earliest and
most impressive systemic approaches to planning U.S. regional development was prepared by Albert Gallatin in his 1808 "Report on Public
Roads and Canals" to Thomas Jefferson, in which the creation of a national transportation system was proposed. Gallatin's plan for a nationally
financed, nationally planned network of roads and canals was rejected by
a Congress concerned with states' rights issues. Yet the federal government did for a brief time make available its considerable resources for a
limited number of state and locally initiated projects.

Assistance to states and localities in the canal era did not represent
an attempt to implement a congressional program or to articulate and
promote national objectives. Yet, there is little doubt that construction of
canals and roads and creation of an internal transportation network in the
period before the Civil War contributed to local economic development;
it is one of the most notable instances of federal assistance to state and
local development.

Two features of these early episodes provide a thread of continuity to the modern period. First, assistance for the purpose of constructing public works infrastructure to facilitate local industrial and commercial growth became an important development strategy. Second, the principle of decentralized participation in spending federal resources remains a vital part of contemporary economic development programs.[2]

Grants for railroad building, river and harbor surveys and improvements, settlement of western land and other measures continued through the nineteenth century. Tariffs boosted the New England economy; railroad and land grants and homesteading opened the western lands. The Morrill Act of 1862 established the land grant college system.

By and large, these programs, particularly those relating to public works and rivers and harbors projects, soon became characterized by "pork barrel" politics, in which decisions were made in line with a legislative necessity to provide benefits for members' constituents and to appease the more influential, rather than on the basis of need or efficiency. In other words projects with potential to redirect economic growth and development patterns were handled as distributive in nature.[3]

Well into the nineteenth century, matters of slavery and free territories, incorporation of new states, trade policies and Reconstruction became involved with regional issues. Other issues were free silver, organization of territories gained from Mexico and other territorial matters. Sometime between the passing of the frontier and the Woodrow Wilson presidency, the sense of a territorial dimension of national policy declined into small-scale concern with particular problems.[4]

However, certain fundamental interregional differences were established in the nineteenth century. The specialization of commercial agriculture was made possible by a host of natural conditions: Rainfall, topography, soil chemistry, temperature variation and accessibility of transportation were the path to well-demarcated patterns of regional specialization, making it possible to identify various agricultural belts—cotton, wheat, corn, tobacco, and others.[5]

Without a national development plan, Congress did move forward on development programs throughout the nineteenth century. Particularly important were land grants for railroad construction, river and harbor improvements and the Homestead Act of 1862, which made it national policy to encourage agricultural development of the West.[6]

Programs

Early in the twentieth century, other forerunners of regional development programs were initiated: the Reclamation Act of 1902, authorizing use of federal funds from and sales for irrigation and reclamation projects; the 1909 report of the Country Life Commission, calling for a program of technical assistance to reduce the vulnerability of a single industry and single crop areas to economic adversity; the Vocational Training Act of 1917, providing support for state programs of education in agriculture and the skilled trades; the construction of a national highway system under the Federal Highway Act of 1916.

In the 1930s, the New Deal led to the creation of new policies and institutions that changed attitudes toward government intervention in regional matters. Though not generously funded, they were generally accepted until the congressional elections of 1994, when a new Republican majority questioned the existence of the New Deal legacy. The first New Deal programs of the 1930s were primarily intended to stimulate aggregate demand. With a national depression and all regions suffering, declining or backward regions did not have to be identified for priority treatment. But the path was cleared for the 1960s regional development programs.

There was a revival of interest in development; emphasis was placed on planning and public works; conservation and systematic development were stressed and the expansion of federal planning activities under the New Deal through such agencies as the Public Works Administration (PWA) and the National Resources Planning Board (NRPB) and its successors, regional planning agencies, and the Tennessee Valley Authority (TVA) to improve the economic base of a rural Southern region. Other large scale projects date from this period, water projects such as Grand Coulee Dam in the Columbia River Valley and the Hoover Dam on the Lower Colorado.

The PWA was established in 1933 to make public works expenditures. It included three types of projects: those undertaken indirectly by federal agencies; those undertaken by state or local bodies, which were meant to be financed in part by grants and in part by loans; and those undertaken by railroads and financed by loans. The Reconstruction Finance Corporation (RFC) established in 1932 subsequently became a lender to state and local governments. These programs had a regional component, either implicit or explicit.

The National Planning Board, established in 1933, was given responsibilities for: (1) preparation of comprehensive regional public works plans; (2) surveys of population distribution and trends, land use, industrial, housing and natural resources and general social and economic trends; and (3) project analysis to ensure coordination in location and sequence.[7] The board took on a number of very broad national planning tasks and went through several name changes. It eventually was incorporated into the executive office of the president as the National

Resources Planning Board (NRPB). During its twenty years of existence, a network of thirteen regional offices and several interagency advisory committees were established. It undertook a variety of social and economic studies as well as physical planning studies on a nationwide basis and stimulated regional, state and local planning all across the nation. The intention of the National Resources Planning Board was to set up multistate and state frameworks for planning public works projects and other economic development activities. By 1937, all but two of the states had established some type of official planning agency.[8]

By 1943, the NRPB had become controversial and was terminated by Congress, which was concerned about too great centralization in the executive branch and angered about interference with the traditional congressional rights to allocate federal pork-barrel largesse, such as river and harbor disbursements. The NRPB was considered nonessential to the war effort and peripheral to the president's immediate needs. Congress let its appropriation lapse and the NRPB was dissolved.[9]

There was an underlying conviction in the period that private sector growth was the ultimate objective of all public development efforts. The primary objective of all federal development programs of the period was the creation of permanent private sector jobs. In fact, job creation, both primary and secondary, became the ultimate criterion for the success of development projects. Since the number of such jobs and cost per job created were difficult to determine, debates on the relative success of federal investments based on these criteria continued into the 1980s.[10]

POST–WORLD WAR II

World War II brought about such great movements of population and industrial development that new as well as old development problems came to the fore. A concern for chronically depressed areas began to emerge in federal policy-making circles, partly because many areas had become dependent on war-related industries and faced especially severe problems of reconversion. Other factors were the depressed areas created in the main by shifts in product demand, depletion of resources and technological change. Extensive pockets of poverty such as Appalachia and the pervasive rural poverty of the South, along with some major industrial areas affected by declining or shifting markets (e.g., coal and textiles), created a new sense of urgency about the dilemma of decline in the midst of the postwar boom.[11]

With the exception of the New Deal policies designed to relieve temporary economic distress in the 1930s, U.S. economic policy before the 1960s largely followed the neoclassical economists' model of growth promotion in the private sector and a laissez-faire stance toward social and spatial distribution of growth. It was assumed workers would move to find jobs and that capital would move to find workers. Any public intervention to affect this flow of labor and capital was deemed an unnecessary and unwelcome intervention into the private sector's domain.[12]

In contrast, regional development specialists contended that market-driven economies stimulated polarized growth. with rich areas gaining at the expense of depressed areas trapped in a cycle of underdevelopment. They advocated a variety of public investment strategies to stimulate new growth in lagging economies and to thereby achieve more balanced growth. These contentions were not taken seriously until the 1960s.[13]

The regional policy debate that emerged in the 1950s centered on how to develop particular weak limbs of the economy, specific local areas with low incomes or high unemployment, so that the entire economy would expand and the transfer payment drain on a healthy national economy could be reduced. Widely dispersed counties were designated on the basis of the social characteristics of their populations, not because they formed viable political entities or theoretically related economic groupings. The framework of the policy discussion, therefore, was national economic efficiency, more effective use of development potential and transfer funds.

Regional equity as an issue was never directly stated, that is, the comparative conditions of different regional and political parts of the country. The emphasis was merely on raising separate and unconnected localities to some national norm, despite the difficulties of these areas being closely involved with the problems of the region and the national economy of which they were a part. Two fundamental questions were overlooked: How was the issue of declining industrial areas to be resolved? And should poor rural areas be redeveloped?[14]

One of the earliest attempts at enacting a program for the economic development of depressed areas was the Hays-Bailey Bill, introduced in Congress in 1946. Its goal of full employment was ultimately embodied in the Employment Act of 1946, but its provisions—designed to promote balanced growth within and among regions, to stimulate the development of markets for products from all regions, to reduce the gap between rural and urban standards of living and to stem the tide of rural migration to overcrowded urban areas—led to criticism that it would result in excessive government intervention in the economy. Also it favored rural over depressed industrialized areas. The Hays-Bailey Bill was defeated.[15]

The post–World War II period (1945–1960) was marked by a single federal action more significant in philosophy than in fact. The Employment Act of 1946 declared there was a role for the federal government in creating an environment for "maximum employment, production, and purchasing power." In 1976, the proposed Full Employment and Balanced Growth Act of 1976 (Humphrey-Hawkins Bill) sought "balanced growth" to achieve long-run economic goals. A much weakened version of the bill was passed in 1978; it contained a commitment to the goal of full employment without mandatory standards or controls.[16]

The 1955 Economic Report of the President, prepared by the Council of Economic Advisors (CEA) for President Eisenhower viewed the problem of depressed areas as one that can be helped somewhat by government programs but stated that "a large part of the adjustment of depressed areas to new economic conditions both can and should be carried out by the local citizens themselves." A year later, in 1956, in the next report, the CEA changed position, stating that "the fate of distressed communities is a matter of national as well as local concern." The CEA concluded that the existing programs were not adequate to resolve the problems of depressed areas and affirmed that bolder measures were needed.[17] From then until the early 1960s there was increased concern for urban and rural areas in economic decline, and until the 1980s, whenever the administration or Congress considered programs to address problems of such areas, debate focused on the familiar theme of the suitability of government action in private sector economic concerns.[18]

In the 1950s, the only regional policy instrument of any note was the 1952 Executive Order known as Defense Manpower Policy No. 4 (DMP4); its intention was to give preference in certain defense contracts to firms in high unemployment areas. The impact was not very substantial since relatively few contracts were involved and preferred firms were required to match the lowest public bid.[19] In the revised policy of 1980, the secretary of Commerce had the responsibility of urging concerns planning new production facilities to consider the advantages of locating in Labor Surplus Areas. The Defense Department consistently opposed placing contracts in Labor Surplus Areas to relieve unemployment.[20]

By 1960, it was clear that the federal government was unwilling to formulate a national development policy as had been discussed by the National Resources Planning Board and the framers of the 1946 Employment Act. But Congress was devoting more attention to the difficulties of particular geographic areas that had high unemployment rates and had not been beneficiaries of the postwar economic growth.[21]

The Democratic electoral victories of 1960 and 1964 created an environment favorable to intervention. An era of regional policy essentially dates from the Kennedy-Johnson administrations in the 1960s well after regional policies were common elsewhere in other industrial nations. No national regional strategy was included. The programs were designed initially for areas of economic distress with high unemployment or with a surplus of low-income residents but to ensure passage by Congress, standards were relaxed.

The year 1965 marked the apex of federal regional policy legislation. The Area Redevelopment Administration was abolished; Congress replaced it by creating the Economic Development Administration, Appalachian Regional Commission and Title V Regional Commissions. They are reviewed in Chapter 19. Since the 1960s, there have been no new focused regional policy initiatives of any magnitude.

The main focus of explicit federal spatial policies in the 1960s was urban and not regional. In response to riots in Watts and other urban areas, the Johnson administration developed a wide range of urban programs summed up in the War on Poverty and Great Society. Typical was the 1966 Model Cities Program.

In the 1970s, sizeable federal resources were devoted to community development, housing, education, job training and job creation. Several federal HUD programs, Community Development Block Grants (CDBGs) and Urban Development Action Grants (UDAGs) were initiated to target economic aid to the most depressed localities. They did not constitute a carefully constructed national or regional economic development plan.

Though new federal domestic initiatives, especially those of a regional nature, were absent, the impact of the federal government on regional economic growth became a major political and economic issue during the 1970s with the Sunbelt-Frostbelt debate. Erosion of the industrial base of the northern and central regions of the country, the rapid growth of the South and West, and the boom in energy-producing states heightened interest in whether federal policies inadvertently were hurting declining states and further boosting economic growth in those regions with the healthiest economies. Currently the location of industry is no longer a question primarily of regional competition within the United States but instead is worldwide.

Jimmy Carter's administration was not overly concerned with regional programs, as expressed in the report issued at the end of its term. Population mobility was the preferred policy. The principal purpose of programs would be to increase mobility in assisting people to follow jobs, rather than concentrating on efforts to direct jobs to where people are.[22]

There has been no change in the 1990s by the federal government to consider and enact spatial economic development legislation. The Clinton administration's major spatial thrust has been to adapt the enterprise zone concept into the Empowerment Zone legislation. The economic development programs of the 1960s, with their already sparse funding, face a precarious future, given the priority on to limiting the role of the federal government and balanced budgets.

NOTES

1. Zane C. Miller, "The Trickiness of Regional Thinking and the Neutralizing of Public Planning and Policy Professionals," *Planning History* 3:1 (1989), p. 3.

2. Patrick G. Grasso, "Distributive Policies and the Politics of Economic Development," in F. Stevens Redburn, Terry F. Buss and Larry C. Ledebur, eds., *Revitalizing the U.S. Economy* (Westport: Praeger Publishers, 1986), p. 93.

3. Ibid., p. 89.

4. John Agnew, *The United States in the World Economy: A Regional Geography* (Cambridge: Cambridge University Press, 1987), p. 355.

5. Ibid., p. 91.

6. Grasso, "Distributive Policies,"p. 89.

7. Merle Fainsod, Lincoln Gordon and Joseph C. Palamountain, *Government and the American Economy* (New York: W. W. Norton & Co., 1959), pp. 732–733.

8. Ibid., p. 733; and Pamela H. Wev, "Economic Development," in Frank S. Sol, Irving Hand and Bruce D. McDowell, eds., *The Practice of State and Regional Planning* (Chicago: International City Management Association and American Planning Association, 1986), p. 377.

9. Fainsod, Gordon and Palamountain, *Government*, p. 733.

10. Wev, "Economic Development,"p. 377.

11. Edward K. Smith, "Introduction," in Edward K. Smith, ed., *New Directions in Federal Economic Development Programs* (National Bureau of Economic Research, Explorations in Economic Research, Occasional Paper 4, Summer 1977), pp. 345–346.

12. Ann R. Tickamyer and Cynthia M. Duncan, "Work and Poverty in Rural America," in Cornelia B. Flora and James A. Christianson, eds., *Rural Policies for the 1990s* (Boulder: Westview Press, 1991), p. 10.

13. Ibid., p. 109.

14. John Zysman, "Research, Politics and Policy: Regional Planning in America," in *The Utilization of the Social Sciences in Policy Making in the United States* (Paris: Organization for Economic Cooperation and Development, 1980), p. 125.

15. Grasso, "Distributive Policies,"pp. 89–90.

16. Wev, "Economic Development,"p. 374.

17. United States, *Economic Report of the President Transmitted to Congress,* January 20, 1955, p. 57, and January 24, 1956, p. 61.

18. Wev, "Economic Development,"p. 375.

19. Harry W. Richardson and Joseph H. Turek, "The Scope and Limits of Federal Intervention," in Harry W. Richardson and Joseph H. Turek, eds., *Economic Prospects for the Northeast* (Philadelphia: Temple University Press, 1985), p. 211.

20. Morris L. Sweet, *Industrial Location Policy for Economic Revitalization: National and International Perspectives* (Westport: Praeger Publishers, 1981), pp. 12–17.

21. Wev, "Economic Development," p. 374.

22. United States, President's Commission on a National Agenda for the Eighties, *Urban America in the Eighties: Perspectives and Prospects and a National Agenda for the Eighties,* 1980.

Chapter 18

U.S. Regional Policy

INTRODUCTION

The United States has no explicit national policy or strategy to deal directly with long-range balanced spatial or geographical economic development. Despite its overall national prosperity, regional economies in the
United States are still highly differentiated and many have deep-rooted
economic problems that they cannot resolve themselves. National concern on the effects of globalization and an ad hoc industrial or sectoral
policy have overshadowed a comparable concern for regional development. Though the political climate may not seem favorable for instituting
an overall regional policy or program, various federal policies and programs indirectly have regional implications that should be considered.
Despite an unfavorable political climate, should there be greater interest
in devising a national regional policy or strategy?

NATURE OF REGIONS

There are significant differences in the physical character, socioeconomic status and the political makeup of regions that cause difficulty in

defining and developing a federal regional policy. Though the United States is becoming more homogeneous in terms of social and political criteria, changing economic processes, such as technology, can differentiate regions.

Regions are seen as loose geographic units smaller than the nation with some objective characteristics of homogeneity. The idea of fixed or static regions, a staple of orthodox American cultural geography, is best avoided. U.S. regions have changed in their de facto if not de jure shape—as well as in importance—over time. Regional economic development in the United States has a particular disadvantage. The federal Constitution recognizes only two levels, federal and state, while regions can involve parts of different states. Though states provide an uneven division of territory, the established pattern is unlikely to be changed. States can have more than one region while many regions are parts of more than one state. An example is New Jersey, between New York and Pennsylvania.

INTERVENTION

A fundamental aspect of debate on regional development is whether government intervention is necessary or useful. There is the contention of proponents of less government intervention that inequalities are inevitable and an individual has the responsibility to take advantage of opportunities. Regional disequilibrium is considered temporary and market forces are supposed to eventually produce balanced conditions nationally. Even among advocates of regional assistance there is a difference on the type of assistance. Should it be for investment in the economic base or in social programs?

National policies for regions have never been enthusiastically accepted in the United States. Even more so, in the climate of the 1990s, the preference is to give the states and localities responsibility for alleviating the plight of economically distressed areas. The rationale is that by devolution those most directly affected and knowledgeable about conditions will be best able to provide solutions, though not necessarily funding.[1]

On the other hand, the concept of regional policy has to embody national concern over economic disparities among geographic areas as well as maintaining economic health. In pursuit of this goal, a successful national regional policy would eliminate or mitigate these economic disparities, which would be reflected in private sector actions. Regional policy carries the connotation of restoring economic vitality and preventing decline. Compared with the United States, the European Union (as well as its individual member states) has devoted sizeable resources to regional development. Canada, though its policy has varied, has had a longstanding federal-provincial commitment to regional development.

REGIONAL POLICIES

Explicit federal regional development policies have never been strong in the United States. The proportion of direct federal expenditures for place-oriented programs is very small compared with macro, sectoral, and people-oriented expenditures. "Given the evidence on differences in regional response to national economic conditions, it may well be that macro-economic policy would in fact be implemented more effectively if it had a regional orientation."[2]

The political structure of the federal government does not easily lead to the formulation and implementation of spatial policies. The nature of the pluralist political system in the United States limits the effectiveness of spatial policies since all regions and states insist on a share of any funding. Allocations can be too small to have a significant impact.

The United States has no strong constituency or consensus on a national regional policy that has no congressional or presidential priority. This can be attributed to faith in the benefits from the automatic adjustment of market mechanisms. Past fiscal crises have reinforced the assertions that regional development programs are ineffectual. The massive tax cuts in the Reagan administration were part of a conscious strategy to create the fiscal stringency and bring about abandonment of such programs.[3] "Old, place-oriented solutions have fallen into intellectual disfavor, having been sharply criticized by academics, the popular press, and conservative and *New Democrat* pundits, who prefer people oriented polices that encourage mobility."[4]

There are doubts about the chances of instituting federal programs when greater priority is given to cutting government expenditures. The dominant political ideology is suspicion of government action, a preference for resource allocation by market forces, and hostility toward government planning. Those groups that in the past would be expected to be strong advocates of a regional policy find themselves constrained by the unfavorable climate for federal government programs as opposed to devolution to state and local levels.

MOBILITY

The question of mobility received much attention with the release of the report in 1980 at the the close of President Carter's term by the President's Commission on a National Agenda for the Eighties. Though the term "urban" was used, the report had broader spatial implications. The report provides a basis for reviewing the concept of mobility as a policy. Should a major long-term goal of federal spatial policy be retraining and relocation assistance linked to economic opportunity, wherever that opportunity might be? Should areas be allowed to decline with minimal government concern? A difference in the political climates of the 1980s and the 1990s is that there is little or no interest by the federal government for spatial economic development legislation.[5]

The 1980 commission found cities to be obsolete as mechanisms by which post-industrial society can be maintained and advanced. It warned that attempts to restore declining industrial cities to "the influential positions they held throughout the industrial era" would not only fail but would have negative effects upon efforts to revitalize the national economy. The Reagan administration reflected a continuation of these policies. Market-forced shifts in people, jobs, capital and income out of older cities and even regions should not be opposed because they raised the wealth of the entire nation. Mobility of labor and capital in the interests of efficiency should be facilitated. Workers should be encouraged to move to areas with labor needs.[6]

The assumption underlying the Reagan policy was that the United States consists of clusters of labor, maintained and reproduced through the production of social consumption goods by local states. The decisions of capital determined the location and duration of these places. In turn, profit-maximizing opportunities and competitive market pressures on firms created by technology determine the movement of capital. In such a system the public goal is to facilitate private investment decisions.[7]

Economic development programs present political problems, especially when industry relocates within the United States or there is interstate or even intrastate competition for foreign investment. For internal moves a federal policy encouraging mobility presents a political dilemma. Transmitting regions are concerned about the loss of population and political power in Congress. A higher rate of outmigration further accelerates decline through a smaller tax base and multiplier effects on local infrastructure and services. A skilled labor force can be the basis for attracting industry, but when an area is bereft of a viable work force, the likelihood of recovery is minimal. The costs of such a mobility policy to the transmitting region are high, with the break-up of family and other social relations and an age gap as the young and more employable are most likely to move. New residents may not be welcome in the receiving regions unless they bring scarce skills and new capital and do not overutilize housing and schools. Extensive movement may alter the character of a region, leaving concentrations of poor, elderly and disabled.

When high levels of unemployment prevail throughout the country, movement from a declining or depressed region to a more prosperous region does not necessarily mean there will be employment in the new region. Positive economic data do not necessarily correlate with employment opportunities for all. The decline of particular regions and the growth of others are not inevitable, nor are these events necessarily reciprocals of each other.

The concept of moving people out of declining areas could be anachronistic in terms of white-collar industries as contrasted to the growth of clusters. The service sector is not bringing people to jobs but sending out jobs to people. Computer-oriented tasks are being transmitted both domestically and worldwide to pools of cheap labor. Distances become less of an obstacle with relatively inexpensive international linkages. Thus, U.S. multinationals have set up shop for data processing and software development in Ireland. As telecommunications costs drop, incentives for location in areas with pools of labor will increase. This could mean the revival of communities with little in the way of accessibility or other advantages. The suitability and cost of the work force is increasingly the key factor in white-collar investment decisions. Assuming there is free and unimpeded flow of information, even a remote area can find itself in demand. However, this type of investment could prove to be short-lived. With alternative labor readily available throughout the world, relocation could be an everpresent phenomenon.[8]

FEDERAL ROLE

Economic growth rates and levels of economic activity vary considerably among states and regions. The search for the source of (and ascribing blame to or seeking relief from) regional economic disparities often leads to the federal government. While much of the variation is caused by private sector forces, federal tax and expenditure policies contribute to regional differences. Federal expenditures and their intentional or unintentional effects have an enormous impact on the economic vitality of regions. In periods of budget cutbacks, the effect on regional economies can be deleterious.

The concern with balanced budgets and budget deficits has reduced the share for economic development. "Given the size of the deficit and the need to reduce it, however, decisions on the future levels of the deficit should be made independently of decisions on the amount of federal spending for investment. It would be unfortunate if, in the process of cutting the deficit to increase private investment, the government reduced federal investment programs. Therefore, within an overall fiscal policy emphasizing deficit reduction, priorities should shift toward well-chosen investment programs."[9]

In the budget the long-term investment character of federal activities is not highlighted. Unlike spending for current consumption, economic development investment can generate future benefits. Differences between investment and consumption activities should be taken into account in allocating federal resources.[10]

Expenditures supporting investment could also be displayed within an investment category to provide a more complete picture of how federal resources devoted to investment benefit the economy. The term "investment" should be applied only to those initiatives, programs or activities that seem likely to increase the productive capacity of the economy.[11]

A factor is the imbalance between revenues the federal government collects from regions and the expenditures made in those regions. Through its appropriation power Congress can serve as a de facto regional development agency. Congress is subject to territorial influences that are pervasive and may override party differences. Depending on the party is in power, certain regions, without regard to need, will benefit most. Seniority in Congress can provide regional preferences. Thus, the poorest and neediest regions often do not get the preference that they could receive in a more bureaucratized, formalized and more technically oriented selection process in which objective criteria would be primary.[12]

The geographic pattern of federal tax and expenditure policies are not necessarily an explicit consideration when programs are adopted or changed. The vast bulk of federal expenditures do not have direct regional distributional objectives. Federal expenditures are motivated by a diverse set of circumstances, such as a desire to stimulate certain activities or, to a lesser extent, to assist a specific region, notably Appalachia, or those with certain characteristics, like the Economic Development Administration (EDA). Programs such as social welfare and Medicaid are directed toward individuals with low incomes regardless of geography. Social Security and Medicare are available to all those qualified. Recipients of trade adjustment assistance and unemployment insurance are tied to unemployment. There is indirect federal involvement spatially through regulation of transportation rates, support of the federal highway system, water resource programs and defense spending. Sectoral policy, tariff changes, and reductions in farm subsidies are examples of federal activities with potentially beneficial or adverse regional implications.

Environmental policy has a potential impact on the location of industry. Disaster and flood control spending is concentrated in areas with certain geographical and topographical characteristics. At times efforts have been made to direct defense spending to obtain the maximum economic or political impact.

The political system in the United States has precluded enactment of any federal regional program unless it ensured a share of benefits to each state, without necessarily giving outright preference to subnational entities most in need of assistance. In the absence of any overwhelming and widely accepted justification for preferential treatment, programs intended to aid backward regions have won passage in Congress by loosely defining eligibility and thus providing a little something to everybody. Yet diffusion minimizes any beneficial impact from the programs.

According to the 1993 Gore Report (National Performance Review), the federal government has no coherent policy for regional development and community dislocation. Instead, it offers fragments and a bureaucratic system of seven programs to assist states and localities. Major programs are the Commerce Department's EDA, HUD's Community Development Block Grant Program, and the Agriculture Department's Rural Development Administration and Rural Electrification Administration. The Defense Department, TVA and the Appalachian Regional Commission (ARC) run smaller programs. Thus, states and communities must turn to many different agencies and programs rather than to a single coordinated system. Communities find it hard to get help, and the dispersion of efforts limits overall funding.

Washington's economic and regional development activities should be reconfigured to suit its customers—states and communities. A Federal Coordinating Council for Economic Development, comprising appropriate Cabinet secretaries and agency heads, to coordinate such activities and provide a central source of information for states and localities created by the president was proposed. The council would provide a unifying framework for economic and regional development efforts, develop a governmentwide strategic plan and unified budget to support the framework, prevent duplication in the various programs, and assess appropriate funding levels for the agencies involved.[13]

The result has been a number of limited administrative improvements that in total have improved the efficiency of programs and responses to clients. Examples are the streamlining of application forms and more customer-friendly services. The Federal Coordinating Council has not been created and most recommendations have not been implemented. But a Community Empowerment Board designed to function as a venue for interagency dialogue on economic development policy and Empowerment Zone-Empowerment Community affairs has been created.[14]

A comprehensive regional development policy has to include a hierarchy of regions combining need and potential. A major deterrent to defining regions for economic policy purposes is that economic criteria and political realities do not always converge. Political boundaries may not necessarily correspond to an economic unit that could effectively implement development programs on a regionwide basis. State boundaries are the result of historical events and it is seldom that these boundaries reflect logical economic units.

An approach to selecting regional units is to use metropolitan areas and groups of nonmetropolitan counties combined into one or more areas within a state. But this fails to take into account functional relationships and recognition that some metro or nonmetro counties in one state may be functionally integrated with an area in another state. Politically it may be more feasible to designate regions that essentially lie within state jurisdictions. Treating the United States as a homogeneous area with programs that are oriented toward some average situation fail to take into account the fact that that the United States is a collection of heterogeneous regions with differing problems and opportunities. By limiting federal subsidies to distressed areas and ending these subsidies when convergence has been attained, permanent or inequitable subsidies can be eliminated. There is a problem as to how such legislation can be enacted without universal geographic coverage as well as how to devise mechanisms for determining when subsidies should be discontinued. Even though various federal programs contain restrictions, they have to be monitored closely to see that recipients of federal assistance do not use the help to encourage relocation of enterprises, particularly to growth regions.

There is a drive in the United States to shift decision-making from the federal level to the local or neighborhood level. Local government entities, though based on historic boundaries, no longer fit today's conditions, making the region a more realistic concept. Employment, shopping, entertainment and education no longer function primarily on the basis of close geographic proximity. Questions have been raised about the ability of small and medium-size cities with severe economic problems to survive. Have they outlived their functional usefulness? Should they be dissolved and incorporated into larger geographic entities? From an economic standpoint, merger or consolidation is not per se going to resolve the problems of a distressed regional economy.

Two important factors in current regional policy are globalism and technology.

GLOBALISM

Regional economies in the United States are highly vulnerable to external influences, notably globalization, from two directions: losses as investment moves outside the United States and gains from foreign direct investment. To what extent has globalization affected the location of industry and thus negated the importance of the regional component?

As companies become global in terms of ownership and markets, neither their highest priority nor their loyalty is concerned with locating production facilities in any one country or region. As globalization or internationalization continues, the question arises as to whether the emphasis in the United States on devolving economic development programs to the lowest government level is the most effective approach. The competition for foreign investment has no limits, whether interstate or between countries. The supranational organizations contain the only means for keeping the competition within bounds, and the federal government is the key player in these organizations.

An optimistic view of globalization is the contention that the world economy will enhance regional distinctiveness. It is undeniable that particular places have become less and less isolated from one another within the world economy. However, the world economy has always provided a backdrop for regional definition and interaction. Regions never did define themselves in isolation from the wider processes of economic and political interaction. Moreover, the impact of global and national processes has always been to create regional distinctiveness rather than to displace it.[15]

The regional distinctiveness has to be expressed in terms of economic differentiation. Can the private sector alone be relied upon to provide this differentiation? The loyalty of much of the private sector to particular regions or countries is weak, shifting the responsibility to certain segments of the private sector as well as the public sector.

TECHNOLOGY

Technological development is not limited to computer-based or telecommunications innovations. Impacts vary by type of innovation; firms no longer are as place-bound. Technology cannot necessarily be expected always to generate sizeable employment increases. Rather it can solidify the economic security of a region in terms of its becoming more technically advanced and competitive. It can also create new industries, such as the manufacture of computers. In terms of research and development, where the nation as a whole benefits, should regional need be a factor in guiding locational decisions unless a specific location is necessary? Preceding the end of the Cold War, federal expenditures for science and technology were largely connected to military and national security. During the Bush administration steps were taken to utilize a share of the substantial federal research and development budget for commercial purposes. The Department of Defense initiated a dual use program, the Technology Reinvestment Program, while the Department of Commerce's National Institute of Standards and Technology (NIST) initiatives were performed under the Advanced Technology Program. The Department of Energy also promoted private sector activity through its Cooperative Research and Development Agreements. Funding for these programs has been precarious.

In 1993, the Clinton administration took the view that technology is the solution to many of the nation's economic problems and the road to the future, and it proposed a major set of initiatives. In terms of the connection to and impact on states and regions, its report, *Technology for America's Economic Growth,* contained a number of minor initiatives with a regional component.[16]

Most important, the Clinton high-technology policy makes no effort to direct high-technology activity spatially. This policy can be seen as a continuation of the policy perspectives espoused by the National Commission on an Agenda for the 1980s and continued by Presidents Reagan and Bush, which held that spatial orientation should be secondary to national economic goals and that national policy should ignore "place."[17]

The Clinton policy would ignore the efforts of subnational entities to develop high-technology industry. High-technology firms on their own without government suasion or incentives tend to select locations without regard to regional needs or balanced economic development. The Clinton administration's major spatially oriented program is the Empowerment Zone program; it has a relatively small resource base and cannot have any significant impact on location for technologically oriented industries.

The needs of high-technology industry are venture capital, specialized production support services, the presence of scientists and engineers and a skilled labor force. In addition to the concern about the location of technology within the United States, there is the overlap with globalization. How can the needs of regions for technological innovation be coordinated with the practices of global firms for diffusion?

Are such programs as the Advanced Technology Program (ATP) necessary to ensure that critical capabilities continue to reside in the U.S. technology base? One viewpoint is that such programs are subsidies that put government managers in the position of picking winners and losers. If successful, such programs might cause foreign governments to increase their support of R&D, leading to a cycle of increasing technological innovation, a process that could make American firms less competitive. How long can innovation be confined to a particular firm? With multinationals, it is unlikely to be kept within the confines of a particular country.

U.S. government support for technology development has favored participation by U.S.-based firms over the affiliates of foreign firms. More often the principle of conditional national treatment has been applied legislatively that permits participation by U.S. affiliates of foreign firms only on the condition that their countries of origin extend reciprocal access for U.S. multinationals. In Europe conditional national treatment has taken the form of requiring firms to establish local R&D operations. This has in effect largely limited participation to European-based companies and a few foreign firms with R&D operations in Europe.[18]

For multinationals, R&D moves overseas much more slowly than does production, sourcing and other business activities. Production facilities often can be established quickly and moved quickly as market conditions change. By comparison, R&D facilities take a long time to set up and, once established, are difficult to move. Thus, most multinationals centralize basic research and product development in the home market, while research oriented toward customization and foreign production support is gradually conducted locally as affiliates move more deeply into local markets.

The tendency of R&D to move overseas slowly in the wake of foreign direct investment, and local production suggests an R&D life cycle. In the initial stages of overseas production, firms tend to use product and process technology developed in the home market. As overseas production units become more established, local R&D activities emerge to customize products in accordance with local market conditions and eventually to support affiliate production operations. In advanced stages, as affiliates become deeply integrated into local economies, they may undertake more substantial forms of R&D to develop products exclusively for the local market. Few firms reach this last stage. However, the degree to which R&D is centralized or decentralized often conforms to different technological and sectoral characteristics.

As with U.S. multinationals, R&D by foreign affiliates in the United States is relatively small, though growing rapidly. In total, most R&D conducted overseas by foreign affiliates is devoted to product customization for local markets or at most to the support of local production facilities.[19]

NOTES

1. For a critical view of devolution see John D. Donahue, "The Disunited States," *Atlantic Monthly* 279 (May 1997), p. 18.

2. Advisory Commission on Intergovernmental Relations, *Regional Growth Historic Perspectives* (Washington, June 1980), p. 91.

3. William Alonso, "Deindustrialization and Regional Policy" in Lloyd Rodwin and Hidehiko Sazanemi, eds., *Deindustrialization and Regional Economic Transformation* (Boston: Unwin Hyman, 1989), p. 230.

4. John Mollenkopf, "What Future for Federal Urban Policy?" *Urban Affairs Review* 30, 5 (1995), p. 658.

5. Robert Warren, "National Urban Policy and the Local State: Paradoxes of Meaning, Action and Consequences," *Urban Affairs Quarterly* 25 (June 1990), p. 548.

6. Ibid.

7. Ibid., p. 549.

8. John Parry, "Hunting Heads in the Global Village," *International Management* 45 (May 1990), pp. 52–53, and Carey Goldberg, "Mainers Say Hello Headsets, Farewell Chicken Plucking," *New York Times*, August 2, 1998, p. 20.

9. U.S. General Accounting Office, Transition Series, *Investment*, GAO/OCG-93-2TR, December 1992, p. 15.

10. Ibid., p. 17.

11. Ibid., p. 18.

12. Ann Markusen, *Regional Planning and Policy: An Essay on the American Exception* (Piscataway, N. J.: Rutgers University, Center for Urban Policy Research, 1989), Working Paper 9, p. 8.

13. The Gore Report on Reinventing Government, *Creating a Government That Works Better and Costs Less: Report of the National Performance Review* (New York: Times Books, 1993), p. 52.

14. National Academy of Public Administration, *A Path to Smarter Economic Development: Reassessing the Federal Role, prepared for the U.S. Economic Development Administration* (Washington: November 1996), p. 40.

15. Neal R. Peirce, "Regional Governance: Why? Now? How?" *University of Virginia Newsletter* 67 (June 1991), p. 4.

16. U.S. President, *Technology for America's Economic Growth: A New Direction to Build Economic Strength*, February 22, 1993.

17. Dennis C. Muniak, "Economic Development, National High Technology Policy and America's Cities," *Regional Studies* 28 (December 1994), p. 803.

18. U.S. Congress, Office of Technology Assessment, *Multinationals and the U.S. Technology Base*, OTA-ITE-612, September 1994, pp. 10–11.

19. Ibid., pp. 87–88, 151.

Chapter 19

U.S. Regional Development Programs

INTRODUCTION

The General Accounting Office (GAO) lists some 340 federal economic development programs administered by thirteen of the fourteen executive departments and numerous agencies. The term "economic development" is used in the broadest sense and only a limited number of programs have a significant spatial or regional impact. Annual core support for economic development in 1995 was $6 billion, including outlays, tax subsidies and the costs of loans and loan guarantees.[1] A second tier of assistance, $7 billion, supports worker training much of which is connected to core economic development.[2] There are some seventy-five separate economic development programs in the various independent agencies and Cabinet departments, including eighteen in the Department of Commerce.[3] Since the 1930s, a number of federal programs have had a direct spatial orientation. First from a clearly regional viewpoint was the TVA, and the latest with a spatial orientation, though below the regional level, is Empowerment Zones. The GAO was unable to find any studies "that established a strong causal linkage between a positive economic effect and an agency's economic development assistance" for The Appalachian Regional Commission (ARC), Economic Development Administration (EDA) and Tennessee Valley Authority (TVA).[4]

RECONSTRUCTION FINANCE CORPORATION (RFC)

Periodically there are calls for a federal financing instrument for public investment, such as a national development bank, using the RFC as a precedent.[5] The RFC, over its quarter-century of existence beginning in 1932, encompassed various components of a national development bank with a potential for regional economic development. A comparison can be made with the European Investment Bank.

History

The justification for the RFC's creation in the Depression was macro-economic stabilization, reduction of unemployment, price stabilization and economic growth. The RFC was created by PL 72-2, January 22, 1932, 47 Stat 5-12.[6] The organization had resources adequate to overcome weaknesses in the credit, banking and railway structures. It was not created to assist any particular industry or region. Thus, most RFC loans went to financial intermediaries and railroads because their economic revitalization would bolster the overall economy. Funding was from the sale of capital stock, borrowing, net profits and sale of assets from terminated programs. On July 21, 1932, the Emergency Relief and Construction Act (PL 72-302, 47 Stat 709-724) authorized an increase in indebtedness to $3 billion and provided up to $300 million in relief loans to state and local agencies and $1.5 billion for public works construction. With approval of the RFC and the governor of a state, a share might be made available to municipalities and other political subdivisions.[7]

Title II authorized loans for various types of self-liquidating or income-producing, self-supporting projects and enabled construction costs to be repaid within a reasonable time by tolls, rents or similar charges except taxes. Self-liquidating loans were authorized for the following purposes:

1. Projects undertaken by states, their political subdivisions or by other public agencies such as public corporations or boards and commissions.
2. Housing construction for families of low income or reconstruction of slum areas.
3. Construction, replacement or improvement of bridges, tunnels, docks, viaducts, waterworks, canals, and markets when undertaken by private limited dividend corporations and devoted to public use.
4. Protection and development of forests and other renewable natural resources when undertaken by private limited dividend corporations if regulated by a state or political subdivision of a state.
5. Construction of publicly owned bridges, the cost of which would be returned in part by means of tolls, fees, rents, or other charges, and the bal-

ance by means of taxes imposed prior to the passage of the Emergency Relief and Construction Act.[8]

Under 1938 amendments the RFC was empowered to make loans through purchase of securities or otherwise to all types of public agencies and bodies to aid in financing projects authorized under federal, state or municipal law. Loans made or securities purchased were to be "of such sound value, or so secured as reasonably to assure retirement or repayment." No statutory limits were placed on the maturity of such loans or securities.[9] The July 1953 Liquidation Act terminated lending power. Operations ceased June 30, 1954 and by 1957 nearly all remaining loans had been liquidated.

Reasons for Termination

The major argument for termination was the improvement in economic conditions after World War II.[10] Another was the contention that private financial markets allocated capital more efficiently. Critics charged that RFC was involved in political favoritism and corruption. Requirements for obtaining a loan gradually became so loose and vague that subjective case-by-case decisions were often made. Yet subjectivity has to be considered in approving unique applications. The position of the RFC relative to other federal agencies and programs was never clearly delineated; consequently there was duplication resulting in waste, confusion and internal administrative conflict.

The RFC finally encompassed varied approaches or policies, macroeconomic, industrial or sectoral, spatial and infrastructure. A legacy is its offspring: Commodity Credit Corporation, Export-Import Bank, Rural Electrification Administration, Small Business Administration and Federal National Mortgage Administration. RFC was responsible for the creation of a number of industries, including aluminum and synthetic rubber.

TENNESSEE VALLEY AUTHORITY (TVA)

In contrast to the RFC, TVA, also a product of the 1930s, had a regional focus, though it was not regarded solely as an instrument of regional development. The regional planning function was initially ignored or considered incidental.[11] Rather, a natural resource-based theory of economic development was implicit in both its legislative history and early policy. The framers anticipated that the development of the land and water resources would provide major leverage for regional economic growth, a view consistent with prevailing 1930s economic thought.[12]

President Franklin Roosevelt asked Congress to create an agency to plan for the use, development and conservation of the Tennessee River Valley; on May 18, 1933, the TVA Act of 1933 created the TVA as a federally owned corporation, covering a number of loosely coordinated programs, largely regional.[13] TVA was not only to produce electric power but to promote non-power-related activities, flood control, navigation improvement, soil replenishment and improvement of agricultural practices. The 80,000 square mile area covers seven states, most of Tennessee and parts of Alabama, Georgia, Kentucky, Mississippi, North Carolina and Virginia.

The area served was possibly the poorest part of the poorest region in the nation and was generally not favored politically. "In short, TVA had unprecedented opportunities for planning and developing one of the most neglected regions in the eastern part of the U.S., a region in which unemployment was endemic, in which the cash income per family in many instances averaged less than $100 per year, in which the mountains had been slashed and forests burned, in which a barter economy, even in a city like Knoxville, was becoming widespread, in which spring flooding was taken for granted."[14]

TVA had a national defense role; it operated the government nitrate and other properties at Muscle Shoals in northern Alabama. Construction for the Muscle Shoals dams started during World War I but never was completed. Chemicals for fertilizer and defense were manufactured; recreational facilities constructed; experimental farms established to test crops, fertilizers and agricultural methods; roads, bridges and model cities were built during the Depression. By 1940, TVA was the largest producer of electric power in the country. TVA is multisectoral in scope and multistate in area coverage, managing two programs: a power system designed to be self-supporting and a set of five nonpower programs supported by congressional appropriations.

Through the nonpower programs, TVA supports an environmental research center, an economic development program, a recreation and environmental education area, and land and water management programs. The environmental research center carries out research in air quality, waste treatment and watershed protection and supports demonstration studies on preventing surface and groundwater contamination.

The economic development program supports strategic and quality planning, business infrastructure development, work-force development, electronic access to a variety of information sources, demographic and economic databases, networks, forecasts and models, industrial site design and planning and project assessment.

The Land Between the Lakes program provides a 170,000-acre outdoor recreation and environmental education facility for the public. The land management program supports the development of a shoreline development and protection strategy, manages 160 public recreation areas and supports environmental conservation. The water management program manages fifty dams on the Tennessee River and its tributaries, controls flooding along the river, manages the navigation system, supports the development of aeration technologies and monitors the river's water quality.

Evaluation

Though TVA was intended to be more than merely a source of electric power, its predominant role has become that of a utility.[15] But the TVA has had a vital impact on the region's economic development. An early evaluation found that it was particularly effective in supplying electric power, flood control and navigation services and fertilizer research, development and education. It suggested that TVA has been less successful or at least less consistent in its role as supplier of other services— industrial location assistance, community development assistance, health and education services and others.[16]

The precarious financial condition of TVA limits an expansion in regional economic development. The GAO has proposed strengthened external control as a solution for the financial problems, such as a regional planning council with representatives from key regional and industrial stakeholders.[17]

A 1997 Congressional Budget Office (CBO) review looked into the merits of continuing federal support of TVA.[18] It concluded that many research projects benefit the private sector while other projects should be merged with those of the Department of Agriculture or Environmental Protection Agency. The Environmental Research Center is uniquely qualified to develop solutions that reflect the environmental, economic and social needs of a large region. Proposed savings from withdrawing federal funding for the programs in recreation, environmental education and local economic development are based on the argument that federal spending for these programs is mostly regional. Funding thus should come from state or local governments or fees levied on private beneficiaries.

Supporters of continued federal funding argue that its removal would damage TVA's ability to meet its federally mandated mission. That mission includes aiding the proper use, conservation and development of the region's natural resources, as well as promoting its economic well-being. TVA is uniquely positioned to develop solutions that reflect a large region's environmental, economic and social needs.

In fiscal year 1997, TVA received federal appropriations for area and regional development of $106 million and revenues from fees.[19] TVA had obligations for economic development of $17 million.

AREA REDEVELOPMENT ADMINISTRATION (ARA)

Following the 1949 and 1955 recessions, each characterized by high unemployment in particular regions, Illinois Senator Paul Douglas led attempts to create a regional development program to assist depressed older, mostly northern, urban areas. With promises made in the 1960 campaign, President John Kennedy wanted special attention for the coal mining areas of West Virginia and eastern Kentucky and enactment of the legislation. By modifying the bill to include both rural and urban areas, Douglas was successful in passing the Area Redevelopment Act of 1961 (Public Law 87-61), the first comprehensive effort to promote economic development directly in lagging areas. It established the Area Redevelopment Administration (ARA), which was placed in the Department of Commerce, but which was short-lived.[20] It lasted until 1965.

The ARA was a significant departure from the federal government's laissez-faire policy. Loans and grants were made for infrastructure or investment directly in enterprises that would locate in depressed areas.[21] The principal impediment to the development of depressed areas, the lack of venture capital, would be addressed with industrial and commercial loans.[22] Funding was available for job training.

Counties with persistent unemployment qualified for aid by producing an Overall Economic Development Plan (OEDP) and providing 50% matching funds. Urban places with established planning teams were more able than rural places to provide matching funds. These criteria were far from stringent since one-third of all counties, covering about one-fifth of the population, qualified. In any state where no area qualified for aid, an appropriate economic development area could be designated based on relative data, such as low incomes, high unemployment or federal assistance rates.[23]

ARA had broad administrative authority to define eligible regions or areas and determine eligibility for aid.[24] The definition of regions was a critical issue for speedy action, which of necessity precluded much background research. By 1963, over a thousand areas had been designated, with at least one in every state. They ranged

---

Table 19.1
Tennessee Valley Authority Appropriations by Program Activity, 1997–1999 (millions of dollars)

	Actual	Estimated	
	1997	1998	1999
Economic development	17	3	1

Source: U.S. Executive Office of the President, *Budget of the U.S. Government for Fiscal Year 1999, Appendix* (Washington, D.C.: Government Printing Office, 1998), p. 1141.

from extreme rural areas with sparse population and few employment opportunities to large urban areas, like Pittsburgh and Detroit, with chronic labor surpluses.[25]

Evaluation

Sums available were so small that, in combination with a large number of qualifying areas, their impact was minimal. Special consideration was not given to areas of high growth potential even in depressed regions and there was excessive emphasis on sewer and water systems. ARA also failed to coordinate its projects with states.[26] Effective planning was hindered by the county-by-county approach, which failed to take account of broader geographic economic interdependencies; poor local development plans upon which ARA depended in assessing the feasibility of projects; and congressional pressures to designate a large number of eligible areas. The program was further hampered by the poor performance of the national economy.[27]

Despite the location of many declining industrial areas in natural resource-exporting regions, there was no consideration of sectors such as coal. The mandate was for troubled communities on their own to find solutions that could involve competing with other communities.[28] The program could have been more successful if an overall strategy had been developed that would have ultimately forced ARA to choose between backward and declining areas and would have broken the alliance behind the legislation. More resources would have improved the quality of technical assistance in communities but would not have resolved problems.[29] "The program, under any circumstances, was really very marginal, and never represented a large commitment. It provided marginal money to marginally alter the situation of some counties, but never confronted the basic competitive forces that produced their problems. It represented, fundamentally, a little largess for the country's poorer areas, but it was little more than gravy."[30]

Achievements were limited; the number of direct jobs created was estimated at only 71,400. Assuming a ratio of two indirect jobs for every three, direct ARA projects helped to provide about 118,000 new jobs between 1961 and 1965.[31] ARA did establish the principle of federal responsibility for promoting the economic development of depressed areas.[32] As a precedent for legitimizing comprehensive regional aid and demonstrating that putting public funds into regions of low incomes and chronic unemployment was both socially acceptable and politically beneficial, the ARA was a significant success.[33] ARA was legislatively recast and expanded in 1965 with EDA.

ECONOMIC DEVELOPMENT ADMINISTRATION (EDA)

One of the few national economic development programs extant is the EDA in the Department of Commerce, administering programs authorized by the Public Works and Economic Development Act of 1965 (PL 89-136) as amended.

EDA and ARA

EDA was created to correct ARA deficiencies but not to innovate and thereby generate strong public and congressional opposition. EDA was given a five-fold budget increase, with greater emphasis on grants than loans. Major human resource programs remained the domain of other federal agencies. Public works grants and loans to improve infrastructures and encourage needed private sector investment were continued.[34] Loans were again authorized on favorable terms for businesses with difficulty obtaining private financing. Technical assistance grants were retained to promote efficient development project selection in target areas, and funds were made available for research, largely responsible for the growth in regional planning and economics within universities during the late 1960s and early 1970s.

EDA emphasized aid to place rather than people and alleviation of poverty.[35] The issue of outmigration was avoided. By providing resources for public works construction, economic development planning at the local level and capital subsidies for industry, Congress hoped to encourage job-producing private investment in areas with lagging growth rates and high levels of structural unemployment.

A key aspect of the act is the restraints on financial assistance, Title 42, §3142, U.S. Code Annotated, later adapted in the Enterprise Zone/ Enterprise Community (EZ/EC) legislation:

Such financial assistance shall not be extended to assist establishments relocating from one area to another or to assist subcontractors whose purpose is to divest, or whose economic success is dependent upon divesting, other contractors or subcontractors of contracts theretofore customarily performed by them: *Provided, however,* That such limitation shall not be construed to prohibit assistance for the expansion of an existing business entity through the establishment of a new branch, affiliate, or subsidiary of such entity if the Secretary finds that the establishment of such branch, affiliate, or subsidiary will not result in an increase in unemployment of the area of original location or in any other areas where such entity conducts business operations, unless the Secretary has reason to believe that such branch, affiliate, or subsidiary is being established with the intention of closing down the operations of the existing business entity in the area of its original location or in any other area where it conducts such operations.

Eligibility

The legislation was not initially intended for distressed urban areas; its focus was on rural areas and small towns. Eligibility criteria made it difficult for cities to qualify. The Bureau of the Budget took a skeptical view of any EDA involvement in large cities.[36] During its first decade, EDA functioned primarily as a rural development agency, providing only 27% of public works and development funds to cities with populations over 50,000.[37]

During the 1967–1969 period, eligibility requirements for cities were relaxed and urban assistance was left to HUD, the poverty programs and other urban-oriented programs. A principal innovation was the provision for more comprehensive geographic planning areas and greater local participation in the planning process. Initially the best-prepared applications received funding, which favored relatively well-off communities; this was followed by an explicit shift to "worst first" strategy favoring severely distressed areas. By the mid-1960s, to prevent riots and destruction the central city rather than the isolated rural community or declining industrial area was the center of attention.

Changes

The Nixon administration supported the principle of federal decentralization and massive general revenue sharing was substituted for area-specific programs. During the 1970s, EDA was weakened by a transfer of powers to states under revenue sharing and the loss of authority for rural development to the Department of Agriculture (Rural Development Act of 1972).[38]

The Reagan administration lodged three complaints against EDA and similar initiatives:

- Lack of targeting: The original purpose of EDA was to provide special assistance to distressed areas, but more than 80% of the nation became eligible.
- Lack of effectiveness: Little evidence was found that these programs induced job development that would not have occurred anyway. To the extent that jobs were induced in distressed localities, they were induced largely at the expense of jobs located elsewhere. That is, jobs were redistributed but not created.
- Hindrance to efficiency: To the extent that programs influenced location of firms and jobs, they reduced the nation's productivity by inducing firms to locate where they could not be most efficient.

Furthermore, the Reagan administration asserted that such programs are superfluous in an environment of general prosperity. Improvements in overall economic conditions gave more hope to distressed areas than do programs that should be ended, it argued.[39] The EDA was also charged in particular with being ineffective and wasteful. Critics in and out of the administration argued that a large amount of money was lost from delinquent loans, that it had not succeeded in advancing the development of chronically depressed areas and wasted money because it promoted development that would have occurred anyway. Even when net jobs were created, they allegedly cost the government too much money.[40]

Though the Reagan administration failed to abolish EDA, Congress sharply reduced the budget, and some semblance of EDA remained. The budget allocation in the last year of the Carter term was $625 million, signifying the further demise of the federal role.[41]

In the Clinton administration, Secretary of Commerce Ron Brown resisted proposals in Vice President Gore's National Performance Review that the EDA be folded into a new, independent, economic development corporation including the Small Business Administration (SBA) and other development programs from the departments of Labor, Agriculture and Defense. Gore's group, in view of Brown's opposition, recommended a weak coordinating council for the different agencies.[42]

In 1995, congressional Republicans sought to eliminate the Department of Commerce and amend EDA by reorganizing it along the lines of the Appalachian Regional Commission (ARC), a federal entity run as a partnership between Washington and the thirteen ARC states. They promoted the ARC model as a virtually bureaucratic-free way of funneling power and money to the states. The ARC has some ten federally paid employees in Washington along with a supplemental staff provided by the states. Some Republicans contended EDA could be reorganized into regional commissions similar to those that existed from 1965 to 1981.[43]

Future

The EDA's future is not promising. In the past it has been rescued by congressional action just as it was on the verge of extinction. Congress members find the agency useful in aiding their constituencies. For 1995, appropriations totaled $440 million. Subsequently the Clinton administration reduced the funding, perhaps effectively ending EDA.

Table 19.2
Economic Development Administration Total Federal Funds Budget Authority and Outlays, 1997–2003 (millions of dollars)

	Actual	Estimated					
	1997	1998	1999	2000	2001	2002	2003
Budget Authority	423	367	398	368	335	306	306
Outlays	410	440	429	415	384	363	347

Source: U.S. Executive Office of the President, *Budget of the U.S. Government for Fiscal Year 1999, Analytical Perspectives* (Washington, D.C.: Government Printing Office, 1998), p. 420.

EDA has seven sparsely funded programs designed to meet its objectives:

Table 19.3

Economic Development Administration Obligations by Program Activity, 1997–1999 (millions of dollars)

	Actual	Estimated	
	1996	1997	1998
Planning Grants	24	24	24
Technical Assistance Grants	10	9	9
Public Works Grants	165	178	160
Economic Adjustment Grants	31	30	79
Research and Evaluation	1	1	1
Defense Economic Conversion	90	89	85
Trade Adjustment Assistance	9	9	10
	330	340	368

Source: U.S. Executive Office of the President, *Budget of the U.S. Government for Fiscal Year 1999, Analytical Perspectives* (Washington, D.C.: Government Printing Office, 1998), p. 188.

Evaluation

The EDA's importance is its role as one of the few federal programs with a direct spatial economic development component. The poorly funded quasi-regional or quasi-sectoral program has never been a key element in a broad national economic strategy. EDA is a small unit in the Department of Commerce, employs a few hundred people and gives out some $300 million to $400 million annually in grants and loans to state and local governments. The limited funding in relation to the large number of eligible areas results in a wide dispersal of funds in relatively small amounts. A minuscule amount of assistance without additional public and private resources is unlikely to result in a meaningful increase in economic activity.

A criticism is that federal assistance should not be provided for activities whose benefits are primarily local. EDA has been criticized for substituting federal credit for private credit and facilitating the relocation of businesses from one distressed area to another through competition among communities for federal funds. Since local governments do not incorporate this minimal aid in their budget plans, eliminating funding would not impose unexpected hardships on communities.[44]

EDA activities bear little resemblance to a coordinated regional development focus and strategy. Though EDA officials have been aware that a logical strategy is a basic prerequisite to any successful attack on the problems of lagging regions, the EDA was never able to implement any consistent strategy or set of strategies. To a large extent this could be attributed to Congress rather than to the EDA. Congress increasingly gave EDA too many responsibilities that had little to do with long-term economic development, and the designation criteria became too broad. The agency has been especially vulnerable to congressional log-rolling whereby legislators manipulate aid formulae to ensure that their districts receive a share of expenditures of a federal aid programs.[45]

The National Council for Urban Economic Development contends that a disproportionate amount of EDA funding has been allocated to rural economic development. This is the result of the overwhelming number of key congress members on the Public Works Committee who come from rural districts.[46]

REGIONAL COMMISSIONS

What might have been a critical turning point for the institutionalization of regional planning never came to fruition. Early in the 1960s, federal aid programs for highways, mass transit, and open space required metropolitan planning as a precondition for obtaining federal action grants. The TVA example helped establish the philosophical basis for passage of the ARC and Title V Regional Commissions in 1965.

A landmark year, 1965, was crucial in terms of the potential for both metropolitan and multistate regionalism; legislation was enacted that could have dramatically changed the governmental structure of the United States by establishing a national system of substate regions between local governments and states as well as multistate regions between the states and the federal government. These regional entities were not really governments, but rather intergovernmental mechanisms designed to fill gaps between existing levels, facilitate the work of the federal, state and local governments and guide the use of implementation powers without creating a fourth level of government.

Title V of the Public Works and Economic Development Act of 1965 (PL89-136 as amended) empowered the president to create multistate commissions with funds for projects to address common economic development issues. The Secretary of Commerce was given designation and funding authority with state cooperation. Once a region was designated, the relevant states participated in a regional commission patterned at least superficially after that provided for Appalachia. The commissions were to serve lagging regions by sponsoring economic development programs designed to move their economies toward the national level.

The term "regional commission" was also applied to smaller areas encompassing metropolitan areas of large cities. These metropolitan coordinating units were commonly termed Councils of Government (COGs) and had different bases than the larger Title V Regional Commissions extending over several states. Some 500 COGs remain in response to the needs of local governments as a heritage of the Title V Commissions.[47]

Title V Commissions were established by the president upon request of the states involved. Though Title V Commissions were created so that groups of states could work together for economic development, they never had the advantages of a range of programs, independence or finances. The Title V Regional Commissions did not achieve any great success before being discontinued in 1981. Five Title II River Basin Commissions (Water Resources Planning Acts of 1962 and 1965), some 150 generally single-purpose regional interstate compacts and ten Federal Regional Councils were also started.[48]

Whereas TVA and ARC boundaries are established specifically and explicitly by federal law, Title V boundaries were first requested by the states and then approved by the federal government. Boundaries had no necessary relationship to multistate statistical analysis regions established by the Census Bureau or Bureau of Economic Analysis. Governors of member states served on a commission with equal status to that of the presidentially appointed federal co-chairman to coordinate federal programs in the respective regions.[49]

The largest share of the Title V funds was used to supplement the federal share for a range of construction projects, such as industrial parks, sewer and water facilities, access roads, airports and vocational schools. Though the Commissions could cover total project costs, they preferred to supplement federal funds rather than replace them. The Commissions, with approval from the secretary of commerce, could also use funds for planning, studies, demonstration projects and training programs. The 1980 budget request was $74 million.[50]

Evaluation

The Title V Commissions were poorly funded. The final three commissions established in 1979 never were funded or activated. No articulated national policy allowed the regions to give context to their plans. Allocation of resources to create jobs or deal with unemployment was minimal and often in competition with those of federal agencies. Congress preferred the direct political feedback from initiating public works projects to the concealed benefits and loss of spending control in block grants to commissions. Nevertheless, Regional Commissions had merits. Apart from data banks, research reports and recommendations, the commissions acted as valuable discussion forums, contributing to a sense of regional identity with which to face major economic and social problems transcending state boundaries.[51]

The commissions are still used as models, such as a replacement for EDA. The Intermodal Surface Transportation Efficiency Act of 1991 (ISTEA) revived the largely moribund metropolitan planning organizations (MPOs). The act required MPOs to set priorities and balance urban and suburban interests, choose among transit and road investments and reconcile mobility with clean air goals. The ability of MPOs to grow into their new role is complicated by confusion over delineation of responsibility, especially in regard to existing state agencies. The law gave some of the power over federal highway funds that had been traditionally held by state departments of transportation to MPOs. Renewal of this provision is questionable even if ISTEA is reauthorized.[52]

Are the ISTEAs a model that can be further applied? Many of the 137 MPOs have developed new and effective administrative capabilities, institutional relationships and methods for performing their new roles. The results of ISTEAs have been to foster increased interstate, state and regional cooperation in transportation planning and decision-making.[53]

APPALACHIAN REGIONAL COMMISSION (ARC)

For almost a century, Appalachian residents lived in a self-sufficient culture and economy with minimal economic activity. As the natural resources base changed, there was an economic fallout with the loss of timber, strip-mining for coal and the water runoff from mined areas leading to contamination and erosion of the land and a high rate of emigration. Agriculture became even more marginal. A smaller share of the profits earned in the region was retained. Low incomes and high unemployment were accompanied by minimal levels of education, health and housing, among the worst nationally.

Overdependence on a single industry and lack of modern infrastructure were common features. The northern part was a major base of the steel industry; the central part was coal based. The problem behind Appalachia's unemployment was not simply an underdeveloped resource potential and lack of a diversified or ample industrial base. There was no labor force with ready aptitudes or diverse skills. A lack of educational resources resulted in a low level of functional literacy, impeding retraining.[54]

The 1960 West Virginia presidential primary focused national attention on long-standing problems of distressed regions such as Appalachia. The Conference of Appalachian Governors wanted an institutional framework to attack common problems of a single region. The ARA program did not meet the special needs of Appalachia and ARA was reluctant to take on the responsibilities for a new Appalachian program.[55]

President Lyndon Johnson signed the Appalachian Regional Development Act (ARDA) of 1965 in memory of assassinated President Kennedy. ARDA established the ARC, a joint federal-state regional development agency based in Washington, serving a thirteen-state region with 399 counties, in Alabama, Georgia, Kentucky, Maryland, Mississippi, New York, North Carolina, Ohio, Pennsylvania, South Carolina, Tennessee, Virginia and all of West Virginia, an area of 195,000 square miles.[56] In 1994, the Appalachian counties had a population of 21.9 million, or 8.8% of the 1990 U.S. population of 248.8 million.

Programs

ARC programs fall into two broad categories: highway and non-highway. The highway program seeks to improve accessibility to the region, reduce highway transportation costs to and within Appalachia and provide highway transportation facilities to accelerate the overall development of the region. The program's goal is to complete a 3,025-mile corridor highway system. Funds for completion will come from the Highway Trust Fund.

The non-highway programs are directed to area development, local development support and technical assistance. The area development program includes three types of activities: physical development, such as basic infrastructure and housing; human development, such as education, child care and health care; and business development, such as strategic planning, tourism and small-business development.

ARC is not a federal agency per se but a cooperative federal-state partnership. The commission consists of the governor of each participating state (or governor's representative) and a federal co-chairman named by the president and confirmed by the Senate and who has one-half the votes on the commission. A co-chairman is selected by the thirteen governors, who have the other half of the votes. ARC is subdivided into regional, state and local development districts. At the regional level, ARC assesses Appalachia's future role in the national economy, its needs in terms of regional public facilities (e.g., highways and airports), and matters related to the socioeconomic well-being of the population. At the state level, ARC identifies specific areas where long-term investment might stimulate growth and development. On a local level, ARC is organized along multicounty lines, which provides a mechanism for citizen participation. Governors act collectively and individually to initiate and approve projects within their respective states. The commission distributes funds competitively, based on such factors as the growth potential, per capita income and rate of unemployment, the financial resources of the state and locality, the prospective long-term effectiveness of the project, and degree of private sector involvement.

Initially, the Reagan administration proposed elimination of funding, except for the portion set aside for highways, to be transferred to the U.S. Department of Transportation. The response from Congress and program recipients was strong, and a relatively low level of funding has kept the ARC afloat.

Table 19.4
Appalachian Regional Commission Budget Authority and Outlays, 1997–2003 (millions of dollars)

	Actual	Estimated					
	1997	1998	1999	2000	2001	2002	2003
Budget authority	161	171	192	92	92	90	92
Outlays	241	166	185	152	120	117	99

Source: U.S. Executive Office of the President, *Budget of the U.S. Government for Fiscal Year 1998, Analytical Perspectives* (Washington, D.C.: Government Printing Office, 1998), p. 553.

In terms of program activity, the highway system has been the major beneficiary of federal funding:

Table 19.5
Appalachian Regional Commission Obligations by Program Activity, 1997–1999 (millions of dollars)

	Actual	Estimated	
	1997	1998	1999
Highway system	99	144	a/
Area development	61	105	
Local development district and technical assistance	6	6	6

a/ Funding will come from the Highway Assistance Trust Fund.

Source: U.S. Executive Office of the President, *Budget of the U.S. Government for Fiscal Year 1999, Appendix* (Washington, D.C.: Government Printing Office, 1998), p. 1033.

In 1995 the commission adopted initiatives to reflect a changed environment. The Internationalization of the Economy initiative is concerned with overcoming the historic isolation of rural Appalachian businesses from international markets. The Telecommunications initiative is designed to ensure the availability and access to the Information Highway. The Leadership and Civic Development initiative has the goal of creating a foundation of civic institutions and local leadership, enabling communities to work cooperatively to resolve local problems and foster economic development.

Evaluation

Although the focus was to be the region, ARC almost exclusively emphasized development of specific local areas. Instead of a regional plan defining objectives of the states and a strategy of growth, each state prepared plans that together substituted for a regional plan.

The only common characteristics were topography and poverty. The region, hundreds of miles from southern New York to Alabama, has large cities, heavy industries, rural settlements and so defined has no economic meaning. From the inception it included declining industrial areas and backward rural areas. "Thus, the Appalachian Region simply reproduces on a smaller scale the national dilemma of regenerating mature areas while promoting growth in rural communities. Moreover, within each of these economic regions one finds areas responsive to several different metropolitan growth centers, thereby fragmenting the Appalachian Region even further. The region could never serve as a focus for joint planning, but only as a means of raising funds to be distributed to the States and communities."[57]

The ARC never had an overall plan for the economic development of the region. It is difficult to see how such a plan could have been prepared given the constitutional role of each state with a variable political stance and new governors every few years. It provides more of a process than a plan to deliver grant aid to rural localities in particular and one that links levels of local, state and federal government through both bottom-up and top-down attempts to develop local resources, human and physical.[58]

The CBO evaluation of ARC found both favorable and unfavorable aspects.[59] Those in favor of termination contend that ARC-supported programs duplicate activities of other federal agencies such as the Transportation Department's highways program and HUD's Community Development Block Grant program. Resources are allocated to poor rural communities, yet they are no worse off than many outside Appalachia and thus no more deserving of special federal attention.

Nevertheless eliminating federal funding would reduce economic development activities in the region; fiscal distress of some states and localities could preclude their offsetting this loss.

ARC is specially popular with governors because: (1) funds are relatively predictable; (2) projects are consistent with their state's development needs, having been selected according to criteria set by governors and not in Washington; (3) state administration of the program gives governors valuable project selection oversight, relatively free of federal intervention.

The Clinton administration's 1999 budget proposal would apply the ARC federal-state partnership economic development model to seven states in the lower Mississippi Delta region. The Delta Regional Commission (DRC) would be established to assist the region's economic development. For 1999, funding of $26 million would be provided. DRC and ARC would share a common staff.[60]

ENTERPRISE/EMPOWERMENT ZONES (EZs)

Background

Enterprise or empowerment zones (EZs) represent one of the few specifically spatially targeted federal programs for distressed areas. EZs are geographically defined economically distressed areas, designated for preferential governmental treatment to promote investment and job creation and designed to increase attractiveness to businesses. Zones contain a minimum population and have certain eligibility criteria, such as unemployment or poverty. Incentives to businesses that hire employees or invest within enterprise zones can be substantial. Improving conditions for zone residents is a higher priority than improving conditions for residents of the surrounding region.[61]

Origins

Origins of EZs go back to Britain, with Peter Hall's 1970s proposal for small selected areas of inner cities to be given a wide range of initiatives, tax reduction and minimal government controls to stimulate firm development and job creation. It quickly became a favorite of Prime Minister Margaret Thatcher.

The Conservative government of Britain introduced enterprise zones in over twenty cities based on the premise that economic development was prevented by bureaucratic city planning and high local taxation imposed by Labor politicians. If physical and financial controls in specific areas of cities were eliminated, enterprise, investment and jobs would be created. Land-use controls and occupational safety regulations were relaxed. Even more important, firms locating in the zones were given exemption from local property taxes for ten years and 100 percent capital allowances on commercial and industrial buildings.[62]

Zones had mixed results without validating the government views on urban regeneration. Twenty thousand jobs were created but the most successful were those with greatest public rather than private sector investment. Also 80 percent of the jobs created were not new but transferred to take advantage of the tax breaks, and these created few new opportunities. As the program cost 180 million pounds in the first five years, the jobs created were expensive and highly subsidized. In light of these criticisms the British government announced in 1988 that no new zones would be created. The government contended that enterprise zones had reached the goals and were no longer necessary.[63]

The British experience did not deter U.S. proponents. Enterprise zones became a much discussed instrument for economic development. Freed-up entrepreneurial capitalism would eliminate urban distress, create jobs and competitive products and result in industrious communities. Government intrusion or involvement in the economic life of inner cities was the basis of urban distress and onerous taxation reduced the financial stimulus to invest. A key to recovery was the fostering of small businesses.[64]

State Enterprise Zones

States and localities took the initiative in setting up zones, some to take advantage of the anticipated federal legislation. States converted existing statutes and programs to anything that could be labeled enterprise zones. In 1995, thirty-five had active programs.[65] States approved far more zones than made economic sense; Louisiana created 473 zones. Incentives became available without recipient businesses making investment and employment commitments.[66] The highly residential nature of some designated areas conflicted with industry needs for cleared sites. Many zones were ambiguous about whether their mission was one of economic development or urban revitalization.[67]

HUD released figures indicating that state programs generated 600,000 jobs and more than $40 billion of business investment in depressed areas. Even proponents of enterprise zones contend that these figures are pretty much fantasy. State EZs do not function in isolation; rather they are components of a much more sizeable economic development structure that encompasses a range of programs in addition to those authorized by the EZ. Though jobs are created in a zone they are not necessarily jobs created by the existence of the zone. It is not simple to distinguish changes for which the zone has been the catalyst.[68]

A GAO analysis of the Maryland enterprise zone program could not show any employment growth demonstrably attributable to the incentives. "Therefore, although these offsets are theoretically possible we could not confirm them empirically. We found neither offsets to program costs nor reductions in welfare dependence among enterprise zone workers. Also, we found that the tax incentives and other inducements typically offered by government to encourage economic development were not seen by firms as especially important factors in their location decisions."[69]

EMPOWERMENT ZONES/ENTERPRISE COMMUNITIES (EZs/ECs)

Congressman Kemp sold the concept to President Reagan that tax breaks to business and reducing regulation would be cheaper and less bureaucratic than maintaining grant programs along the lines of EDA. Enterprise zones were popular politically since they did not involve new spending but called for tax cuts. A minimal federal enterprise zone program was incorporated in the 1987 Housing and Community Development Act as Title VII. Signed by Reagan on December 5, 1988, it involved coordination and expedited processing of existing programs.

Empowerment zones became the principal urban initiative of the Clinton administration overlooking regional initiatives. Legislation for empowerment zones (EZs) and enterprise communities (ECs) was included in the Budget Reconciliation Act of 1993, PL 103-66, Section 13301, approved August 10, 1993. It was not as broad in scope as its adherents wanted; government deregulation is not the key component.

Summary of the Empowerment Zone/Enterprise Communities Program
• 9 empowerment zones: 6 urban, 3 rural
• 95 enterprise communities: 65 urban, 30 rural
• HUD designates urban zones and communities
• Agriculture Department designates rural zones and communities
• Maximum 10-year designation periods

Pervasive poverty, unemployment and general distress

Maximum population of nominated areas (no minimum requirement)
• 200,000 for jurisdiction of 2 million or more
• 10% of population for a jurisdiction between 500,000 and 2 million
• 50,000 for a jurisdiction of up to 500,000
• 30,000 for rural zones

Maximum size and boundary requirements
• Urban zone
    20 square miles
    located entirely in no more than two contiguous states
    either a continuous boundary or no more than three non-contiguous parcels
        that each have a continuous boundary
• Rural zone
    1,000 square miles
    located entirely within no more than three contiguous states
    if in more than one state, must have one continuous boundary
    if in one state, can have up to three noncontiguous parcels with one continuous boundary for each parcel

Legislation includes approximately $2.5 billion in new tax incentives. ECs are eligible for new tax-exempt facility bonds for certain private business activities. Businesses in EZs will also be afforded an employer wage credit of up to $3,000 per year per employee for wages and training expenses for employees who are zone residents. And zone businesses will be afforded an additional Section 179 expensing deduction under the internal revenue code of up to $20,000 (for an annual total of up to $37,500). In addition, although they are not limited to EZs or ECs, individual investors are eligible for a 50% exclusion of capital gains for investments in certain small businesses.

Included was $1 billion in flexible social service block grant funds for promoting economic self-sufficiency. Designated areas receive federal grant funds and substantial tax benefits and access to other federal programs. An enterprise community can receive approximately $3 million in EZ/EC–social service block grant funds. An empowerment zone can be awarded up to $40 million for each rural zone and up to $100 million for each urban zone in the empowerment zone.

Urban empowerment zones are eligible for a state pass-through of $100 million for each zone, along with a package of targeted tax assistance (including wage credits and use of tax-exempt bond financing) and limited pledges of federal regulatory relief. Urban ECs receive a much smaller package involving $3 million each in social service block grants and use of tax-exempt facility bonds.

The EZ/EC initiative contains new funding estimated at some $1 billion annually, the bulk for the nine empowerment zones. The resource base is heavily dependent on a shift of ongoing program funding. EZ/EC areas receive preference in the competition for federal grant funds in related economic, physical, environmental, public safety and human resource areas. In this respect the program of interagency cooperation resembles the 1960s Model Cities program. The limited funding may not be adequate for depressed urban areas. For second-tier ECs, resources are even more limited.

Contrary to earlier proposals, for which relief of government statutes and regulations was a key component, this legislation alerts applicants not to anticipate receiving waivers or changes in federal statutes and regulations.[70] The legislation differed from earlier proposals by not giving tax breaks for numerous areas; the lion's share of the $3.5 billion in tax incentives and grants goes to just six cities and three rural areas. Instead of the proposed sweeping capital gains tax relief, the main benefit is wage credits for businesses in the zones, but sufficient profit is required to take advantage of the wage credits.

Patterned after the EDA provision, Section 1391(F) similarly contains limits on assistance to businesses for relocation.

Evaluation

Predominantly residential areas are not ideal for industry, yet a basis for designation is the number of eligible residents. There is limited financing for basic infrastructure. Many target areas contain aging multistory facilities poorly suited for modern industrial operations. Narrow streets make it difficult for freight-carrying trucks. EZs do not directly address the conditions conducive to doing business in the zone.[71] The program is based on the assumption that inner-city areas can best turn themselves around by empowering grass-roots efforts and the federal role is in supporting rather than displacing these efforts.[72] This is an instrument of limited community revitalization rather than metropolitan or regional revitalization. Economic development can be futile unless carried out within a framework of actions designed to break down political boundaries.

Zenia Kotval and John Mullin contend that all industry is regional and the concept of jobs locally for residents has lost its validity and is less likely today. Support for industrial expansion in the county or region merits support. The concept of well-planned, large scale industrial clusters located outside established communities has far greater merit than local, small-scale industrial parks. Workers may not prefer to have industrial uses within their communities.[73] A strong proponent of the cluster concept avers that the most exciting prospects for the future of inner-city economic development lie in capitalizing on nearby regional clusters.[74] A crucial ingredient is a metropolitan or regional transportation system.

Merely locating employment close to low-income residents does not guarantee that they will be hired. Unless there is a qualified work force, meaningful local hiring requirements or tight labor markets, employers will feel free to hire outside the zone.[75] Growth industries are no longer labor-intensive. Those living just outside the zone and otherwise eligible could be justifiably resentful for zone residents being given preference. Relying on the growth of small businesses in the zones can be a long and hazardous strategy.[76]

If the zone is located in a declining region, resolving the region's problems should have priority over assistance to a zone within the region. The case for enterprise zones is more convincing as a means of equalizing economic development within regions than as an instrument for combating interregional shifts. Enterprise zones could be most effective in dealing with pockets of stagnation in rapidly growing regions.

Incentives

A growing body of literature affirms that business and industry today are less sensitive to the kinds of tax and other financial incentives provided by the zones. Enterprise zones cannot recreate through tax expenditures the economic dynamics that brought firms to specific urban/rural locations in the past.[77] The effect of the credits is modest and does not compensate for myriad more crucial influences on investment and location decisions. Declining regions would benefit from policies or programs that improve physical and social infrastructure as well as narrowing interregional cost differentials while giving entrepreneurs considerable leeway in deciding where in subregions and specific sites to locate. If workers have accessibility in the region, the need for EZs is minimized.[78]

A problem is the conflict between emphasis on economic development or social services. Should zones be concerned with improving the economic base or assisting individuals through substance abuse centers, health and child care services? Though the two are not mutually separate, there is insufficient funding for both.[79]

TECHNOLOGY

Technology (and not only information technology) is a key component lacking in the previously discussed economic development programs. To what extent have current federal technology programs been concerned with regional economic development? Funding for the following programs has not been munificent but their spatial impact should be considered. President Clinton stated that with the approach of the twenty-first century, U.S. technology programs must be strengthened and reoriented to emerging sectors. The president cited public investment in technology through the Advanced Technology Program and the Manufacturing Extension Partnerships in the Department of Commerce and the Technology Reinvestment Project at the Department of Defense. These are reviewed in terms of their regional impact.[80]

NATIONAL INSTITUTE OF STANDARDS
AND TECHNOLOGY (NIST)

The National Bureau of Standards was established in 1901 to perform research and development needed to develop uniform standards and physical measurements. Title V of the Omnibus Trade and Competitiveness Act (Public Law 100-418, 1988), which established the Advanced Technology Program (ATP), transformed the National Bureau of Standards into NIST and expanded its mission and responsibilities. Its primary mission shifted to promoting economic growth by working with industry to develop and apply technology measurements and standards. The fiscal 1989 authorization created the Technology Administration and the position of under-secretary for technology in the Department of Commerce.[81]

NIST is only one component of the federal R&D policy. It is also related to the Defense Department's Advanced Research Projects Agency (ARPA), which directs defense R&D toward a dual-use technology base. NIST is the only U.S. government agency whose sole mission is directly helping U.S. industry to strengthen its competitiveness. It is responsible for assisting industry in the development of measurements, standards and technologies needed to improve product quality, to modernize manufacturing processes and to facilitate rapid commercialization. Its annual federal funding is less than $1 billion, with funding from other sources.

Table 19.6
National Institute of Standards and Technology Budget Authority and Outlays, 1997–2003 (millions of dollars)

	Actual	Estimated					
	1997	1998	1999	2000	2001	2002	2003
Budget Authority	565	673	716	757	793	819	793
Outlays	681	649	655	677	722	761	794

Source: U.S. Executive Office of the President, *Budget of the U.S. Government for Fiscal Year 1999, Analytical Perspectives* (Washington, D.C.: Government Printing Office, 1998), p. 424.

The four major NIST programs are Advanced Technology Program (ATP), Manufacturing Extension Partnership (MEP), NIST Laboratory Programs, and Malcolm Baldrige National Quality Award Program (BNQP). ATP and MEP account for most of the NIST obligations.

ATP invests in cost-shared projects in companies or industry-led joint ventures to develop enabling, high-payoff technologies with broad economic potential that otherwise would not be pursued because of technical risks and other obstacles that discourage private investment.

The MEP's goal is to improve the competitiveness of smaller manufacturers, over 381,000 companies with fewer than 599 employees that account for about 95% of all U.S. manufacturing plants. The objective has been to set up a cost-shared, integrated nationwide network of manufacturing extension centers to help small and medium-size manufacturers modernize their production capabilities.

The Laboratory Programs focus on meeting U.S. industry's infrastructural technology needs, including standards, measurements and measurement technologies, evaluating data, manufacturing process models, product performance tests and quality-assurance techniques.

BNQP provides awards whose criteria have become the U.S. standard of quality achievement in industry and a comprehensive guide to quality improvement, assessing quality management and competitiveness and sharing information on successful strategies.

Advanced Technology Program

Program resources are used for technology areas with significant potential for stimulating economic growth. A program is a major research direction with technology and business goals that generally involve a broad range of specific technology development tasks, involving multiple projects by single companies and joint ventures. Programs are not funded, but a specific research project can receive ATP funds.[82]

ATP provides funds for the early phases of technology development through cooperative research agreements with single business or industry-led joint ventures and research consortia. Awards to individual companies may not exceed $2 million and projects must be completed within three years. Projects by joint ventures may run as long as five years, and the ATP can fund up to 50% of the project. Cost-sharing is required for all projects.[83]

Matching funds may include contributions from state, county, city, company or other nonfederal sources, which gives wealthier entities an advantage. However, the intent of the matching-fund requirement is to secure the recipient's commitment to pursue commercialization. Congress intended that business bear the majority of the risk. A tenet of ATP since 1990 has always been that research priorities should be set by industry rather than the government, making it unlikely that regional economic conditions would be a factor.[84]

One factor in an evaluation is the potential broad-based economic benefits and the measurement of long-term economic impacts, but no mention is made of regional or spatial considerations. However, profiles of applicants and recipients, technologies and projects have included a geographic distribution of ATP participants.[85] ATP focuses only on assistance to for-profit companies. This distinguishes ATP from other federal R&D expenditures on basic university research or for federal laboratories. Selection criteria include:

1. Scientific and technical merit of the proposal (30%)
    - improvements in manufacturing costs, product quality and time to market
2. Potential broad-based economic benefits of the proposal   for the nation (20%) (nothing about geographic criteria)
    - potential to improve U.S. economic growth
    - creation of new industries or new industrial capabilities
    - increased worldwide market share
    - timeliness of the proposal, that is, the potential project   results will not occur too late or too early to be competitively useful
    - degree to which ATP support is essential for thee achievement of the broad-based benefits from the proposed R&D and appropriateness of the proposed R&D for ATP support
3. Adequacy of the plans for eventual commercialization (20%)
4. Proposer's level of commitment and organizational structure (20%)
5. Experience and qualifications of the proposing organization (10%).[86]

Until 1994, ATP used general competitions for proposals in all areas of technology as its sole investment mechanism. In 1994 another element was added—focused program competition. Focused programs are a mechanism to give critical mass support for high-risk technologies in special technology areas identified by U.S. industry as providing particularly important opportunities for economic growth.

ATP requires participants to provide a substantial portion of a project's costs, and many R&D projects involve a consortia of companies within an industry. ATP received its first appropriation, $10 million, in 1990. Through October 1995, the program has funded a total of 276 projects, awarding nearly $1 billion to companies and technology coalitions around the country to foster cutting-edge research with large potential economic benefits for the United States. Companies have provided approximately $1 billion in matching funds.[87] As with similar programs, ATP funding is not expanding.

Table 19.7
Advanced Technology Program Obligations, 1997–1999 (millions of dollars)

1997 Actual	1998 Estimated	1999 Estimated
351	313	376

Source: U.S. Executive Office of the President, *Budget of the U.S. Government for Fiscal Year 1999, Appendix* (Washington, D.C.: Government Printing Office, 1998), p. 216.

Evaluation

The GAO has questioned NIST's reports on the impact of ATP in that the short-term results overstated or lacked adequate support.[88] In July 1995, the GAO concluded that it was too early to determine ATP's long-term effect.[89] Department of Commerce critics see ATP as a notable example of a wasteful dispenser of corporate welfare that provides aid to some of the nation's largest firms.[90]

The CBO determined it was too early to assess the commercial success of ATP-funded projects because even after a project has been completed, additional research is required for product development and commercialization. Opponents question the federal government's ability to select projects with the greatest potential for technological and commercial success. Furthermore, they say, if they were clearly potential winners, they would have been funded privately. Proponents suggest that ATP encourages the formation of joint ventures which increases cooperation between academia and firms. ATP support of generic technologies is not likely to be supplanted by the private sector.[91]

Manufacturing Extension Program

Direct federal involvement in the MEP began with the 1988 Omnibus Trade and Competitiveness Act after states already had taken the lead. NIST was selected to help smaller manufacturers adopt and apply performance-improving technologies necessary to confront intensifying domestic and global competition.

MEP is a nationwide network of manufacturing extension services that provides small and medium-size manufacturers with technical assistance to modernize operations and increase competitiveness. The MEP plans called for organizing a comprehensive yet locally responsible system to help small and medium-size manufacturers upgrade their equipment, techniques and operations. MEP carries out a variety of regional, national and program development activities. On a regional basis MEP cooperates with states or local organizations to set up manufacturing extension centers or expand existing services that assist smaller manufacturers.

Components of the network are not financed to perform manufacturing R&D but rather to concentrate totally on the diffusion of appropriate technologies to accelerate industrial modernization.[92] The primary mission is to give "hands-on" technical assistance to manufacturers through use of appropriate technologies, often in partnership with other business assistance providers such as Small Business Development Centers, community colleges and federal laboratories. There are centers in all fifty states and Puerto Rico.[93]

Following its predecessor, Manufacturing Technology Centers (MTCs), MEP has not ignored regional or spatial factors. The MTCs, which were incorporated into MEPs, were regionally based, nonprofit institutions or organizational centers that provided local manufacturing industries with technical and management assistance. Each center had its individual area of expertise, depending on the needs of the industry in that geographical area. For example, the Ohio MTC dealt with fabricated metal products and the California MTC with the aerospace defense industry.[94]

The centers are nonprofit organizations that are partially funded but not owned by the federal government. The model was the Agricultural Extension Centers established early in the century to help farmers learn about modern farming technology.[95]

MEP's State Technology Extension Program (STEP) provides funding and technical support for planning, implementation and regional linkages to strengthen industrial extension efforts in states and communities. Regional activities are a large part of the STEP program. STEP-funded projects enable states to build their own infrastructure for business and technology outreach services by planning extension systems or technical and business assistance programs.

Funding of the MEP centers is initially divided among federal, state and local partners. Federal funding is furnished either directly through the NIST or through the Advanced Research Projects Agency in the Defense Department. Federal funding is always matched by state or local funding, service fees and industry contributions. MEP estimates the network that it has helped fund since 1988 reached a total of 25,000 small and medium-size manufacturers as of March 1995.[96]

NIST is authorized to award funding for up to six years to U.S.-based nonprofit organizations for establishing and operating MTCs, predecessors of MEPs. While NIST could provide up to 50% of an MEP center's capital and annual operating and maintenance costs during the center's first three years, the center's operator was expected to contribute an increasing percentage of the costs in the last three years. NIST's declining levels of funding were intended to ensure that the centers would no longer need NIST financial support by the seventh year. NIST found, however, that revenues generated by the centers would not be sufficient to cover the costs of operating services to small manufacturers. In response, Congress in Commerce's fiscal 1995 appropriation (PL 103-317) allowed NIST to provide up to one-third of a center's total annual costs for additional periods that were not to exceed the three years to any one center. This provision changed the character of the program from offering time-limited incentives to states to provide technology assistance to creating a possible longer-term federal role in providing such assistance.[97]

Federal MEP appropriations through NIST grew in 1994 dollars from some $6.1 million in fiscal 1988 to $138.4 million in fiscal 1995. The limited funding controls the scope of the program.[98]

Table 19.8
Manufacturing Extension Partnership Program Obligations, 1997–1999 (millions of dollars)

1997 Actual	1998 Estimated	1999 Estimated
98	114	107

Source: U.S. Executive Office of the President, *Budget of the U.S. Government for Fiscal Year 1999, Appendix* (Washington, D.C.: Government Printing Office, 1998), p. 216.

Japan has some 169 regional centers, *kohsetsushi*, managed by the governments of the various prefectures while the national government sets the guidelines, furnishes some funding and runs a national register for qualified consultants who work with the centers to assist their client small businesses, firms with under 300 employees. The centers are involved in testing, technical assistance training and technology dissemination.[99] Japan's population of some 125 million is about half the U.S. population of 250 million. In terms of size, Japan's 146,000 square miles is slightly smaller than California, and considerably smaller than the U.S., with 125 million square miles.

DEPARTMENT OF DEFENSE

The Technology Reinvestment Project (TRP) was established in the Department of Defense (DOD) in 1993 to support consortia that would develop and disseminate dual-use (civilian and military) technologies. The program was designed to help break down barriers between the two sectors and promote end innovation. Half of a project's funding would come from industry. Republican members of Congress considered the program inappropriate and wasteful; the funding projects had little military value and did not merit DOD support after 1995. Industry representatives favored coninuation of the program.[100]

In 1997 TRP was replaced by the Dual Use Applications Program (DUAP) to focus on technologies potentially useful to the military. The 1997 budget of $123 million is considerably less than the 1995 TRP budget of some $500 million. In 1998 the program became the DUAP and Commercial Operations and Support Savings Initiative (COSSI). DOD would be enabled to use commercial technologies, products and services more widely, reflecting the Clinton administration's desire to increase the direct involvment of the military in every aspect of the program.[101]

Table 19.9
Dual Use Applications Program/Commercial Operations and Support Savings Initiative Budget Authority, 1997–1999 (millions of dollars)

1997 Actual	1998 Estimated	1999 Estimated
123	120	158

Source: U.S. Executive Office of the President, *Budget of the U.S. Government for Fiscal Year 1999* (Washington, D.C.: Government Printing Office, 1998), p. 100.

NATIONAL AERONAUTICS AND SPACE ADMINISTRATION (NASA)

NASA, over years of developing space exploration technology, has developed projects and ideas and put together an array of research that could be applied in other areas. The NASA Field Centers assist industry in accessing NASA technology and form research and development partnerships.[102]

The National Technology Transfer Network (NTTN) is a national network of regional centers that help transfer federal information to U.S. private industry and thus enhance the competitiveness of U.S.business. NTTN was created to assist federal agencies in complying with federal-wide technology transfer mandates and exchanges of information and developments. NTTN functions as the national base for federal technological transfer, maintaining connections among federal resources, industry and firms.[103] NTTN consists of the National Technology Transfer Center (NTTC) and six Regional Technology Transfer Centers (RTTCs).[104]

RTTCs furnish information and analysis for reports that are concerned with the technological needs of business and industry. The centers offer access to information for products, services, technical expertise and current information on new technologies. Industry is given assistance in developing technical transfer initiatives.[105]

NOTES

1. National Academy of Public Administration, *A Path to Smarter Economic Development: Reassessing the Federal Role*, prepared for the U.S. Economic Development Administration (Washington: 1996), p. 1; and U.S. General Accounting Office, *Community Development Comprehensive Approaches and Local Flexibility Issues*, GAO/T-RCED-96-53, December 5, 1995, pp. 5–6.

2. National Academy, *A Path*, p. 13.

3. National Academy, *A Path*, Appendix I, p. 65.

4. U.S. General Accounting Office, *Economic Development Limited Information Exists on the Impact of Assistance Provided by the Three Agencies*, GAO/RCED-96-103, April 1996, p. 2.

5. Ira Hirschman, "Can We Pay for What We Plan? Infrastructure in the New York Region," *Metro Planner*, Metropolitan Chapter of the American Planning Association 9 (November/December 1996), p. 10; U.S. Congress, House Committee on Public Works and Transportation, Subcommittee on Investigations and Oversight, *Hearings on Infrastructure Financing*, Testimony by Felix G. Rohatyn, 103rd Congress, 2d session, Serial Number 103-62, July 13, 1994. For a different view, see Walker F. Todd, "The Reconstruction Finance Corporation: A Bad idea Whose Time Seems To Have Come," paper presented at Jerome Levy Economics Institute, Bard College, Annadale-on-Hudson, NY, November 22, 1991.

6. William J. Tobin, *Public Works and Unemployment: A History of Federally Funded Programs*, (Washington: U.S. Department of Commerce, Economic Development Administration, 1974), p. 5.

7. Ibid., p. 5.

8. Ibid., p. 6.

9. U.S. Secretary of the Treasury, *Final Report of the Reconstruction Finance Corporation*, n.d.

10. U.S. Congress, House Committee on Banking, Finance and Urban Affairs, Subcommittee on Economic Stabilization, *Hearings on Industrial Policy*, Part 4, Statement of Felix G. Rohatyn, 98th Congress, 1st session, Serial Number 98-47, September 1983, p. 110.

11. Harry W. Richardson and Joseph H. Turek, "The Scope and Limits of Federal Intervention," in Harry W. Richardson and Joseph H. Turek, eds., *Economic Prospects for the Northeast* (Philadelphia: Temple University Press, 1985),

p. 211.

12. Vernon W. Ruttan, "The TVA and Regional Development," in Erwin C. Hargrove and Paul K. Conklin, eds., *TVA—Fifty Years of Grass Roots Bureaucracy* (Urbana: University of Illinois Press, 1983), p. 4.

13. James S. Olson with Susan Wladever-Morgan, *Dictionary of United States Economic History* (Westport, CT: Greenwood Press, 1992), p. 535.

14. Richard Lowitt, "The TVA, 1933–45," in Erwin C. Hargrove and Paul K. Conklin, eds., *TVA—Fifty Years of Grass Roots Bureaucracy* (Urbana: University of Illinois Press, 1983), p. 37.

15. Scott Campbell, *Integrating Economic and Environmental Planning: The Regional Perspective* (Piscataway: Rutgers University, Center for Urban Policy Research, 1992), Working Paper 43, p. 18.

16. Ruttan, "The TVA,"p. 157.

17. U.S. General Accounting Office, *Tennessee Valley Authority Financial Problems Raise Questions About Long Term Viability*, GAO/AIMD/RCED-95-134, August 1995, pp. 70–71.

18. U.S. Congress, Congressional Budget Office, *Reducing the Deficit: Spending and Revenue Options*, March 1997, pp. 162–163.

19. U.S. Office of the President, *Budget of the U.S. Government Fiscal Year 1999 Analytical Perspectives* (Washington, D.C.: Government Printing Office, 1998), p. 572.

20. Patrick G. Grasso, "Distributive Policies and the Politics of Economic Development," in F. Steven Redburn, Terry F. Buss and Larry C. Ledebur, eds., *Revitalizing the U.S. Economy* (Westport: Praeger Publishers, 1986), p. 83.

21. Ann R. Tickamyer and Cynthia W. Duncan, "Work and Poverty in Rural America," in Cornelia B. Flora and James A. Christianson, eds., *Rural Policies for the 1990s* (Boulder: Westview Press, 1991), p. 106.

22. Niles Hansen, "Economic Development and Regional Heterogeneity: A Reconsideration of Regional Policy for the U.S.," *Economic Development Quarterly* 21 (May 1988), p. 107.

23. Richardson and Turek, "The Scope and Limits,"p. 211.

24. John H. Cumberland, *Regional Developments Experience and Elements in the U.S. of America* (The Hague: Mouton, 1971), p. 71.

25. David Clark, *Post-Industrial America: A Geographical Perspective* (New York and London: Methuen, 1985), p. 194.

26. Richardson and Turek, "The Scope and Limits,"p. 211.

27. Niles Hansen, Benjamin Higgins and Donald J. Savoie, *Regional Policy in a Changing World* (New York: Plenum Press, 1990), p. 123.

28. John Zysman, "Research Politics and Policy: Regional Planning in America," in *The Utilization of the Social Sciences in Policy Making in the United States* (Paris: Organization for Economic Cooperation and Development, 1980), p. 144.

29. Ibid.

30. Ibid.

31. Clark, *Post-Industrial America*, p. 196.

32. Hansen, "Economic Development," p. 108.

33. Clark, *Post-Industrial America*, p. 196.

34. John Rees and Bernard Weinstein, "Government Policy and Industrial Location," in John W. House, ed., *United States Public Policy: A Geographical View*

(Oxford: Clarendon Press, 1983), p. 213.

35. Cumberland, *Regional Development*, p. 84.

36. Jeffrey L. Pressman and Aaron Wildavsky, *Implementation: How Great Expectations in Washington Are Dashed in Oakland*, 3rd ed., (Berkeley: University of California Press, 1984), pp. 11, 154.

37. Timothy Barnekov, Robin Boyle and Daniel Rich, *Privatization and Urban Policy in Britain and the United States* (New York: Oxford University Press, 1989), p. 27.

38. John W. House, "The Policy Arena," in John W. House, ed., *United States Public Policy: A Geographical View* (Oxford: Clarendon Press 1983), p. 64.

39. Marc Bendick Jr., "Employment, Training and Economic Development," in John L. Palmer and Isabel V. Sawhill, eds., *The Reagan Experiment* (Washington: Urban Institute Press, 1982), p. 264.

40. Barnekov, Boyle and Rich, *Privatization*, p. 111.

41. Maia Kelly and Steven Maynard-Moody, "Policy Analysis in the Post-Positivist Era: Engaging Stakeholders in Evaluating the Economic Development District," *Public Administration Review* 43 (March–April 1993), pp. 138, 145.

42. John B. Judis, "Sleazy Genius," *The New Republic*, May 15, 1995, p. 25.

43. "EDA Reform," *News and Views*, American Planning Association, Economic Development Division, September 1995, p. 10.

44. U.S. Congress, Congressional Budget Office, *Reducing the Deficit: Spending and Revenue Options*, February 1995, p. 156.

45. Hansen, Higgins and Savoie, *Regional Policy*, pp. 129, 142–143.

46. "Reauthorization of EDA in Peril," *News and Views*, American Planning Association, Economic Development Division, October 1994, p. 4.

47. Deborah A. Miness, "Regional Planning: An Update From the Field," *Landlines*, Lincoln Institute of Land Policy 6 (May 1994), p. 3.

48. House, "The Policy Arena,"p. 64.

49. Michael Bradshaw, *Regions and Regionalism in the United States* (Hampshire, England: MacMillan Education, 1988), p. 135.

50. U.S. Congress, House Committee on Public Works and Transportation, Subcommittee on Economic Development, *Hearings on Proposals to Extend Economic Legislation*, 96th Congress, 1st Session, March 1979, p. 742.

51. House, "The Policy Arena," p. 71.

52. "Devolution Ready or Not, Here Comes Regional Power," *Governing* 5 (April 1992), p. 67 and David Luberoff, "The Road Ahead for Public Works," *Governing* 10 (January 1997), p. 58.

53. "Napa's Standing Panel on the Federal System, Devolution: Making It Work," *Public Administration Times* 20 (April 1997), p. 9.

54. Pressman and Wildavsky, *Implementation*, p. 152.

55. James L. Sundquist, *Politicians and Policy: The Eisenhower, Kennedy and Johnson Years* (Washington: The Brookings Institution, 1968), p. 101.

56. Grasso, "Distributive Policies," p. 90.

57. Zysman, "Research Politics," p. 147.

58. Bradshaw, *Regions and Regionalisms*, p. 152.

59. Congressional Budget Office, *Reducing the Deficit*, p. 159.

60. U.S. Executive Office of the President, *Budget of the U.S. Government for Fiscal Year 1999, Appendix* (Washington, D.C.: Government Printing Office, 1998)

p. 1035.

61. Richard J. Reeder, *Rural Enterprise Zones in Theory and Practice: An Assessment of Their Development Potential* (U.S. Department of Agriculture, Agriculture and Rural Economy Division, Economic Research Service, March 1993), p. 17.

62. Michael Parkinson, "Political Responses to Urban Restructuring: The British Experience under Thatcherism," in John R. Logan and Todd Swanstrom, eds., *Beyond the City Limits: Urban Policy and Economic Restructuring in Comparative Perspective* (Philadelphia: Temple University Press, 1990), p. 100.

63. Ibid., pp. 100–101.

64. Barnekov, Boyle and Rich, *Privatization*, p. 119.

65. Margaret G. Wilder and Barry M. Rubin, "Rhetoric versus Reality: A Review of Studies on State Enterprise Zone Programs," *Journal of the American Planning Association* 62 (Autumn 1996), p. 473.

66. Michael Allan Wolf, "Enterprise Zones: A Decade of Diversity," *Economic Development Quarterly* 4 (February 1990), pp. 5, 11.

67. Ibid., p. 10.

68. William Fulton and Morris Newman, "The Strange Career of Enterprise Zones," *Governing* 7 (March 1994), p. 34.

69. Eleanor Chelimsky, *Statement on Enterprise Zones Before the House of Representatives*, U.S. General Accounting Office, GAO/T-PEMD-90-5, October 17, 1989, p. 3.

70. David Rapp, "Clinton and the Country Sort of Quiet on the Urban Front," *Governing* 6 (August 1993), p. 88.

71. Nicholas Lemann, "The Myth of Community Development," *New York Times Magazine*, January 9, 1994, pp. 30–31.

72. Allen D. Wallis, "Inventing Regionalism: A Two-Phase Approach," *National Civic Review,* (Fall–Winter 1994), p. 466.

73. Zenia Kotval and John R. Mullin, "The Coming Crisis in Industrial Land: A Planning Perspective," *Economic Development Quarterly* 8 (August 1994), p. 303.

74. Michael E. Porter, "The Competitive Advantage of the Inner City," *Harvard Business Review* 73 (May–June 1995), p. 60.

75. Philip Kasinitz and Jan Rosenberg, "Missing the Connection: Social Isolation and Employment on the Brooklyn Waterfront," *Social Problems* 43 (May 1996), pp. 193–194.

76. Jennifer Pitts, "Twilight Zone," *New Republic,* September 7 and 14, 1992, p. 25.

77. Elizabeth M. Gunn, "The Growth of Enterprise Zones: A Policy Transformation," *Policy Studies Journal* 11 (Autumn 1993), p. 446.

78. Neil S. Mayer, "HUD's First Thirty Years: Big Steps Down a Long Road," *Cityscape, A Journal of Development and Research* (HUD) 1 (September 1995), p. 15.

79. Charles Mahtesian, "E-Z Money," *Governing* 9 (October 1995), p. 40.

80. U.S. Office of the President, *Economic Report of the President*, transmitted to Congress together with the Annual Report of the Council of Economic Advisers (Washington, D.C.: Government Printing Office, 1996), pp. 32–33.

81. U.S. Congress, House Committee on Space, Science and Technology, American Technology Preeminence Act of 1991: report together with additional and dissenting views to accompany H.R. 1989, 102d Congress, 1st session, House

Report 102–134, June 26, 1991 and American Technology Preeminence Act of 1991, PL 102–245.

82. U.S. Department of Commerce, National Institute of Standards and Technology, Technology Administration, *Advanced Technology Program*, October 1994, p. 5.

83. U.S. Department of Commerce, National Institute of Standards and Technology, Technology Administration, *Setting Priorities and Measuring Results at the National Institute of Standards and Technology*, January 31, 1994, p. 11.

84. U.S. Department of Commerce, National Institute of Standards and Technology, Technology Administration, *Advanced Technology Program Proposal Preparation Kit*, November 1996, p. 23.

85. Department of Commerce Technology Administration, *Setting Priorities*, pp. 12–15.

86. Department of Commerce Technology Administration, *Proposal Preparation Kit*, p. 1.

87. Silber and Associates, *Survey of Advanced Technology Program 1990–1992 Awardees: Company Opinion About the ATP and Its Early Effects*, (Clarksville, MD: January 1996).

88. U.S. General Accounting Office, *Performance Measurement Efforts to Evaluate the Advanced Technology Program*, GAO/RCED-95-68, May 1995, p. 8.

89. U.S. General Accounting Office, *Government Reorganization Observations on the Department of Commerce*, GAO/T-GGD/RCED/AIMD-95-248, July 25, 1995, p. 9.

90. "The New Daley Machine," *The Economist* 342 (February 1, 1997), p. 34.

91. Congressional Budget Office, *Reducing the Deficit*, pp. 139–140.

92. Department of Commerce Technology Administration, *Setting Priorities*, pp. 25–26.

93. U.S., Department of Commerce, National Institute of Standards and Technology, Technology Administration, *Quick List of Manufacturing Centers*, May–June 1997.

94. William A. Delphos, *Capitol Capital: Government Resources for High Technology Companies* (Washington: Venture Publishing, 1993), p. 10.

95. Jacques S. Gansler, *Defense Conversion: Transforming the Arsenal of Democracy* (Cambridge: MIT Press, 1996), p. 64.

96. U.S. General Accounting Office, *Manufacturing Extension Programs: Manufacturers' Views of Services*, GAO/GGD-95-26BR, August 1995, p. 11.

97. U.S. General Accounting Office, *Government Reorganization*, p. 10.

98. U.S. General Accounting Office, *Manufacturing Extension Programs*, p. 13.

99. Bennett Harrison, *Lean and Mean: The Changing Landscape of Corporate Power in the Age of Flexibility* (New York: Basic Books, 1994), p. 238.

100. David Hanson, "House Votes to Kill Technology Programs," *Chemical and Engineering News*, February 27, 1995, p. 9.

101. U.S. Executive Office of the President, *Budget of the U.S. Government for Fiscal Year 1999*, 1998, p. 102.

102. Delphos, *Capitol Capital*, p. 16.

103. Delphos, *Capitol Capital*, p. 17.

104. Delphos, *Capitol Capital*, p. 17.

105. Delphos, *Capitol Capital*, p. 82.

Chapter 20

States (U.S.)

EVOLUTION OF POLICY

Though the emphasis in this chapter is on states, the term "state" could be a proxy for "region." The traditional federalist position was that the national government ought to exercise restraint in helping solve problems hitherto viewed as a state responsibility and generally oppose help for state policy objectives. To justify federal action a strict test of national purpose would be applied:

- spillovers or external effects—costs or benefits from activities that cross jurisdictional borders
- efficiency advantages of centralized coordination
- poor distribution of resources, especially for certain disadvantaged groups or regions.[1]

Governmental functions should be assigned to those jurisdictions best able to perform them at reasonable cost and higher level of effectiveness. This approach resembles the European Union's subsidiarity policy.

Prior to the Civil War states had much greater impact than did the federal government. Capital in the form of loans and credits was made available for new industries.[2] Post–Revolutionary War manufacturing industries needed capital as profit opportunities were greater in commerce, agriculture and transportation. However, the 1812 War cut off imports from Europe and capital involved in trade and shipping became available for manufacturing. After the war, British merchants and manufacturers sought to regain markets by sending enormous quantities of goods. Domestic manufacturers turned to the federal and state governments for relief. State governments were more responsive as a financing mechanism was already in place.

Loan programs were limited by the paucity of state financial resources and legal restrictions on providing public assistance to private organizations. The restrictions, whose legacy remains, arose not from any undue expansion or lack of soundness in the manufacturing loans but from loans to private parties for internal infrastructure improvements, principally canals and railroads. After the 1837 depression, as canals and railroads were unable to meet their obligations, states defaulted on debt repayment, resulting in constitutional amendments limiting borrowing.

Thus the law governing public fiscal affairs has been pervasively influenced by the 19th century experience, which also pointed up countervailing policy considerations to be balanced against the desire to devote public funds to the attraction of industry. The progeny of the restrictions developed at that time constitute the legal limitations with which state and local governments must presently confine their attempts to induce industrial location.[3]

An example of the restrictions on gifts or loans of state credit or money still in existence is Article VII, Section 8.1 of the New York State Constitution. "The money of the state shall not be given or loaned to or in aid of any private corporation or association, or private undertaking; nor shall the credit of the state be given or loaned to or in aid of any individual, or public or private corporation or association, or private undertaking, but the foregoing provision shall not apply to any fund or property now held or which may hereafter be held by the state for education, mental health or mental retardation purposes." Subsequent changes, in section 8.3, allow lending or loan guarantees to be made indirectly for business activities.

States have demonstrated considerable ingenuity in financing within the framework of the controls. Tax exemption was used as early as the seventeenth century and has continued as a key factor in the competitive struggle for industry. During the colonial period direct subsidies or bounties were more prevalent than tax exemption.[4] Subsequently it became customary, particularly in New England, to grant tax exemptions on the property of manufacturing enterprises during the early years. States were so generous in giving exemptions that on occasion the towns with the factories protested.[5]

With the 1930 Depression, the economic power of states was eclipsed. No subnational entity could do without federal assistance. The massive federal spending of World War II laid the basis for an economic expansion benefiting all states and reinforced the federal dominance. Specific regional or subnational economic development federal legislation began during the Kennedy-Johnson administrations (e.g., ARA, EDA and ARC).

Federal initiatives gave communities federal funds, often bypassing state governments. In the late 1970s, the situation changed significantly. Devolution of the national government's responsibilities was not accompanied by any transfer of funds. Federal economic development programs are now relatively unimportant in the aggregate compared with state economic development policies and programs.[6] Reagan's budget cuts and the deep recession in 1981–1982 convinced states and communities that they were on their own when it came to economic development.

FEDERAL AND STATE ROLES

The United States lacks the political and economic centralization of European countries, where primary responsibility for economic development rests with the national government. In the United States decentralization is more feasible because of the country's size. There are advantages to subnational hegemony. Subnational jurisdictions are better able to respond to variances in natural endowments and historic industrial development. More knowledgeable of local conditions, they can better fill gaps in broad federal policies, programs and target incentives, and are better able to experiment and innovate.

Subnational programs are subject to criticism. Strategies typically evolve incrementally without an underlying economic justification except that more jobs are good and fewer jobs are bad.[7] Many programs are poorly administered with too liberal use of subsidies. Another issue is whether these programs are too fragmented and redundant to operate economically.

State development programs should be judged not only by benefits to states but nationally as well. States are not concerned about whether jobs are drawn from other states. The long-term effectiveness of incentives is of secondary concern to elected officials. The competitive process raises subsidy costs for all states. From a national perspective, subnational programs promoting productivity and economic growth are preferred to those designed to draw companies from other areas.

There are clear limits as to what can be expected at the state level. States cannot deal with problems affecting industries crossing state and national lines. Regulation of capital markets is national in scope. International trade is beyond the control of state governments. Because state governments are competing, there are severe pressures to keep taxes low, which makes it difficult to fund needed investment; those needing most investment have the least financial capability. If resources are to be redistributed, the federal government must be the agent.[8] National policies can set uniform standards and take into account spillover effects. The federal government can provide the breadth of data gathering and analysis necessary to help governments at all levels formulate economic development policies and programs.

Subnational entities cannot be compared with national governments. With globalization, even national governments are less self-contained. Nations can apply tariffs and change the value of currencies. States are not units sealed off from such exogenous developments.[9]

Foreign Investment

States are active in efforts to attract foreign investment and promote exports. In 1959, North Carolina Governor Luther H. Hodges' trip to Europe to attract foreign investment was a critical turning point, if not an embryonic impetus, for state involvement in international affairs.[10] The benefits of state promotion programs are questionable on grounds of national economic policy; they bid up the cost of subsidies to attract foreign investment and can impinge on federal treaty obligations such as WTO and NAFTA. In contrast, the British government coordinates promotional and competitive activities of the regional development agencies in seeking foreign investment. The responsibility is assigned to the Invest in Britain Bureau of the Department of Trade and Industry.[11]

Industrial Development Bonds

The federal government does not have unlimited power over subnational entities but has influence through financial controls and incentives.[12] Federal tax law permits issuance of local and state government federally tax-exempt bonds, industrial development bonds (IDBs) for private activities at substantially lower rates than private market interest rates. Their value is compounded by state and local tax exemption. In the 1970s and early 1980s, IDBs grew to be the economic development tool of choice and represented 90% of local economic development activity.[13]

Efforts to limit their use were ineffective until passage of the 1986 Tax Reform Act. The total dollar amount that could be issued in a single year was reduced significantly. Power to allocate private activity bond authority (within federally imposed ceilings) was shifted from local governments to states, increasing their power over local public finance. The volume of IDBs has shrunk sharply.[14]

Federal responsibility ideally should be leadership, that is, when problems transcend the capabilities of states.[15] Federal intervention could be helpful in finance, such as an RFC-type of institution to support infrastructure. Federal efforts in terms of technology and job training benefit the whole country.[16] If historical patterns hold true, the federal government will eventually adapt successful state programs and innovations as with the New Deal.[17] But there is no certainty as to when and in what form the national role will re-emerge.[18] Federal fiscal and monetary policies have differing effects on industries and regions. Federal expenditures, while not specifically labeled economic development, have spatial impacts, such as defense spending.

STATE POLICIES AND PRACTICES

Incentives

In 1917, Kentucky provided tax exemption to manufacturers for machinery and raw materials. Between 1920 and 1930, six other Southern states followed with their own tax-exemption plans: Arkansas, Georgia, Louisiana, Mississippi, South Carolina and Virginia. In 1930, only three Northern states had provisions for any type of tax exemption, and in two of these instances, exemption was limited to specific towns or counties.

Mississippi's historic Balance Agriculture with Industry (BAWI) program, initiated in 1936 and revised in 1944, was the first concerted state effort to sell itself to industrialists. Municipalities were permitted to acquire land and construct buildings for lease to private employers and to issue general obligation bonds. It was an immediate success. Within ten years there were twelve BAWI subsidized plans in operation, accounting for 14 percent of the state's industrial work force.[19] BAWI represented a breakthrough in offering incentives, but wide utilization of these devices cancelled any state advantage.

Use of tax-exempt bonds to attract industry was joined by gifts of land, money and services. To entice prospective employers, communities would extend sewer and water lines to the industrial site and build roads to the site or finance railroad spur lines.[20] In 1949, Maine authorized the first statewide business development corporation. In 1955, New Hampshire created the first state industrial finance authority to guarantee industrial loans or make direct loans of state funds to businesses.[21]

An explosion of business incentives came as an aftermath of the
1970s employment crisis and the recession of the early 1980s. States
became so competitive in offering incentives that the expression "The
Second War Between the States" came into wide use.[22]

During the 1970s, technological advances and world market changes
led to increasing vulnerability to foreign competition. "The progressive and
nationally-oriented and globally-oriented business community" has limited
interest in traditional or parochial boundaries.[23] The components of a positive business climate became education, physical infrastructure, regulation,
taxation and modernization. Investment in education is a key prerequisite.[24]

With few programs or accompanying funds from Washington, governors were largely on their own to formulate development strategies.
States have created new programs, expanded existing ones, developed
trade contacts abroad and established an array of agencies, advisory
boards and councils devoted to economic development. In addition states
have partnerships with universities, the private sector and other states.
The partnership metaphor is popular with both policymakers and schol-
ars because it captures the collaborative and interdependent nature of
economic development policy.[25]

By the mid-1980s, more than 15,000 state and local officials had
domestic economic development activity as their primary responsibility
and countless others dealt with development problems in tangential or
episodic fashion. Lacking national leadership, an entirely new public policy industry centered on problems of economic development was created.[26] How much the nation spends on local economic development is
unknown because funds come from varied sources not easily calculated,
tax expenditures (preferences and exemptions) as compared with direct
expenditures. A conservative 1990 estimate places total expenditures at
over $10 billion.[27] A subsequent estimate for total state and local support,
including tax expenditures for economic development, in 1992 came to
$12 billion.[28]

Between 1984 and 1994 spending by state economic development
agencies more than quadrupled. In 1994, their budgets came to $1.7 bil-
lion. Some 46% of their support came from federal sources, 34% from
state appropriations and 20% from such sources as fees and donations.[29]

State governments in competing for foreign direct investment have
been generous in offering incentives. Their competition is with other states
as well as other countries. Examples of subsidies are the 1993 incentives
given by Alabama to Mercedes-Benz, valued at $168,000 per employee for
a total $300 million, and the 1994 incentives given by South Carolina to
BMW, valued at $108,000 per employee.[30] Though attracting foreign
investment is a valuable contribution to national prosperity, these efforts
can produce "destructive interjurisdictional competition."[31]

Development Policies

Development policies are frequently classified as supply and demand but are not necessarily confined to one. The supply category encompasses the traditional approach of location incentives, financial and tax, to stimulate investment and/or relocation and outbid other states. The supply side relies on low factor costs to attract businesses.

A change occurred during the 1980s when most states shifted their emphasis from the supply to the demand side to obtain maximum returns from economic development, for example, expanding demand by increasing exports or decreasing imports.[32] Demand-side incentives are designed to create or sustain businesses, to increase aggregate output and demand through activities targeted to specific industries. On the supply side, government follows and supports private sector decisions; on the demand side, government helps identify new investment opportunities that private firms may have overlooked or have been reluctant to pursue.[33]

Differences between demand and supply sides are not easily distinguished.[34] Enterprise zones have elements of both but the supply side predominates since the zones depend on subsidies to compensate for locational disadvantages. When there is interjurisdictional competition for a sizeable facility, particular supply and demand factors are less important and incentives become a key component of the competitive strategy.[35] A variation is the maintenance strategy (direct subsidies, cost reduction, recruitment) compared with a creation strategy (product development and commercialization, equity-based financial assistance and university-industry linkages).

Another school believes in a Third Wave. Underlying programs include investment in job training and education, industrial modernization, community-level economic development planning and encouragement of industrial clusters. The primary goal is to establish broad institutional or individual capability.[36] The Third Wave entails heavy government involvement, especially funding with tangible outcomes.

In the 1990s, the private sector assumed a strengthened role in providing direct economic development services. The focus has shifted away from a public sector concern with declining geographic areas and creation of jobs to an emphasis on the business climate and competitiveness.[37]

A 1996 KPMG Peat Marwick survey of 203 Fortune 1000 companies measured the competitive climate and reflected the importance of the supply side. Seventy percent (160 firms) had received some form of state or local incentive for placing facilities in a particular location. The most popular benefits were property tax rebates (51%), income and franchise tax rebates (48%), sales tax rebates (35%), job training (11%), employment or payroll tax credits (9%) and utility rebates (8%).[38]

COMPETITION

Is there federal power to limit state economic development powers? The Constitution and Supreme Court rulings provide guidelines. The United States has no federal law against subnational subsidies. States cannot countervail the subsidies of other states, though foreign subsidies can be countervailed.[39]

One viewpoint is that competition is without question unalterably American and is thus unavoidable.[40] Another viewpoint avers that interstate competition can be controlled and that it is time for Congress to exercise its Commerce Clause power to end the economic war. Justice Benjamin Cardozo stated that an objective of the framers of the Constitution in granting Congress power to regulate interstate competition was to create an economic union especially by ending the trade war among the states that prevailed under the Articles of Confederation (*Baldwin v. G.A.F. Seelig, Inc.*, 294; U.S. 511, 523, (1934). While there has been no court ruling on the constitutionality of this competition, the court has stated that these activities may be admirable (*Metropolitan Life Insurance Company v. Ward*, 470 U.S. 869, 879, 1985) and may fulfill a legitimate public purpose.[41]

Can Congress fashion legislation to prevent states from using incentives to attract businesses? Congress could tax recipients on the direct and imputed value of benefits, deny tax-exempt status on outstanding state debt or deny federal funding otherwise payable to these states as highway funds are denied to states failing to meet federal pollution standards. But it is difficult to enact and enforce legislation that covers the various avoidance techniques states can devise.[42]

The Commerce Clause grants Congress the right to regulate "commerce...among the several States"(Article I, Section 8, Clause 3) but does not expressly prohibit states from interfering with interstate commerce.[43] The Supreme Court can only decide cases that come before it and cannot create legislation to implement the Commerce Clause. Only Congress has the power to enact legislation and set competition rules.[44] Competition clauses have been incorporated in EDA and EZ/EC legislation.

Any assessment of constitutionality has to rely on what the Supreme Court has indicated in applying the judicially constructed "dormant" or "negative" Commerce Clause. In these cases the court has defined the grant of power to Congress to regulate "commerce among the states" as implicitly mandating a policy of free interstate markets; local economic measures not outlawed by Congress are nonetheless unconstitutional if they unduly burden interstate commerce. In these cases, the court has viewed the local economic activity as inconsistent with the policy of the Commerce Clause only where out-of-state interests are burdened for the benefit of local interests, for example, by a tax that discriminates against out-of-state goods. Accordingly, in *West Lynn Creamery Inc. v. Healy*, 114 S. Ct 2205, 2214 (1994), the court suggested that "a pure subsidy funded out of general revenues ordinarily imposes no burden on interstate commerce, but merely assists local businesses," which confirms the 1985 *Metropolitan Life* decision.[45]

The constitutional problems can be overcome. Confirmation is required that the subsidies are contributing to a national problem for which federal intervention is needed. If Congress enacts legislation there will be appeals to the court, enabling it to adjudicate the constitutionality. To support the court's decision, the statute should include detailed congressional findings.[46]

State Tax Incentives

A firm viewpoint on state tax incentives is that restraints can be supported constitutionally.[47] Since the inception of constitutional history, the Supreme Court has "expounded the view that eventually became central to the whole constitutional scheme: the doctrine that the Commerce clause, by its very own force and without implementing congressional legislation, places limits on state authority and these limits may be enforced by the courts…. [T]he Court has never precisely delineated the scope of the doctrine forbidding discriminatory state taxes. Nevertheless the central meaning of discrimination as a criterion for adjudicating the constitutionality of taxes affecting interstate commerce emerges unmistakably from the Court's numerous decisions addressing the issue."

A tax that by its scope places greater burdens on out-of-state goods, activities or enterprises than on competing in-state goods, activities or enterprises will be terminated under the Commerce Clause. State tax incentives, whether in the form of credits, exemptions, abatements or other preferential treatment, typically have two aspects that discriminate against interstate commerce. First, state tax incentives select for favorable treatment activities, investments or other actions that take place within the taxing state. Second state tax incentives as key components of the state's taxing apparatus are closely connected to the coercive power of the state. They therefore fall readily into the realm of state action to which the Commerce Clause is directed.

While the Commerce Clause does not prohibit all state action designed to give state residents an advantage in the marketplace, the Supreme Court observed in *New Energy Co. v. Limbach* (486 U.S. 269, 1988); it clearly applies to "action of that description in connection with the States regulation of interstate commerce." The court has recognized in scores of cases that state tax laws affecting activities carried on across state lines are "plainly connected to the regulation of interstate commerce" (*Oregon Waste Systems, Inc. v. Department of Environmental Quality,* 114 S.Ct. 1345, 1994).[48]

Federal Policy

As federal economic development funds are curtailed, the ability of the federal government to limit the use of incentives is reduced. The federal government cannot eliminate competition but can encourage more rational competition.

Federal policy could encourage and support economic development incentives in high-unemployment areas, where the social benefits are greater. Federal policy could encourage experiments with small business assistance, which may increase productivity. Finally, federal policy could support more consistent information on and evaluation of state and local development policies. Better information on the size and effects of incentives, and other economic development policies, should put pressure on state and local governments to adopt more rational policies.[49]

"The problems of economic development competition reinforce the argument that the federal government should have primary responsibility for redistributional policies." The traditional wisdom in public finance is that income redistribution should be a federal responsibility because the mobility of households and business makes this task difficult for state and local governments and is now increasingly relevant.[50]

Another skeptical view of state and local subsidies was enunciated by the Congressional Budget Office (CBO):

Unless state development programs serve to increase productivity and improve adjustment to market forces, they would, from a national perspective, only cancel each other out by competing, through subsidies, for the location of a fixed amount of economic activity. To the extent that the states only offset each other's policies, no net national benefit results from the vast number of development incentives offered by the states. National economic goals are more likely to be served if programs either create new economic activity or enhance the efficiency of market performance.[51]

A strong federal role is a remote possibility. The call for federal involvement has largely emanated from advocacy groups lacking any support from elected officials.[52] Members of Congress are not prone to putting national interests above parochial concerns and alienating local constituencies. The favorable attitude toward devolution runs counter to any efforts to give the federal government additional power.[53]

Yet there are signs of a growing attitude shift. State officials have requested the federal government to limit disastrous interstate competition. In May 1996, the Ohio Senate unanimously passed a resolution calling for federal assistance in stopping the interstate competition for industry. Subsequently the Ohio legislature funded a $500,000 study to evaluate economic incentive programs. In Maryland, as part of a 1996 job-creation tax-credit bill, a provision was attached directing the governor to negotiate a cease-fire agreement with counterparts in Delaware, North Carolina, Pennsylvania and West Virginia. Federal intervention was not requested. The Minnesota legislature passed a resolution advocating a federal law to eliminate any federally funded programs used to lure businesses from one state to another.[54]

Several jurisdictions have unsuccessfully sought truces in the bidding wars. In 1988, Michigan held a "midwestern summit" in an effort to get its neighbors to stop handing out tax breaks. One state balked (reportedly Illinois), and the idea was dropped.[55] In August 1993, the National Governors Association Conference adopted voluntary guidelines to limit state tax breaks and subsidies to companies. States should limit and be able to recoup public funds misplaced in companies not meeting their obligations.[56] The Committee for Economic Development has urged states to cooperate on a regional basis and a moratorium on corporate raiding has been discussed by policymakers in the Great Lakes states.[57]

There is growing skepticism about the effectiveness of incentive programs and the ability of businesses to play states off against each other. One approach is to focus efforts on business loans instead of grants; by providing training, roads, sewers and similar infrastructure, the local economy is permanently enhanced even if the recipient company should downsize or depart.[58] To monitor deals and publicize costs and benefits, federal agencies, states and the private sector should establish a nonprofit organization, the Alliance for Smart Recruiting. Information on incentives is incomplete, unreliable and not widely used.[59]

Mirroring the competition among states, a survey of county-sponsored industrial development agencies across New York state conducted by Cornell University researchers concluded that county oversight of such programs is weak and in many cases does not extend to tracking the jobs created.[60]

Taxes

Tax incentives have been criticized on the grounds that tax considerations play a limited role in location decisions. Surveys have ranked taxes relatively low compared with other locational factors. All state and local taxes combined may make up a small share of the cost of doing business and reduce profits only to a limited extent.[61] But the conventional wisdom that tax incentives are insignificant compared with other cost factors affecting location decisions is questioned. With sophisticated modeling and statistical methods, studies have identified significant relationships between taxes and development. Earlier surveys may have concentrated on traditional manufacturing industries, for which availability of labor and market access were more crucial than tax benefits.

More recent surveys are wider in scope and include service and other nontraditional industries, such as high-tech. Products are relatively lighweight and cheap to transport, lessening the importance of transportation links and proximity to markets. "Hence, taxes may play a relatively larger role in location decisions today than in earlier years."[62]

Tax breaks deprive states of needed revenue. Without adequate resources states cannot improve their education systems, enhance their infrastructure and retain or attract the requisite industries. Businesses using temporary tax rebate programs may relocate when the incentives expire. State and local governments cannot control all factors that affect a company's decisions to close a facility.

Clawbacks

A concept of private sector responsibility to workers, community and government is the clawback clause.[63] States include them in incentive agreements requiring companies to repay subsidies when they fail to meet job targets. Companies in a strong bargaining position seek the least onerous clawback agreements and are skilled at pitting governmental entities against each other. New Mexico Senator Jeff Bingaman called for the U.S. Department of Commerce to decide whether companies that receive tax benefits should be required to file cost-benefit analyses and stand behind their job pledges.[64]

STATES, REGIONS AND METROPOLITAN AREAS

Economic growth in central cities, suburbs and rural areas can best be addressed from a regional or metropolitan perspective. Shifts in economic activity from central cities to suburbs, exurbia and beyond are strong and perhaps irreversible. In 1980, President Carter's Commission on Urban America in the Eighties stated that social and economic migration to the suburbs was a natural, even beneficial phenomenon and should not be discouraged. In the 1990s, the economic survival of both central cities and suburbs depends on cooperation and a regional approach to development.

Suburbs and central cities have a common interest in a prosperous metropolitan and regional economy. Cities and suburbs as well as adjacent towns and rural areas form a single, informal, interdependent regional economy. Their economic welfare and futures are joined. Yet despite the fact that 80% of the population resides in metropolitan areas, only 3% live under a single metropolitan government.[65]

Federal policy should recognize this reality and address the common needs of these regional economies.[66] The economic performance of each region has an impact on the performance of the national economy. In turn a regional economy is not self-contained and immune to national and global developments.[67]

"In many urban regions, public authorities have, in the 1990s, become the central organizational instruments for advancement of state and local government economic agendas."[68] Some 6,400 public authorities are operating in the United States, mostly within metropolitan regions. In 1990, they were responsible for more than $900 billion in public debt.[69] Technically they are independent of state and local governments. Yet governing bodies are largely appointed by the governments from which they are supposed to be legally and financially independent. The authorities usually have powers of eminent domain, and can issue tax-exempt bonds with certain restrictions. Resources come from fees, assigned taxes and grants.

Public authorities have become increasingly important participants in metropolitan, more so than overall regional economic development. Initially the authorities were instrumental in providing key infrastructure such as transportation, water and sewers and port facilities, expanding to tourism, sports facilities, technology and convention centers. State economic development authorities and local industrial development agencies generally serve as financing mechanisms rather than becoming directly involved in operations. The authorities are a means of removing jurisdictional obstacles.

Community- and Neighborhood-Based Development

Local government entities based on historic boundaries are not independent economic entities; the region is a more realistic economic concept. Communities are components of the regional economies within which they function. But will giving priority to the region as the key to stimulating economic development be accepted in view of the preference for a locally based orientation? Community-based organizations have lacked the internally generated financial resources, technical expertise and the appropriate outlook to cope effectively with economic development problems. It is no exaggeration to state that they do not possess the necessary theoretical or conceptual basis for evaluating economic development at the lowest local level.[70] As to the benefits and costs of local economic development policies, the benefits have generally been overrated and the costs largely ignored.[71] They are unlikely candidates upon which to build economic development policy and are best viewed as social communities.[72]

TECHNOLOGY

A difficulty in remaining competitive is the disappearance of what have been considered strengths as technology removes locational advantages. For example, the economic base of areas whose strength has been the availability of low-cost labor is vulnerable to improvements in communications and transportation, which improve accessibility to lower-cost areas.[73]

How can the existing economic base be maintained while shifting toward a more technological orientation? Programs have to be formulated that focus on maintaining a competitive advantage based on the region's strengths. Traditional industries can be still be valuable and should be assisted in modernization.

The concentration of high-tech industries in particular areas raises serious questions about the potential of modifying or expanding the spatial pattern of technology-based employment. Those states with an existing base of high-tech infrastructure will be most attractive to other high-tech firms (clusters). Key in the development of a strong technological base has been the federal role. Silicon Valley and Route 128 had limited state and local government support; crucial was the federal support from major defense expenditures. A good part of the success of the Research Triangle Park in North Carolina comes from federal facilities. Yet, when the results of R&D go into mass production, production is done in a different region, possibly outside the country. Tight budgets can limit state efforts to recruit high-tech investment. Such states as Georgia and North Carolina have been willing to risk tens of millions of dollars to build up high-tech industries in their states.[74]

State funding programs for technology generally fall under four categories:

- research and development funding
- venture capital in the form of investments (debt, equity, or royalty agreements)
- traditional development incentives (tax benefits, industrial revenue bonds)
- partial subsidies (incubator facilities, industrial retraining).[75]

Seed and venture capital programs for high-technology industry emphasize funding for the early stages of production. They exist alongside more traditional state and local small-business support programs such as industrial revenue bonds, loan guarantees and training programs for workers. They give priority to job creation for small companies that have difficulty obtaining capital from traditional financial sources.[76]

Equity investment programs provide funding for small high-tech companies. These programs are generally executed on a cost-sharing basis with the state agency in exchange for royalties, common or pre-ferred stock or convertible debt. Some programs also offer loans or loan guarantees to qualifying companies.[77]

Manufacturing Extension Services (MESs) provide a lead in indus-trial modernization. State support of MESs predates the federal Manufacturing Technology Centers (MTCs) now incorporated into the federally funded Manufacturing Extension Partnership (MEP) network. The main purpose of the state-sponsored MESs was to upgrade manu-facturers' capabilities, especially small businesses, which on their own lacked the professional expertise to remain competitive. An MES pro-vides state officials with the opportunity to demonstrate their interest in economic/industrial development, obtain available federal resources and distribute benefits to their constituents.[78] With the establishment of the MEP, there has been a shift from the state to the federal level.

Sector-specific MESs suit the changing industrial environment. By concentrating activities in a limited number of sectors, MESs can be the core of a cluster. An MES should concentrate on three areas: assessment and planning, technology demonstration, and education and training. By demonstrating proven technologies and offering training information and training, costs can be reduced and an environment can be created that is conducive to using technological know how. Over time an MES should offer fewer assessment and planning services and more technolo-gy demonstration and educational services.[79]

EVALUATION

As state governments seek innovative programs to meet new eco-nomic realities, they have to take into account structural shifts in the national and international economies, major technological change, global competition and changes in corporate and government finance. Too fre-quently, state programs respond to perceptions reflecting the general state of the art in other states rather than an outgrowth of particular research, analysis and complex decision-making processes, and they evaluate their development programs on a short-term basis.[80]

Without incentives states will be adversely affected in terms of their ability to attract and retain businesses. Yet a high level of subsidies within a state shifts costs to businesses that do not receive benefits. The long-standing criticism of using incentives to recruit industry is that they are essentially a zero-sum game from a national perspective. But not all state and local economic development programs are zero-sum games if they provide net national benefits or if activity is shifted from prosperous to distressed areas without a deleterious impact on the prosperous area.

In contrast to the competition through incentives, a more beneficial policy is the provision of physical and social infrastructure and research and development. A legacy remains when a recipient firm leaves. Positive programs have a spillover effect on other states and nationally.

Can states abandon development strategies that from a national perspective are considered inefficient and expensive? It is likely that states will continue to devote resources into attracting and retaining firms until the unlikely event that such programs are restricted nationally.[81] Following the example of the EU, can a mechanism be devised whereby states can only offer justifiable incentives or subsidies? However, there is no indication that the federal government is interested in or inclined to take such action.

NOTES

1. U.S. Congress, Congressional Budget Office, *The Federal Role in State Industrial Development Programs,* July 1984, p. 45.

2. Ibid.

3. "Legal Limitations on Public Inducements to Industrial Location," *Columbia Law Review* 59 (1959), p. 623. Copyright (1959) by the Directors of the Columbia Law Review, Inc.

4. Claude W. Stimson, "The Exemption of Property From Taxation in the United States," *Minnesota Law Review* 18 (March 1934), p. 417.

5. Claude W. Stimson, "The Stimulation of Industry Through Tax Exemption," *The Tax Magazine* 11 (May 1933), p. 169.

6. John Sidor, *Put Up or Give Way: States, Economic Competitiveness, and Poverty* (Washingto: Council of State Community Development Agencies), November 1991, p. 9.

7. Mary Jo Waits, Karol Kahalley and Rick Heffernon, "Organizing for Economic Development: New Realities Call for New Rules," *Public Administration Review* 52 (November/December 1992), p. 612.

8. David Osborne, *Laboratories of Democracy* (Boston: Harvard Business School Press, 1988), pp. 284–285.

9. Paul Brace, *State Government and Economic Performance* (Baltimore: Johns Hopkins University Press, 1993), p. 18.

10. Curtis Ventries, "The Internationalization of Public Administration and Public Policy: Implications for Teaching," *Public Policy Review* 8 (Summer 1989), p. 898.

11. Kevin R. Cox and Andrew M. Wood, "Local Government and Local

Economic Development in the United States," *Regional Studies* 28 (October 1994), p. 640.

12. Harold Wolman and Gerry Stoker, "Understanding Local Economic Development in a Comparative Context," *Economic Development Quarterly* 6 (November 1992), p. 406.

13. John E. Petersen, "Interstate Meat Markets: The High Price of Buying Jobs," *Governing* 7 (October 1993), p. 60.

14. U. S. General Accounting Office, *Federal State Local Relations: Trends of the Past Decade and Emerging Issues,* GAO/HRD 90-34, March 1990, p. 22.

15. Timothy J. Bartik, *What Should the Federal Government Be Doing about Federal Urban Economic Development?* (Kalamazoo, MI: W. E. Upjohn Institute for Employment Research, April 1994), Staff Working Papers 94-25, p. 1.

16. Ibid., p. 37.

17. R. Scott Fosler, "The New Economic Role of American States," in R. Scott Fosler, ed., *The New Economic Role of American States: Strategies in a Competitive World Economy* (New York: Oxford University Press, 1988), p. 329.

18. Richard P. Barke, "Technology and Economic Development in the States: Continuing Experiments in Growth Management,"in Jurgen Schmandt and Robert Wilson, eds., *Growth Policy in the Age of High Technology: The Role of Regions and States* (Boston: Unwin Hyman, 1990), p. 438.

19. Thomas A. Lyson, *Two Sides to the Sunbelt: The Growing Divergence Between the Rural and Urban South* (Westport, CT: Praeger, 1989), p. 4.

20. Ibid., pp. 4–5.

21. Roger Wilson, *State Business Incentives and Economic Growth: Are They Effective? A Review of the Literature,* Council of State Governments, Division of Policy Analysis Services, 1989, p. 2.

22. Ibid., p. 3; and "The Second War Between the States," *Business Week,* May 17, 1976, pp. 92–114.

23. Neal R. Peirce, "Regional Governance: Why? Now? How?"*University of Virginia Newsletter* 8 (June 1991), p. 3.

24. Brian Dabson, Carl Rist and William Schweke, "Business Climate and the Role of Development Incentives," *The Region* (Federal Reserve Bank of Minneapolis) 10 (June 1996), pp. 47–48.

25. DeLysa Burnier, "State Economic Development Policy: A Decade of Activity," *Public Administration Review* 51 (March–April 1991), p. 2.

26. Thomas J. Anton, "Exploring the Politics of State Economic Development Policy," *Economic Development Quarterly* 3 (November 1989), p. 343.

27. John M. Levy, *Economic Development Programs for Cities, Counties and Towns,* 2d ed. (Westport, CT: Praeger, 1990), p. 1.

28. Timothy Bartik, "Better Evaluation for Economic Development Programs," *Economic Development Quarterly* 8 (May 1994), p. 106.

29. National Academy of Public Administration, *A Path to Smarter Economic Development: Reassessing the Federal Role,* prepared for the U.S. Economic Development Administration (Washington: November 1996), p. 16.

30. "Uncommercial Travellers," *The Economist* 342 (February 1, 1997), p. 25; and Alan Erenhalt, "The Devil in Devolution," *Governing* 10 (May 1997), p. 7.

31. "State and Local Governments in International Affairs, ACIR Findings and Recommendations," *Intergovernmental Perspectives* 20 (Fall 1993–Winter 1994),

p. 37.

32. Sidor, "Put Up or Give Way,"p. 84.

33. Brace, *State Government*, p. 126.

34. Harold Wolman and David Spitzley, "The Politics of Local Economic Development," *Economic Development Quarterly* 10 (May 1996), p. 127.

35. Kevin E. Cullinane, "Kentucky and Ohio Compete for Jobs With Aggressive Relocation Incentives," *Wall Street Journal*, July 21, 1992, p. A2.

36. Peter Eisinger, "Development in the 1990s: Politics and Policy Learning," *Economic Development Quarterly* 9 (May 1995), p. 153.

37. Judith A. Kossy, "Economic Restructuring and the Restructuring of Economic Development Practice: A New York Perspective, 1985–1995," *Economic Development Quarterly* 10 (November 1996), p. 302.

38. Peter Morici, "Resolving the North American Subsidies War," *Canadian-American Public Policy* 27, (September 1996), p. 10.

39. U.S. Congress, Congressional Budget Office, *How the GATT Affects U.S. Antidumping and Countervailing Duty Policy*, September 1994, p. 22.

40. William Fulton, "The Sadness of the Giveaway," *Governing* 8 (August 1995), p. 78.

41. Melvin L. Burstein and Arthur J. Rolnick, "Congress Should End the War Among the States," *The Region* (Federal Reserve Bank of Minneapolis) 9 (March 1995), pp. 3, 4.

42. Ibid., p. 10.

43. Ibid., p. 11.

44. Ibid., p. 15.

45. Philip P. Frickey, "The Congressional Process and the Constitutionality of Federal Legislation to End the Economic War among the States," *The Region* (Federal Reserve Bank of Minneapolis) 10 (June 1996), p. 59.

46. Ibid., p. 89.

47. Walter Hellerstein, "Commerce Clause Restraints on State Law Incentives," *The Region* (Federal Reserve Bank of Minneapolis) 10 (June 1995), p. 60.

48. Ibid., pp. 60–61.

49. Timothy J. Bartik, "Eight Issues for Policy toward Economic Development Incentives," *The Region* (Federal Reserve Bank of Minneapolis) 10 (June 1996), p. 45.

50. Ibid., p. 46.

51. Congressional Budget Office, *The Federal Role*, p. 8.

52. Charles Mahtesian, "Romancing the Smokestack," *Governing* 8 (November 1994), p. 40.

53. Graham S. Toft, "Doing Battle Over the Incentives War: Improve Accountability but Avoid Federal Noncompete Mandates," *The Region* (Federal Reserve Bank of Minneapolis) 10 (June 1996), p. 38.

54. Charles Mahtesian, "Saving the States for Each Other," *Governing* 10 (November 1996), p. 15; and Charles Mahtesian, "Resisting the Lure of the Smokestack," *Governing* 10 (May 1997), p. 76.

55. Robert Guskind, "The Giveaway Game Continues," *Planning* 56 (February 1990), p. 9.

56. Petersen, "Interstate Meat Markets,"p. 60.

57. Russell L. Hanson, "Bidding for Business: A Second War Between the States," *Economic Development Quarterly* 7 (May 1993), p. 184.

58. Michael M. Phillips, "More States Reassess Business Incentives," *Wall Street Journal*, March 20, 1997, p. A2 and Robyn Meredith, "Chrysler Wins Incentives From Toledo," *New York Times*, August 12, 1997, p. D3.

59. John DeWitt, "Where Is Rural Policy Headed?" *Annals of the American Academy of Political and Social Science* (September 1993), p. 24.

60. "Cuomo Vetoes Bill to Make Businesses Accountable," *Newsday*, July 29, 1994, p. A49.

61. Robert G. Lyncy, *Do State and Local Tax Incentives Work?* (Washington: Economic Policy Institute, 1996), p. 1.

62. Richard J. Reeder, *Rural Enterprise Zones in Theory and Practice: An Assessment of Their Development Potential*, U.S. Department of Agriculture, Agriculture and Rural Economy Divisin, Economic Research Service, March 1993, pp. 7–8.

63. Alan M. Peters, "Clawbacks and the Administration of Economic Policy Development in the Midwest," *Economic Development Quarterly* 7 (November 1993), p. 328.

64. John Greenwald, "A No-Win Between the States," *Time*, April 8, 1996, p. 45.

65. Michael Lind, "A Horde of Lilliputian Governments," *The New Leader*, May 5, 1997, p. 6.

66. Larry C. Ledebur and William J. Barnes, *Metropolitan Disparities and Economic Growth*, rev. ed. (Washington: National League of Cities, September 1992), p. 17.

67. Ibid., p. 18.

68. Dennis C. Muniak, "Letter from America, Public Authorities and Economic Development in Metropolitan Regions," *Regions: The Newsletter of the Regional Studies Association* 192 (August 1994), p. 9.

69. Ibid., p. 10.

70. Michael B. Teitz, "Neighborhood Economics: Local Communities and Regional Markets," *Economic Development Quarterly* 3 (May 1989), p. 113.

71. Timothy Barnekov and Daniel Rich, "Privatism and the Limits of Local Development Policy," *Urban Affairs Quarterly* 2 (December 1989), p. 214.

72. Teitz, "Neighborhood Econoomics,"p. 111.

73. Mark S. Rosentraub and Michael Przyblski, "Competitive Advantage, Economic Development and the Effective Use of Local Public Dollars," *Economic Development Quarterly* 10 (November 1996), p. 316.

74. Greg Jafe, "States Compete to Recruit Top Scientists Spending Surges to Develop High-Tech Industries," *Wall Street Journal*, April 23, 1997, p. A2.

75. William A. Delphos, *Capitol Capital: Government Resources for High Technology Companies* (Washington: Venture Publishing, 1993), p. 104.

76. Ibid., p. 105.

77. Ibid., p. 110.

78. Ross J. Gittell and Allen Kaufman, "State Government Efforts in Industrial Modernization: Using Theory to Guide Practice," *Regional Studies* 39 (August 1996), pp. 479, 484.

79. Ibid., pp. 485–486.

80. Robert D. Behn, "The Benefits of the Private Sector," *Governing* 8 (June 1995), p. 103.

81. Keon S. Chi and Drew Lestherly, *State Business Incentives: Trade and Options for the Future*, Executive Summary (Lexington, KY: Council of State Governments, 1997), pp. 14–16.

Selected Bibliography

Andrews, James H. "Metro Power." *Planning* 62 (June 1996): p. 8.

Bachtler, John, and Rona Michie. "A New Era in European Union Regional Policy Evaluation? The Appraisal of the Structural Funds." *Regional Studies* 29 (December 1995): p. 745.

Bartik, Timothy J. *Who Benefits From State and Local Economic Development Policies?* Kalamazoo, MI: W. E. Upjohn Institute, 1991.

Bingham, Richard D., and William W. Bowen. "The Performance of State Economic Development Programs: An Impact Evaluation." *Policy Studies Journal* 22 (Autumn 1994): p. 501.

Blakely, Edward J., and Philip Shapira. "Industrial Restructuring: Public Policies for Investment in Advanced Industrial Society." *The Annals, American Academy of Political and Social Science* 475 (September 1984): p. 96.

Boeckelman, Keith. "Governors, Economic Theory, and Development Policy."*Economic Development Quarterly* 10 (November 1996): p. 342.

Breagy, Jim. "Metro Units Cooperating in Global Marketplace." *Economic Developments* (National Council for Urban Economic Development) 21 (April 15, 1996): p. 4.

Breckenridge, Robert E. "Integration From Below: Transnational Regionalism in Europe and North America." Paper presented at the Fourth Biennial International Conference of the European Community Studies Association, Charleston, SC, May 1995.

Browne, Harry. "BECC and NADBank." In Sarah Anderson, John Cavanaugh and David Ranney, eds., *NAFTA'S First Two Years The Myths and the Realities.* Washington: Institute for Policy Studies, March 1996, p. 30.

Bucar, Bojko. "International Cooperation of European Subnational Regions." Paper presented at the Fourth Biennial International Conference of the European Community Studies Association, Charleston, SC, May 1995.

Charles, Anne, Consul General of Canada, Detroit. "Remarks on the Canadian Experience." Presented at Conference sponsored by Federal Reserve Bank of Chicago, Institute for Development Strategies, Indianapolis, October 15, 1992, p. 15.

Chinitiz, Ben. "What Role for the Economic Development Administration in the New Economy?" *Economic Development Quarterly* 9 (August 1995): p. 203.

Cini, Michelle. *European Community Competition Policy*, European Dossier Series 24. London: University of North London Press, 1993.

Colgan, Charles S. "Brave New World: International Regulation of Subsidies and the Future of State and Local Development Programs." *Economic Development Quarterly* 9 (May 1997): p. 107.

Daneke, Gregory A. "Technological Entrepreneurship as a Focal Point of Economic Policy: A Conceptual Assessment." *Policy Studies Journal* 17 (Spring 1989).

Delagram, Leslie. "Regional Development Subsidies in Canada-U.S. Trade Negotiations." Occasional Paper 8 in Bruce Fountain et al., eds. *Symposium on Subsidies under the FTA*, Vol. III. Manufacturing and Regional Studies, Legal Studies Center, Canada–United States Trade Center, University of Buffalo, 1990, p. 14.

Delamaide, Darrell. *The New Superregions of Europe*. New York: Dutton, 1994.

DeMestral, Armand, and Jan Winter. "Dispute Settlement Under the North American Free Trade Agreement and the Treaty of European Union." *Journal of European Integration* 17 (Winter–Spring 1994): p. 235.

Drozdiak, William. "Revving Up Europe's Four Motors: Up-and-Coming City-States Are Driving the Continent's Economy." *Washington Post* March 27, 1994, p. C3.

Erenhalt, Alan. "Cooperate or Die." *Governing* 8 (September 1995): p. 28.

Estes, Ralph, with M. Jeff Hamond, "Enterprise Zones: A Critical Analysis." Briefing Paper. Washington: Institute for Policy Studies and Center for Advancement of Public Policy, March 1993.

European Union, Commission. *The Community's Finances Between Now and 1997.* COM (92) 2001 final, March 10, 1992.

———. "The European Union's Regional Policy: Objectives, Ways and Means." *Frontier-free Europe* 1 Supplement (January 1995): p. 1.

———. (London). *Innovation for Growth and Development in Europe*, Background Report B7/97, April 1997.

———. (London). *State Aids.* Background Report ISEC/B3/95, March 1995.

European Union. European Investment Bank. "The EIB and Regional Development." Information No. 82, November 1994.

Flynn, Patricia M. "Technology Life Cycles and State Economic Development Strategies." *New England Economic Review* (Federal Reserve Bank of Boston) (May–June 1994): p. 551.

Fountain, Bruce. "Subsidies in Manufacturing: The Myths and Realities." Occasional Paper 8 in Bruce Fountain et al., eds., *Symposium on Subsidies under the FTA*, Vol. III, Manufacturing and Regional Studies, Legal Studies

Center, Canada–United States Trade Center, University of Buffalo, 1990, p. 3.

Gottlieb, Gideon. "Nations Without States." *Foreign Affairs* 73 (May/June 1994): p. 100.

Gray, Charles. "Committee of the Regions." *Commentary* 11:33 (C. D. Howe Institute), October 1991.

Grayson, George W. *The North American Free Trade Agreement Regional Community and the New World Order.* Lanham, MD: University Press of North America, 1995.

Grinspun, Ricardo, and Maxwell A. Cameron. "The Political Economy of North American Integration: Diverse Perspectives, Converging Criticism." In Ricardo Grinspun and Maxwell A. Cameron, eds., *The Political Economy of North American Free Trade.* New York: St. Martin's Press, 1993, Chap. 1.

Hama, Noriko. *Disintegrating Europe.* Westport, CT: Praeger Publishers, 1996.

Harvie, Christopher. *The Rise of Regional Europe.* London: Routledge, 1994.

Howes, Candace, and Ann R. Markusen, eds. "Trade Industry and Economic Development." In Helzi Noponen, Julie Graham and Ann R. Markusen, eds., *Trading Industries Trading Regions.* New York: Guilford Press, 1993, Chap. 1.

Isserman, Andrew, and Terence Rephann. "The Economic Effects of the Appalachian Regional Commission: An Empirical Assessment of 26 Years of a Regional Development Plan." *Journal of the American Planning Association* 61 (July 1995): p. 345.

Izzo, Somonetta. "The Juridical Nature of the European Investment Bank." *Journal of Regional Policy* 1.2 (January–March 1992): p. 123.

James, Robert P. "Fears That U.S. Could Lose Trade Sovereignty Cloud New GATT's Propects in Congress." *Traffic World* 239 (August 1, 1994): p. 25.

Jensen, Finn B., and Ingo Walter. *The Common Market Economic Integration in Europe.* Philadelphia and New York: J. B. Lippincott, 1965.

Kahler, Miles. *International Institutions and the Political Economy of Integration.* Washington, D.C.: Brookings Institution, 1995.

Kaplan, Robert D. "History Moving North." *Atlantic Monthly* 279 (February 1997): p. 21.

Koprowski, Gene. "NIST Director Defends Advanced Technology Program From GOP." *R&D Magazine* 36 (February 1995): p. 37.

Krause, Lawrence B. "Regionalism in World Trade: The Limits of Economic Interdependence." *Harvard International Review* 13 (Summer 1991): p. 4.

Kresl, Peter Karl. *The Urban Economy and Regional Trade Liberalization.* Westport, CT: Praeger Publishers, 1992.

———. "The Impact of Free Trade on Canadian-American Border Cities." *Canadian-American Public Policy* 16, (December 1993).

Kuttner, Robert. "Another Great Victory of Ideology Over Prosperity." *Atlantic Monthly* 268 (October 1991): p. 32.

Leycegui, Beatriz, William B. P. Robson and S. Dahlia Stein, eds., *Trading Punches: Trade Remedy Law and Disputes Under NAFTA.* Report 279. Washington: National Planning Association, 1995.

Lipowicz, Alice. "Private-Sector Jobs, Investment Powering Empowerment Zones." *Crains New York Business,* February 1, 1997, p. 31.

McAleavey, Paul. *The Political Logic of the European Community Structural Funds Budget: Lobbying Efforts by Declining Industrial Regions.* Working Paper RSC

94/2. Florence: Robert Schuman Centre, European University Institute Working Paper RSC No. 94/2, May 1994.

McGaughey, William, Jr. *A U.S.-Mexico Free-Trade Agreement: Do We Just Say No?* Minneapolis: Thistlerose Publications, 1992.

MacLaren, Roy. "A Hemispheric Trade and Investment Strategy to Move the World." *North American Outlook* (National Planning Strategy) 5.6 (Winter 1995/1996): p. 64.

McLean, Beverly M. "Studying Regional Development: The Regional Context of Economic Development." *Economic Development Quarterly* 10 (May 1996): p. 188.

Michaelis, Michael. "Science and Technology in the Cities: Views and Comments." In S. George Walters, Morris L. Sweet and Max D. Snider, eds., *Marketing Management Viewpoints Commentary and Readings*, 2d ed. Cincinnati: South-Western Publishing, 1970, Chap. 7.

Michelmann, Hans J., and Panarotis Soldatos, eds. "Comparative Integration in the European Union and the North American Free Trade Area: A Comparative Approach." *Journal of European Integration* 17 (Winter–Spring 1994).

Migue, Jean-Luc. "The Balkanization of the Canadian Economy: A Legacy of Federal Policies." In Filip Palda, ed., *Provincial Trade Wars: Why the Blockade Must End*. Vancouver: Fraser Institute, 1994, p. 107.

Morici, Peter. "Regionalism: Motivations and Risks." In Richard S. Belous and Rebecca S. Hartley, eds., *The Growth of Regional Trading Blocs in the Global Economy*. Washington: National Planning Association, 1990, p. 134.

Moussis, Nicholas. *Access to European Union Institutions and Policies*, 4th rev. ed. Rixensart, Belgium: Edit-Eur (Eurconfidential), 1994.

Nagel, Jerry. "The Future of Borderless Communities." *ASPA Times* 16 (November 1993): p. 10.

Nesbitt, Lois E. "In State: Suburbia on Edge." *Rutgers Magazine* 73 (Winter 1993): p. 10.

Netzer, Dick. "An Evaluation of Interjurisdictional Competition Through Economic Development Incentives." In Daphne A. Kenyon and John Kincaid, eds., *Competition Among States and Local Governments Efficiency and Equity in American Federalism*. Washington, D.C.: Urban Institute Press, 1991, Chap. 13.

New York City Housing and Redevelopment Board. *Industrial Development in New York City*. Report 10, May 1964.

Ohmae, Kenichi. "The Emergence of Regional States: The Disappearance of Borders." *Survey of Regional Literature* 23 (March 1993): p. 2.

———. *The End of the Nation State*. New York: Free Press, 1995.

Oughton, Christine. "Growth, Structural Change and Real Convergence in the European Community." In Kirsty S. Hughes, ed., *European Competitiveness*. Cambridge: Cambridge University Press, 1995, Chap. 9.

Pierce, Neal R. "There's a New Way to Define Regions." *National Journal* 25 (14 August 1993): p. 2045.

Robinson, Ian. "How Will the North American Free Trade Agreement Affect Worker Rights in North America?" In Maria Lorena Clark and Harry C. Katz, eds., *Regional Integration and Industrial Relations in North America*. Ithaca, NY:

Institute of Collective Bargaining, New York State School of Industrial Relations, Cornell University, 1994, p. 105.

Ross, Doug, and William Schweke. "The Emerging Third Wave: New Economic Development Strategies in the 1990s." *News and Views* (Economic Development Division, American Planning Association), February 1991.

Russell, Brian R. "Industrial Policy, Subsidies, and Trade Law: Troubling the Waters of Trade." In A. R. Riggs and Tom Velk, eds., *Beyond NAFTA: An Economic, Political and Sociological Perspective.* Vancouver: Fraser Institute, 1993, p. 251.

Schwanen, Daniel. "One Market, Many Opportunities: The Last Stage in Removing Obstacles to Interprovincial Trade." *Commentary* 60 (C. D. Howe Institute) (March 1994).

Shuman, Michael H. "GATTzilla v. Communities." *Cornell International Law Journal* 27 (1994): p. 101.

Smith, Murray G. "Overview of Provincial and State Subsidies: Their Implications for Canada-U.S. Trade." *International Economic Issues* (Institute for Research on Public Policy) (April 1990): p. 1.

Smith, Neil. "The Region Is Dead, Long Live the Region." *Political Geography* 7 (April 1988): p. 141.

Spaak, Paul-Henri. *The Continuing Battle: Memoirs of a European.* Boston: Little, Brown and Co., 1971.

Swann, Dennis. *The Economics of the Common Market,* 6th and 7th eds. London: Penguin Books, 1988 and 1992.

Sweeney, G. P. *Innovation, Entrepreneurs and Regional Development.* New York: St. Martin's Press, 1987.

Sweet, Morris L. "Mandating Industry to Locate in the Northeast." Paper presented to the New England Business and Development Conference, Wakefield, MA, November 1977.

————."Codetermination and the Location of Industry in Impacted Regions." Paper presented to New England Business and Economic Association Conference, Newport, RI, October 1978.

————. "Industrial Location Policy: Western European Precedents for Aiding U.S. Impacted Regions." *Urbanism Past and Present* 70 (Winter 1978–1979): p. 1.

————. "State Plant Closing Legislation." Paper presented to the New England Business and Economic Conference, Boston, MA, October 1979.

————. *Industrial Location Policy for Economic Revitalization: National and International Perspectives.* Westport, CT: Praeger Publishers, 1981.

————. "The United States and Canada." In Michael Cross, ed., *Managing Workforce Reduction: An International Survey.* Westport, CT: Praeger Publishers, 1985, Chap. 2.

Sweet, Morris L., and S. George Walters. *Mandatory Housing Finance Programs: A Comparative International Analysis.* Westport, CT: Praeger Publishers, 1976.

Talbot, R. B. "The European Community's Regional Fund: A Study in the Politics of Redistribution." *Progress in Planning* 8 (3) Oxford: Pergamon Press, 1977.

Tannenwald, Robert. "State Business Climate: How Should It Be Measured and How Important Is It?" *New England Economic Review* (Federal Reserve Bank of Boston) (January–February 1996): p. 22.

U.S. Congress, Congressional Budget Office. *A Budgetary and Economic Analysis of the North American Free Trade Agreement,* July 1993.

U.S. Congress, House. Subcommittee on International Economic Policy and Trade and Subcommittee on Europe and the Middle East. Study paper by C. Randall Henning. "Management of Economic Policy in the Economic Community." In *Europe and the United States: Competition and Cooperation in the 1990s* (June 1992): p. 16.

U.S. Department of Commerce, Office of Economic Research, Economic Development Administration. *Regional Economic Development and Federal Legislation.* March 1970.

U.S. General Accounting Office. *The General Agreement on Tariffs and Trade Uruguay Round Final Act Should Produce Overall U.S. Economic Gains,* Volumes 1 and 2. GAO/GGD-94-83b, July 1994.

———. *U.S.-Canada Free Trade Agreement Factors Contributing to Controversy in Appeals of Trade Remedy Cases to Binational Panels.* GAO/GCD-95-175, June 1995.

———. *Economic Development Programs.* GAO/RCED 95-251R, July 28, 1995.

———. *International Trade Implementation Issues Concerning the World Trade Organization.* GAO/T-NSIAD-96-122, March 13, 1996.

Van Young, Eric. "Introduction: Are Regions Good to Think." In Eric Van Young, ed., *Mexico's Regions Comparative History and Development.* San Diego: Center for U.S-Mexican Studies, 1992, Chap. 1.

Wallis, Allen D. "Evolving Structures and Challenges of Metropolitan Regions." *National Civic Review* 83 (Winter–Spring 1994): p. 40.

———. "Inventing Regionalism: The First Two Waves." *National Civic Review* 83 (Spring–Summer 1994): p. 159.

———. "The Third Wave: Current Trends in Regional Governance." *National Civic Review* 83 (Summer–Fall 1994): p. 290.

———. "Inventing Regionalism: A Two-Phase Approach." *National Civic Review* 83 (Fall–Winter 1994): p. 447.

Walters, S. George, and Morris L. Sweet. "Can Private Enterprise Manage Economic and Social Programs." Paper presented to the New England Business and Economic Association Conference, Newport, RI, October 1978.

Wishlade, Fiona. "Achieving Coherence in European Community Approaches to Area Designation." *Regional Studies* 28 (February 1994): p. 79.

Wolf, Michael Allan. "Enterprise Zones: A Decade of Diversity." In Richard D. Bingham, Edward W. Hill and Sammis B. White, eds., *Financing Economic Development.* Newbury Park, CA: Sage Publications, 1990, Chap. 8.

World Trade Organization. *Regionalism and the World Trading System.* Geneva, April 1995.

Index

About the Author

MORRIS L. SWEET is an economic development specialist currently doing independent research. His publications include *Industrial Location Policy for Economic Revitalization* (Praeger, 1981).

ISBN 0-275-95617-2

HARDCOVER BAR CODE